Translated Texts for Byzantinists

The intention of the series is to broaden access to texts of interest to Byzantinists from 800 CE, enabling students, non-specialists and scholars working in related disciplines to access material otherwise unavailable to them. The series will cover a wide range of texts, including historical, theological and literary works, all of which include an English translation of the Byzantine text with introduction and commentary.

Liverpool University Press gratefully acknowledges the generous continued support of Dr Costas Kaplanis, alumnus of King's College London, who was instrumental in setting up the series.

General Editors
Judith Ryder, Oxford
Tim Greenwood, St Andrews

Editorial Committee
Anne P. Alwis, University of Kent
Zachary Chitwood, Johannes Gutenberg-Universität Mainz
Mary Cunningham, Nottingham
Charalambos Dendrinos, Royal Holloway
Niels Gaul, Edinburgh
Judith Herrin (Founding Editor), King's College London
Anthony Hirst, London
Liz James, Sussex
Michael Jeffreys, Oxford
Costas Kaplanis, King's College London
Marc Lauxtermann, Oxford
Fr Andrew Louth, Durham
Brian McLaughlin, Independent Scholar
Rosemary Morris, York
Leonora Neville, University of Wisconsin-Madison
Charlotte Roueché, King's College London
Teresa Shawcross, Princeton
Mary Whitby, Oxford

Editor Emerita
† Elizabeth Jeffreys

A full list of published titles in the **Translated Texts for Byzantinists** series is available on request. The most recently published are shown below.

The Laws of the Isaurian Era: The Ecloga and its Appendices
Translated with an introduction and commentary by MIKE HUMPHREYS
Volume 3, 208pp., ISBN 978-1-78694-008-7 limp

Nicholas Mesarites: His Life and Works
Translated with notes and commentary by MICHAEL ANGOLD
Volume 4, 376pp., ISBN 978-1-78694-204-3 limp

An Early Ottoman History: The Oxford Anonymous Chronicle (Bodleian Library, Ms Marsh 313)
Historical Introduction, translation and commentary by DIMITRI J. KASTRITSIS
Volume 5, 272pp., ISBN 978-1-78962-074-0 limp

The Chronicle of Constantine Manasses
Translated with commentary and introduction by LINDA YURETICH
Volume 6, 344pp., ISBN 978-1-78962-158-5 limp

The Chronicle of the Logothete
Translated with Introduction, Commentary and Indices by STAFFAN WAHLGREN
Volume 7, 320pp., ISBN 978-1-78962-807-4 limp

Gregory Palamas: The Hesychast Controversy and the Debate with Islam
Translated with an introduction and notes by NORMAN RUSSELL
Volume 8, 504pp., ISBN 978-1-80207-747-6 limp

Narrating Martyrdom: Rewriting Late-Antique Virgin Martyrs in Byzantium
Translated with introduction and notes by ANNE P. ALWIS
Volume 9, 224pp., ISBN 978-1-80207-748-3 limp

The Tale of Livistros and Rodamne: A Byzantine Love Romance of the 13th Century
Translated with an introduction by PANAGIOTIS A. AGAPITOS
Volume 10, 208pp., ISBN 978-1-80085-603-5 limp

The De Thematibus ('on the themes') of Constantine VII Porphyrogenitus
Translated with introductory chapters and notes by JOHN HALDON
Volume 11, 296pp., ISBN 978-1-80207-843-5 limp

The Disputatio of the Latins and the Greeks, 1234
Introduction, Translation and Commentary by JEFF BRUBAKER
Volume 12, 224pp., ISBN 978-1-83553-669-8 limp

Epiphanios the Monk: Life of Mary, the Theotokos, and Life and Acts of St Andrew the Apostle
Introduction, Translation and Commentary by MARY CUNNINGHAM
Volume 13, 224pp., ISBN 978-1-80207-853-4 cased

Germanos II, Patriarch of Constantinople (1223–1240): Select Sermons
Introduction, Translation and Commentary by MICHAEL ANGOLD
Volume 14, 368pp., ISBN 978-1-80207-459-8 cased

For full details of **Translated Texts for Byzantinists**, including prices and ordering information, please contact: Liverpool University Press, 4 Cambridge Street, Liverpool, L69 7ZU, UK (Tel +44-[0]151-794 2233. Email janet.mcdermott@liverpool.ac.uk, http://www.liverpooluniversitypress.co.uk).

Translated Texts for Byzantinists
Volume 13

Epiphanios the Monk

Life of Mary, the Theotokos, **and**
Life and Acts of St Andrew the Apostle

Introduction, Translation, and Commentary by
Mary B. Cunningham

Liverpool
University
Press

First published 2023
Reprinted with corrections 2024
Liverpool University Press
4 Cambridge Street
Liverpool, L69 7ZU

This paperback edition published 2025

Copyright © 2025 Mary B. Cunningham

Mary B. Cunningham has asserted the right to be identified as the author of this book in accordance with the Copyright, Designs and Patents Act 1988.

All rights reserved. No part of this book may be reproduced, stored in a retrieval system, or transmitted, in any form or by any means, electronic, mechanical, photocopying, recording, or otherwise, without the prior written permission of the publisher.

British Library Cataloguing-in-Publication Data
A British Library CIP Record is available.

ISBN 978-1-80207-853-4 (hardback)
ISBN 978-1-83553-798-5 (paperback)

Typeset by Carnegie Book Production, Lancaster

CONTENTS

Abbreviations	vii
Acknowledgements	x
Preface	xi
Introduction	1
1 The Life of Mary, the Theotokos	75
2 The Life and Acts of St Andrew the Apostle	107
Appendix A	147
Appendix B	155
Maps	159
List of Manuscripts Cited in Book	161
Bibliography	163
Index	185

ABBREVIATIONS

AA	*Acts of Andrew* (see Primary Sources)
AAMt	*Acts of Andrew and Matthias* (see Primary Sources)
AASS	*Acta Sanctorum*, 68 vols (1643–1940) (Brussels: Société des Bollandistes)
AB	*Analecta Bollandiana*
ACO	*Acta Conciliorum Oecumenicorum*, Series I, ed. E. Schwartz and J. Straub (Berlin: De Gruyter, 1922–84)
BBOM	Birmingham Byzantine and Ottoman Monographs
BHG	F. Halkin, ed. (1957), *Bibliotheca Hagiographica Graeca*, 3 vols (Brussels: Société des Bollandistes)
BHG^a	F. Halkin, ed. (1969), *Auctarium Bibliothecae Hagiographicae Graecae* (Brussels: Société des Bollandistes)
BHL	*Bibliotheca Hagiographica Latina Antiquae et Mediae Aetatis*, 2 vols (1898–1901); repr. 1949; H. Fros (1986), *Novum Supplementum* (Brussels: Société des Bollandistes)
BHO	*Bibliotheca Hagiographica Orientalis* (1910), Subsidia Hagiographica 10 (Brussels: Société des Bollandistes)
BZ	*Byzantinische Zeitschrift*
CANT	*Clavis Apocryphorum Novi Testamenti*, ed. M. Geerard (1992) (Turnhout: Brepols)
CCSA	Corpus Christianorum Series Apocryphorum (Turnhout: Brepols)
CPG	*Clavis Patrum Graecorum*, 5 vols, ed. M. Geerard (1983–87) (Turnhout: Brepols)
CPL	*Clavis Patrum Latinorum*, ed. E. Dekkers and A. Gaar (3rd edn, 1995) (Turnhout: Brepols)
CSCO	Corpus Scriptorum Christianorum Orientalium (Louvain: Secrétariat du Scriptorum Christianorum Orientalium)

DHGE	L. Courtois, F. Keygnaert, and E. Louchez, eds (rev. edn 2015–19), *Dictionnaire d'histoire et de géographie ecclésiastiques*, 5 vols (Turnhout: Brepols)
DOML	Dumbarton Oaks Medieval Library (Cambridge, MA: Harvard University Press)
DOP	*Dumbarton Oaks Papers*
DOS	Dumbarton Oaks Studies (Washington, DC: Dumbarton Oaks Research Library and Collection)
DS	M. Viller, ed. (1937–95), *Dictionnaire de spiritualité: ascétique et mystique: doctrine et histoire*, 17 vols (Paris: Beauchesne)
EO	*Échos d'Orient*
FOTC	Fathers of the Church (Washington, DC: Catholic University of America Press)
GCS	Die griechischen christlichen Schriftsteller der ersten Jahrhunderte
HTR	*Harvard Theological Review*
JECS	*Journal of Early Christian Studies*
JÖB	*Jahrbuch der Österreichischen Byzantinistik*
JTS	*Journal of Theological Studies*
LAA	Epiphanios the Monk, *Life and Acts of Andrew* (see Primary Sources)
Lampe	G.W.H. Lampe (1961), ed., *A Patristic Greek Lexicon* (Oxford: Clarendon Press)
LS	H.G. Liddell and R. Scott, eds (9th edn, 1977), *A Greek-English Lexicon* (Oxford: Clarendon Press)
LVM	Epiphanios the Monk, *Life of the Virgin Mary* (see Primary Sources)
LXX	Septuagint (see Bibliography, Primary Sources)
OCA	Orientalia Christiana Analecta (Rome: Pontifical Institute of Oriental Studies)
OCP	*Orientalia Christiana Periodica*
ODB	A. Kazhdan, et al., eds (1991), *Oxford Dictionary of Byzantium*, 3 vols (Oxford and New York: Oxford University Press)
ODCC	F.L. Cross and E.A. Livingstone, eds (3rd edn, 1997), *The Oxford Dictionary of the Christian Church* (Oxford: Oxford University Press)

ABBREVIATIONS

PBE	Prosopography of the Byzantine Empire, ed. John Martindale, King's College London, at http://www.pbe.kcl.ac.uk
PG	J.-P. Migne, Patrologia Graeca
PO	Patrologia Orientalis (Paris: Éditions du Cerf, 1904–; repr. Turnhout: Brepols)
PTS	Patristische Texte und Studien (Berlin and New York: Walter de Gruyter)
SC	Sources Chrétiennes (Paris: Éditions du Cerf, 1942–)
ST	Studi e Testi
Suppl. VC	Vigiliae Christianae Supplement
SynaxCP	H. Delehaye, ed. (1902), Synaxarion of Constantinople. Propylaeum ad Acta Sanctorum Novembris. Synaxarium Ecclesiae Constantinopolitanae (Brussels: Société des Bollandistes)
TIB	Tabula Imperii Byzantini
TLG	Thesaurus linguae graecae (a digital library of Greek literature), at http://stephanus.tlg.uci.edu/
TM	Travaux et Mémoires (Paris: Centre national de la recherche scientifique)
TTB	Translated Texts for Byzantinists (Liverpool: Liverpool University Press, ongoing)
TTH	Translated Texts for Historians (Liverpool: Liverpool University Press, ongoing)
TU	Texte und Untersuchungen zur Geschichte der altchristlichen Literatur (Leipzig)
VC	Vigiliae Christianae (Leiden: Brill)

ACKNOWLEDGEMENTS

It is a pleasure to thank Judith Herrin, the late Elizabeth Jeffreys, and Judith Ryder, along with their Editorial Committee, for encouraging me to submit this book for publication. Clare Litt (Commissioning Editor) and Sarah Warren (Senior Production Editor) generously provided advice throughout its production. I am also grateful to Nicholas Wilshere in the Department of Classics at the University of Nottingham for checking my translations at an early stage and helping to eliminate errors and infelicities of English style. Father Maximos Constas and Christos Simelidis shared their knowledge of the Marian literary tradition and John Geometres' tenth-century *Life of the Virgin* in private correspondence with me. I am also grateful to them both for allowing me to read their translation of that work while it was still in preparation. Elizabeth Jeffreys and Marc Lauxtermann (who acted as readers for the TTB series), along with Judith Ryder (as General Editor), provided further corrections and suggestions. I would also like to thank the colleagues and friends (who are too numerous to mention by name) who have helped me to think about Byzantine hagiography and the Marian literary tradition over the years.

On producing this revised version of the publication so soon after the first edition appeared, there are further people to thank. These include Christos Simelidis (once again) and Archimandrite Nikodemos, *hegumenos* of the Monastery of the Panagias Chryssopodaritisses near Patras in Greece. These scholars informed me of the modern Greek translation of the *Life and Acts of St Andrew*, thanks to the work of the monks at that monastery, and of the Russian critical edition of the text that was produced by Andrey Vinogradov in 2005. My ignorance of his work became clear just one month after the publication of the first edition of the present book. I am deeply grateful to the editors of TTB and to Liverpool University Press for allowing me to revise my introduction and translation in this second edition. I would also like to take this opportunity to thank Dr Vinogradov for his fine work on the Greek literary tradition associated with the apostle Andrew. He also offered valuable comments and corrections during the final phase of my revisions. Any errors that remain are my own.

PREFACE

This project grew out of my recent research on the Virgin Mary in Byzantium, which introduced me to the early ninth-century writer, Epiphanios the Monk, and his intriguing narratives about the Theotokos and the 'first-called' apostle, Andrew. The two accounts diverge in significant ways from canonical and apocryphal sources, thus raising the question whether Epiphanios possessed an active imagination or whether he was drawing on apocryphal sources that have been lost or remain uncovered.

A few words about my decisions concerning the presentation of Epiphanios the Monk's two *Lives* in English translation are appropriate. In choosing how to transliterate Greek names (both of people and places), I have usually followed the conventions that are set out in the *ODB*. Those names that are well known to English readers in their anglicised forms (such as 'John Chrysostom' or 'Andrew of Crete') follow this convention. Translations from other literary sources, including the Septuagint and New Testament, are my own – often because Epiphanios diverges from the standard versions in his rendering of biblical passages. The meanings of unusual words are discussed in the commentaries for each text. Readers may sometimes disagree with my choices, but no translation should ever be regarded as definitive.

It is also worth noting that Andrey Vinogradov's critical edition of the *Life and Acts of St Andrew the Apostle* is not, to my knowledge, widely available in European and American academic libraries. Readers may therefore find it difficult to check my translation against the original Greek and should bear in mind that Vinogradov's text diverges in significant ways from Albert Dressel's 1843 edition. As they read my translation and commentary, however, I hope that they will recognise the excellent philological work that is currently being carried out in Russia and remind their libraries to obtain the relevant publications.

INTRODUCTION

Epiphanios, a monk and priest who probably lived in Constantinople at the end of the eighth and beginning of the ninth century, was also a pilgrim and author who wrote of his travels in search of saints and their relics in Asia Minor, the Pontos, and other regions.[1] The two hagiographical texts that he composed, which celebrated the Virgin Mary and the 'first-called' apostle Andrew, reflect Epiphanios's interest in establishing the 'facts' concerning the lives and deaths of his holy subjects.[2] Our hagiographer based his work not only on the Greek canonical and apocryphal narratives that circulated in this period, but also on chronicles, homilies, and oral accounts which he was able to collect in the course of his travels. Epiphanios was aware that some narratives were considered unreliable, or even heretical, as he compiled his own versions of Mary's and Andrew's stories; for this reason, he was careful to list his literary sources at the beginning of each oration.[3] However, Epiphanios also considered that his work was innovative. In the prologue to his *Life of the Virgin Mary* (hereafter *LVM*) he suggests that he is the first hagiographer to provide a comprehensive and accurate account

---

1 On the association of Epiphanios with the Monastery of Kallistratos in Constantinople, which has been accepted by most scholars, see below, n. 30. Following the titles provided in most surviving manuscripts containing his texts, I have chosen to call our author 'Epiphanios the Monk' throughout this study.

2 Epiphanios the Monk, *LVM* and *LAA*, ed. Dressel 1843, 13–82. The *LVM* was also edited by Mingarelli 1783, repr. PG 120, 185–216B. Albert Dressel's edition of the *LAA* is reproduced in PG 120, 216C–260B, with some emendations in punctuation and capitalisation. Andrey Vinogradov published a critical edition of the *LAA* in 2005, providing both versions of the text. For further discussion of this edition and the two versions, see below, 35–36, 70–73. Although I was unfortunately unaware of Vinogradov's work in the first edition of my book, this omission has been corrected in the present one. All references to the *LAA* now follow the Vinogradov edition.

3 Epiphanios the Monk, *LVM*, ed. Dressel 1843, 13–15; PG 120, 185–89A; Epiphanios the Monk, *LAA*, ed. Vinogradov 2005, 236. 6–18; see Chap. 1, 1; Chap. 2, 1. It is noticeable, however, that Epiphanios does not list all of the sources that he used.

of her life from birth to death.⁴ Following Christos Simelidis' convincing attribution of the Georgian *Life of the Virgin* to the late tenth-century translator and writer, Euthymios the Athonite, and the elimination of its (or its Greek prototype's) possible date in the early seventh century,⁵ it is indeed likely that Epiphanios the Monk was the first Greek hagiographer to attempt a full-length biography of the Mother of God.⁶ As for his *Life and Acts of Andrew* (hereafter *LAA*), Epiphanios compiled material from a variety of literary sources, but also added original elements of his own. To quote the prologue of his *LVM*, our author aimed 'to provide something in simple language for those who long for the [facts] about her'.⁷ The same statement would apply to the *LAA* – with a bonus being that the text contains even more stories of miracles, a martyrdom, and other dramatic elements.

The two *Lives* that are translated in this volume are also important from wider historical, literary, and theological perspectives. Although it is impossible to date them precisely, most scholars agree that they were composed in Constantinople during the first decades of the ninth century – a period of religious and political upheaval which has received considerable study in recent years.⁸ After the suppression of holy images especially during the reign of Constantine V (741–75), an iconophile interregnum took place between the seventh Ecumenical Council of Nicaea in 787 and the reintroduction of Iconoclasm in 815 under the emperor Leo V (813–20). Probably writing during the years that followed this reversal of official religious policy,⁹ Epiphanios reveals his personal reactions to the controversy in the *LAA*. His interest in the apostles and early martyrs, to

---

4 Epiphanios the Monk, *LVM*, ed. Dressel 1843, 13–14; PG 120, 185B; see Chap. 1, 1.

5 Simelidis 2020. For a response to this article, which argues for an earlier date for the Georgian *Life of the Virgin*, see Shoemaker 2023. I remain unconvinced by Shoemaker's arguments for contextual and historical reasons, but the controversy is ongoing.

6 *Pace* M. van Esbroeck and S.J. Shoemaker in the Introductions to their separate editions of Euthymios the Athonite ((ps-) Maximos the Confessor), *Georgian Life of the Virgin*; for references, see below, n. 66.

7 Epiphanios the Monk, *LVM*, ed. Dressel 1843, 14; PG 120, 188B (...ἁπλαῖς ταῖς λέξεσιν τοῖς ποθοῦσιν τὰ περὶ αὐτῆς παραστήσομεν); see Chap. 1, 1.

8 Most recently in Humphreys 2021; Humphreys 2015; Brubaker and Haldon 2011. However, see also Bryer and Herrin 1977; Gero 1973; Gero 1977; Cormack 1985, 95–140; Barber 2002.

9 The key evidence here is a passage in Epiphanios the Monk's *LAA*, in which he says that he and his companion (a monk named James) 'fled from communion with the icon-fighters', having already noted that the iconoclasts of the reign of Constantine V belonged to a previous generation; see Epiphanios the Monk, *LAA*, ed. Vinogradov 2005, 239. 24–26; see Chap. 2, 9.

INTRODUCTION 3

the extent that he travelled widely in order to venerate their holy relics and images, manifests itself especially in this text. After visiting the city of Sinope on the southern coast of the Black Sea, the hagiographer describes how he saw a marble icon of the saint which, according to a local witness, had been attacked (unsuccessfully) by iconoclasts during the reign of Constantine V.[10] Epiphanios thus provides us with a precious, albeit personal, perspective concerning the religious climate of the period in which he lived.[11] Having experienced both iconoclast and iconophile policies imposed by the emperors of the late eighth and early ninth centuries, he associated himself with those Christians – especially from monastic backgrounds – who defended the veneration of icons during the period of second Iconoclasm. His high regard for the Virgin Mary, or Theotokos, which led him to write his account of her conception, birth, life, and death may reflect changing attitudes towards this holy figure during the eighth and ninth centuries.[12] Scholars still debate whether the iconoclasts actively suppressed veneration of the Mother of God, along with the saints and their relics, during the first and second periods of Iconoclasm.[13] Epiphanios provides evidence in his *LVM* that, in addition to her Christological importance, she was regarded as a figure of virtue and power especially by iconophiles such as himself.

Information about the geographical regions that are covered in both texts, which include Palestine and Jerusalem, Asia Minor, the Pontos, the Caucasus, Crimea, Thrace, and the Peloponnesian peninsula, is potentially valuable.[14] Nevertheless, it can be difficult to disentangle the textual and material evidence that Epiphanios presents concerning distant places from hearsay or legend. His descriptions of the Holy Land in the *LVM*, for example, reflect his ignorance of this region: he suggests in one passage that Bethlehem lies on higher ground than Galilee and in another that Sion and

---

10 Epiphanios the Monk, *LAA*, ed. Vinogradov 2005, 238. 3–12; see Chap. 2, 6.
11 This is also noted by Kazhdan 1999, 307. On the interaction between hagiographers and their holy subjects, see Hinterberger 2014a, esp. 214–15.
12 For background on the development of the cult of the Virgin Mary during the period of Iconoclasm, see Kalavrezou 1992; Tsironis 2000; Cunningham 2021, 14–17.
13 Parry 1996, 191–201; Tsironis 2000, esp. 28. For a thoughtful re-evaluation of the literary evidence, see Krausmüller 2021, esp. 466–77.
14 Cyril Mango used the text as a basis for identifying cities and shrines around the coast of the Black Sea; see Mango 2002. I have supplemented his study with Kahl 1989, Janin 1975, and various volumes of *TIB* in my commentary for the *LAA* below.

Gethsemane are in the same place in Jerusalem.[15] The accounts of various cities along the Black Sea, as well as in the Caucasus and the Crimea, are sometimes based on ancient narratives that populate these areas with cannibals, demon worshippers, and other uncivilised peoples. However, Epiphanios supports the descriptive sections of the *LAA* by the claim that he, accompanied by another monk named James, actually visited them.[16] Cyril Mango accepts the historical reality of this journey on the grounds that 'he provides here and there local detail that appears to be genuine.'[17] In summary, the two texts present us with a combination of fact and fiction which reflects an approach to historical narrative that is common to many Byzantine chroniclers and hagiographers.

The literary qualities of Epiphanios the Monk's two *Lives* are also worthy of study. Our hagiographer employs a simple, or koine, style of Greek, which may either reflect his level of education or aim deliberately to attract a wider readership.[18] The two orations are framed as narratives, following prologues in which Epiphanios sets out his didactic intentions and cites his literary sources. Whereas the *LVM* mostly adheres to this narrative structure, keeping speeches, ekphraseis, and other rhetorical interventions to a minimum, that of Andrew offers more variety. In keeping with the form of the original *Acta Andreae* (hereafter *AA*), which probably dates from the second or third century,[19] Epiphanios adds descriptive passages and long speeches (usually in the form of homilies delivered by his holy subject) to the composition. Narrative sections, such as the story about the proconsul Aigeates and his wife Maximilla towards the end of the *LAA*,[20] add affective power to the work.[21] Earlier sources, including

---

15 Epiphanios the Monk, *LVM*, ed. Dressel 1843, 23, 38; PG 120, 200B, 212B; see Chap. 1, 12, 27. These errors are also noted in Dräseke 1895, 351; Darrouzès 1963, 614.

16 See especially Epiphanios the Monk, *LAA*, ed. Vinogradov 2005, 239. 20–240. 7; see Chap. 2, 9.

17 See Mango 2002, 256.

18 According to I. Ševčenko's classification of Byzantine texts into three styles, high, middle, and low, I would classify both *Lives* as belonging to the 'low' category. The literary style is close to that of the New Testament, with few, if any, classical quotations or attempts at grammatical complexity. See Ševčenko 1981, 291–92. For further evaluation of the literary quality of the *LAA*, see Vinogradov 2005, 43–44. Background on the form, style, and likely audiences of Byzantine *Lives* of saints appears in Browning 1981; Høgel 1997; Hinterberger 2014b; Alwis 2020.

19 See below, 45–49, 62–68. On the likely date of the *AA*, see *Actes*, trans. Prieur 1995, 51–54.

20 Epiphanios the Monk, *LAA*, ed. Vinogradov 2005, 158.23–164.12; see Chap. 2, 36–44.

21 For discussion of this section of the *Life*, see *AA*, ed. Prieur 1989, 45–55.

the *AA*, employ rhetorical devices including exclamatio, prosopopoeia, and anaphora in order to intensify the drama.[22] The *LAA*, which displays its composite background even more than does the *LVM*, moves from travelogue to novel in its second half.[23] The latter section of the text, which describes the apostle's arrival in Patras, friendship with the local consul's wife Maximilla, arrest, and execution, contains a complex tale of shifting personal loyalties among the various protagonists. The unfortunate consul, Aigeates, whom Maximilla shuns following her conversion to Christianity, eventually kills himself by jumping from a high place – not because he regrets the execution of Andrew but because he misses his wife.[24] This section of the text, which is largely dependent on the earlier *AA*, must have provided readers or auditors with entertainment as well as moral teaching.

Turning to the theological content of the two *Lives*, we find a mixture of orthodox Christological doctrine and ascetic reflection. As I have already noted, Epiphanios adopts a more narrative than panegyrical approach to Mary, the Theotokos, in his account of her terrestrial life. However, the divine providence that chose her as the virginal mother of Christ is revealed in aspects of the story that are borrowed from the early apocryphal text known as the *Protevangelion of James*: Mary was conceived after her aged and previously sterile parents, Joachim and Anna, experienced visions, and was raised in the Jewish Temple before being betrothed (following a miraculous sign) to Joseph.[25] In portraying the Virgin as a pious and

---

22 On these rhetorical devices and their persuasive impact, see Kennedy 1983, 52–103; Lanham 1991, 11, 61, 123–24; Rowe 1997, 131, 143–44.

23 A. Kazhdan calls the work a 'perverse romance', perhaps because it deals with conjugal love on the part of Aigeates but celebrates his rejection by Maximilla; see Kazhdan 1999, 307. As already noted, and to be discussed below, 45–49, the final section of Epiphanios's *LAA* is based closely on the early *AA*. Several scholars have associated the latter, along with other early *Acts* of the apostles, with the ancient genre of novel; see Bovon 2003, 170; Pervo 1987, 122–31.

24 Kazhdan notes a vivid detail in a version of the text that appears only in Cod. Vat. 824 where Aigeates is described as getting up at the dead of night, when 'there was a deep silence', and throwing himself off the roof of the praetorium; Kazhdan 1999, 308; Epiphanios the Monk, *LAA*, ed. Dressel 1843, 81; PG 120, 260A. This detail has however been borrowed from an earlier anonymous narrative in praise of St Andrew; see anon., *Narratio* 36, ed. Vinogradov 2005, 196. 7–10. It is not included in Vinogradov's edition of the *LAA* since it does not feature in any other manuscripts that contain either version of that text. For further discussion, see below, 67.

25 *Protevangelion of James*, ed. de Strycker 1961; Tischendorf 1876/1987; trans. Elliott and Rumsey 2022.

virginal ascetic throughout her life, Epiphanios revives a tradition which began during the early centuries of Christianity but was superseded by Christological considerations in liturgical texts from the early fifth century onward.[26] As in his *LAA*, the monastic hagiographer seizes elements in the earlier literary tradition that might appeal to his largely celibate audience. Both the Virgin Mary and Andrew are portrayed as models of asceticism, praying constantly, wearing simple clothing and, above all, remaining virginal. The Encratite tendencies of the earlier apocryphal *Acts* of this apostle (along with those of his colleagues), which had attracted condemnation from early Christian leaders including Jerome and Augustine, could thus be adapted to fit the aspirations of middle Byzantine monastic readers.[27] Epiphanios's iconophile tendency is revealed not only in his references to icons and relics in the *LAA*, but also in his whole approach to the holy subjects. Although he devotes only one short passage to healings and miracles which Mary was said to have performed towards the end of her life in Jerusalem, he stresses physical reminders of her sojourn on earth such as the imprints of her knees on the marble floor of the house that she occupied on Mt Sion in Jerusalem – a reference that he borrowed from one of Andrew of Crete's homilies on the Dormition.[28] The *LAA* is replete with sermons which the apostle is supposed to have preached in the course of his travels around the Black Sea, other parts of Asia Minor, and Greece. Some of these texts begin by describing the goodness of God's creation, followed by his dispensation for salvation following the expulsion of Adam and Eve from paradise. Such emphasis on creation, as the imprint of an immanent or incarnate God, reflects the influence not only of apostolic sources such as 1–2 Clement (along with passages in the pseudo-Clementine literature), but also the theology that was worked out – or reiterated – by contemporary theologians including John of Damascus, Andrew of Crete, and others during the first and second periods of Iconoclasm.[29] In summary, although

---

26 Cunningham 2019b, 321; Cunningham 2021, 30–31.

27 On the appeal of the early *AA* to Encratite, Apotactite, Manichaean, and other communities during the early Christian centuries, see J.-M. Prieur's introductory remarks for an English translation of the text in Schneemelcher 1992, vol. 2, 101–3; *Actes*, trans. Prieur 1995, 18–23, 49–54.

28 Epiphanios the Monk, *LVM*, ed. Dressel 1843, 38; PG 120, 212A; Chap. 1, 27 and n. 156. The homily which the hagiographer quotes here is Andrew of Crete, *Homily I on the Dormition*, PG 97, 1073A.

29 On the influence of 1–2 Clement and the pseudo-Clementine texts, see Chapter 2, n. 3; on iconophile theology, see Louth 2007, 41–66; Barber 2002.

the theology of the two *Lives* is simply expressed, especially by means of narrative or panegyric, it provides a coherent didactic message that reflects the monastic and iconophile background in which Epiphanios flourished.

More detailed analysis of the historical, literary, and theological content of the two texts is provided below. Before turning to the individual features of each *Life*, however, it is worth examining the historical and literary background of the author.

Epiphanios, priest and monk – perhaps of the Monastery of Kallistratos

What we know about this rather obscure Byzantine writer appears in the titles of his works, along with hints within the texts about his cultural and religious milieu. He is called 'Epiphanios, monk and presbyter' in most of the manuscripts that contain the *Lives* of the 'supremely holy Theotokos' and of the 'first-called of the apostles, Andrew'. The monk's association with the Constantinopolitan Monastery of Kallistratos is attested only in a few late manuscripts, including Vat. gr. Ottob. 415 (14th–15th c.) and Cod. Queriniana Brescia A.III.3 (16th c.).[30] J. Darrouzès suggests a further link, namely, that a hermit belonging to the Monastery of Mt Auxentios in Bithynia (to whom another early ninth-century hagiographer, Stephen the Deacon, dedicated his *Life of St Stephen the Younger*)[31] later became abbot of the Monastery of Kallistratos and authored the *Lives* of the Virgin

---

30 F. Diekamp supplies this information in his edition of Hippolytos of Thebe's *Chronicle* (1898), 136. Cod. Vat. Ottob. gr. 415 (14th–15th c.), f. 291, provides the following title for the *LVM*: Διήγησις Ἐπιφανίου μοναχοῦ μονῆς τῶν Καλλιστράτων περὶ τῆς... Θεοτόκου; Cod. Bresc. gr. A.III.3 (16th c.), f. 424, reads: Ἐκ τοῦ βίου καὶ ἀνατροφῆς τῆς Θεοτόκου διήγησις Ἐπιφανίου μοναχοῦ μονῆς τοῦ Καλλιστράτου. Subsequent scholars have largely accepted the association of Epiphanios with the Monastery of Kallistratos: see Flamion 1911, 70; Jugie 1944, 258–59; Vinogradov 2005, 41; Mimouni 2011, 89; Efthymiadis 2011b, 107; Cunningham 2019b, 309; Domínguez 2020. It is only since writing the latter study (Cunningham 2019b) that I began to explore the basis for Epiphanios's link with the Monastery of Kallistratos. The unquestioning acceptance of the title 'Epiphanios of Kallistratou/os' may reflect scholars' reliance on a theory that has been transmitted mainly (apart from the two late manuscripts) in the secondary literature.

31 *The Life of St Stephen the Younger*, ed. and trans. Auzépy 1997, 5, 9–10, 87. 2, 175. 27. See also the Prosopography of the Byzantine Empire (PBE), hosted by King's College London, 'Epiphanios 25', at http://www.pbe.kcl.ac.uk/data/nmnm/index.htm.

Mary and of the apostle Andrew.[32] St Auxentios, who had founded the monastery in Bithynia and whose relics were celebrated on 14 February at the Monastery of Kallistratos, offers further evidence of a link between the two monasteries.[33]

The view that Epiphanios the Monk flourished in the late eighth and early ninth century is based on his own statements about the activities of iconoclasts during the reign of Constantine V in the *LAA*. As stated above, the hagiographer travelled to Sinope where he saw an icon which had survived the image fighters' attempts to deface it.[34] Epiphanios narrates the story as if the first period of Iconoclasm had recently ended; it also appears, however, that the iconophile interregnum had been overturned. When describing their travels through Asia Minor, he states that he and the monk James 'fled from communion with the icon-fighters'.[35] The hagiographer was thus active, at least when he composed the *LAA*, after Leo V's reintroduction of iconoclastic policies after 815. It is likely, not only according to this passage, but also more broadly in relation to Epiphanios's interest in the Virgin Mary, saints, relics, and icons, that he was himself a committed iconophile.[36]

Epiphanios the Monk should not be confused with Epiphanios 'Hagiopolites', a contemporary writer who composed a kind of guidebook (*Diegesis*) for Syria and Jerusalem.[37] Our hagiographer, although well travelled, has probably not visited the Holy Land since he commits basic

---

[32] 'Pour la biographie d'Épiphane il faut peut-être rapprocher son nom de celui d'un higoumène du mont S.-Auxence, auquel le biographe d'Étienne le Jeune dédie son œuvre en 808 (PG 100, 1067, 1184); le monastère de Callistrate à Constantinople possédait en effet les reliques de S. Auxence et gardait peut-être des rapports avec le monastère fondé par ce saint en Bithynie. Les deux Épiphanes, celui de Callistrate et celui de S.-Auxence, pourraient être identiques'; Darrouzès 1963, 614–15. It is also worth noting that Byzantine historians cited the Monastery of Kallistratos as one of a few establishments in Constantinople which Constantine V either destroyed or sold during his reign; see Domínguez 2020, 406.

[33] *Synax CP*, ed. Delehaye 1902, 465. 16–18.

[34] Epiphanios the Monk, *LAA*, ed. Vinogradov 2005, 238. 3–12; see Chap. 2, 6.

[35] Epiphanios the Monk, *LAA*, ed. Vinogradov 2005, 239. 24–240. 7; see Chap. 2, 9.

[36] See, however, S. Mimouni's doubts on this question on the basis that Epiphanios underplays the miraculous aspects of the Virgin Mary's life – to the extent that the text meets criteria outlined by I. Ševčenko and M.-F. Auzépy for identifying iconoclast saints' *Lives*; see Mimouni 2011, 91–92; cf. Ševčenko 1977; Auzépy 1992.

[37] Epiphanios Hagiopolites, *Diegesis of a Journey to Syria and Jerusalem*, ed. Dressel 1843, 1–12; PG 120, 259–72; trans. Wilkinson 1977, 117–21.

INTRODUCTION 9

errors concerning its topography in his *LVM*.[38] Epiphanios Hagiopolites, possibly a monk living in Jerusalem, is thought to have flourished at the end of the eighth century. His guidebook, which is intended for pilgrims, describes the most important biblical sites in the order in which they should be visited both in Jerusalem and surrounding regions. On the grounds that the author describes the Holy Land as it appeared before the Frankish ruler, Charlemagne, established a Christian protectorate there, it is likely that the text was composed before about 807.[39]

Scholars have also debated whether the same author, named Epiphanios, composed both the *LVM* and the *LAA*.[40] Although most accept the single authorship of both texts, it is worth considering the arguments for and against the hypothesis carefully. First, the rather vague title 'monk and presbyter' which appears in the titles for both works in most of the surviving manuscripts does little to identify this shadowy figure. However, the wording of the title is consistent enough to suggest an identifiable epithet; further, this humble designation would offer little attraction as a pseudonym to most aspiring authors. Second, as we shall see in the analysis of each of the two *Lives* that follows, similarities in content and literary style suggest a single hagiographer. Epiphanios expresses his desire in the prologues of both works to offer coherent narratives that are based on reliable sources. Although he is aware of the 'heretical' reputations of some apocryphal works, he nevertheless employs these along with accepted biblical, apostolic, and patristic texts. Our hagiographer is eager to supplement his literary sources with material evidence. In the *LVM*, he mentions physical signs of his subject's terrestrial life in the Holy Land, including the Evangelist John's house on Mt Sion where she was believed to have lived after Christ's ascension into heaven and, as we saw above, the marble floor on which the imprints of her knees could still be seen.[41] The mention of the marble icon and two seats (or thrones) which Epiphanios

---

38 Dräseke 1895, 350; Kazhdan 1999, 307–8; Mimouni 2011, 89. Although these three scholars accept the different identities of Epiphanios 'monk and presbyter' and Epiphanios 'Hagiopolites', E. Kurtz argued that they were the same author; see Kurtz 1897, 216.

39 J. Darrouzès 1963, 615.

40 Most notably by Kurtz, who placed the author of the *LVM* in the eleventh century on the basis of the dates of surviving manuscripts; see Kurtz 1897, 216.

41 On John the Evangelist's ownership of the house on Mt Sion in Jerusalem where Mary was believed to have lived during the final years of her life, see Epiphanios the Monk, *LVM*, ed. Dressel 1843, 35; PG 120, 209A; Chap. 1, n. 137. On the imprint of her knees on the floor of the house, see above, n. 28.

claims to have seen in Sinope, according to the *LAA*, is followed by that of many other holy relics which he was able to venerate in the course of his travels around Asia Minor.[42]

As for the literary qualities of the two *Lives*, Epiphanios employs a simple, paratactic style in both works. Sentences and phrases are frequently linked by conjunctions while longer parentheses are avoided. This colloquial style sometimes leads to ambiguity in meaning, but readers and auditors would probably have been able to follow the narratives thanks to their conventional structure and dramatic quality. The separate subject matter of the two works, with the *LVM* providing a panegyrical biography and the *LAA* offering an account of the apostle's journey and mission, followed by his martyrdom in Patras, helps to explain some discrepancies between them. I have not been able to identify distinctive words or expressions that might help to identify an authorial style, but it is noticeable that Epiphanios sometimes employs recondite phrases or words such as ἀγυρτώδης ('characteristic of a beggar or imposter')[43] and δασύς ('hairy' or 'shaggy', meaning 'a copse').[44] He uses alliteration, as in a sentence with four adjectives beginning in 'a': ἁπλῆν... ἄδολον... ἀμνησίκακον... ἀγαθόν.[45] Wordplay may also feature, as in the use of the pun ἄμισος ('agreeable' or 'not hateful') for the city of Amisos.[46] Both *Lives* offer opportunities for ekphrasis, or description, which may be employed in connection with the appearances of biblical personages, including Christ and Mary, or for geographical locations.[47] Epiphanios provides a vivid description of the Sea of Galilee, for example, in his *LVM*, in which he mentions the lush trees that surround its northern end and the abundance of fish that it contains.[48] One obstacle to systematic comparison of the two *Lives* is the extent to which Epiphanios copies, or plagiarises, the earlier, now lost, *AA* – or a later version of the text.[49] This problem will be examined in more detail

---

42 See above, n. 10; on Epiphanios's veneration of other holy relics during his travels, especially in Bithynia, see idem, *LAA*, ed. Vinogradov 2005, 239. 20–240. 25; Chap. 2, 9.
43 Epiphanios the Monk, *LAA*, ed. Vinogradov 2005, 246.15; see Chap. 2, 18, n. 78.
44 Ibid., ed. Vinogradov 2005, 248.8; below, Chap. 2, 22, n. 85.
45 Ibid., ed. Vinogradov 2005, 242.19–20; below, Chap. 2, 12, n. 59.
46 Ibid., ed. Vinogradov 2005, 240.31; below, Chap. 2, 10, n. 47.
47 For further discussion of the physiognomic descriptions in Epiphanios's texts, see below, 17–18.
48 Epiphanios the Monk, *LVM*, ed. Dressel 1843, 32; PG 120, 205D–208A. On the derivation of this passage from Josephus's *The Jewish War*, see Chap. 1, 21, n. 122.
49 *AA*, ed. Prieur 1989; MacDonald 1990. It is worth noting that Stephanos Efthymiadis

below, but for the purposes of this comparative section it is simply worth noting that a large section of the text, which deals with Andrew's activities and martyrdom in Patras, is based on the earlier apocryphal narrative (or a later version of this).[50] This means that analysis of Epiphanios the Monk's literary style must involve some differentiation between aspects that are original and those that are borrowed.

In summary, I agree with the scholarly consensus that Epiphanios, known in manuscripts as 'monk and presbyter' (and occasionally 'of the Monastery of Kallistratos'), wrote the *LVM* and the *LAA* at the beginning of the ninth century but was not the author (known as Epiphanios Hagiopolites) of a contemporary work called the *Diegesis of a Journey to Syria and Jerusalem*. Narrative and stylistic similarities between the *LVM* and *LAA* suggest that they were composed by one author, but differences in the structure and purpose of each text make this difficult to prove. In the sections that follow, I will examine the two texts separately, analysing their content, purpose, and style, along with the literary sources and material evidence that Epiphanios employed in each case. Following this, it is also worth discussing the dissemination and reception of each text, not only in Byzantium, but in the Latin-speaking West and other surrounding regions. Both texts contributed in important ways to the development of Byzantine Mariology and hagiography in the course of the ninth century and beyond.

The *LVM*: context, content, and didactic purpose

Epiphanios the Monk's oration on the life and conduct of Mary, the all-holy Theotokos, follows an explosion of Marian liturgical praise which had begun during the first decades of the fifth century and continued especially in the seventh and eighth centuries.[51] Although scholars increasingly question the theory that the Council of Ephesus (431) played a pivotal role in the rise of the cult of the Virgin,[52] there can be no doubt that it contributed to her

---

confuses the Late Antique *AA* with Epiphanios the Monk's ninth-century *LAA*; see Efthymiadis 2011b, 132. It is the former text, not the latter, which appears in *AA*, ed. Prieur 1989.

50 *AA*, ed. Prieur 1989, 18–20, 121–22.

51 For background on this tradition, see Daley 1998, 1–45; Cunningham 2019a; eadem 2021.

52 See, for example, Price 2004; Shoemaker 2016a, 3–5; Price 2019.

growing importance in both Eastern and Western Christian spirituality. Homilies and hymns celebrated Mary's Christological importance as the virgin who gave birth to Christ, the Son and Word of God.[53] She supplied him with his human nature but also, thanks to her physical and moral purity, was worthy of containing the One who could not be contained. The Theotokos was thus the crucial link that allowed God to become man. This doctrine, which was slowly worked out with the help of theological discussions and councils that took place from the fifth century onward, was enhanced by increasing reflection on Mary's maternal relationship with her son. Hymnographers, including especially Romanos the Melodist, explored the Virgin's human qualities with dramatic depictions of her emotions in response to the conception, birth, life, death, and resurrection of Jesus Christ.[54] The intercessory power of the Mother of God, who could intervene with God on behalf of humanity, is also reflected in Byzantine liturgical orations and poetry from about the late fifth or early sixth century onward.[55] The introduction of feast days, which celebrated events in the Virgin's life according to both apocryphal and canonical sources and were added to the Constantinopolitan liturgical calendar between about the middle of the sixth and end of the eighth century, provided further opportunities for Marian praise.[56] It is likely that Epiphanios was inspired by this burgeoning liturgical and devotional tradition when he undertook to write his *LVM*. The oration, which is transmitted mostly in later menologia or panegyrika (collections of hagiographical and homiletic texts for the entire liturgical year),[57] appears to have been used as a reading either for the feast of Mary's Nativity (8 September) or Dormition (15 August).[58] It is impossible to determine the audience or occasion for which the *LVM* was first composed; however, it is likely that Epiphanios intended it primarily for monastic readers or auditors and that he may have delivered it to them on one of the great feasts of the Mother of God.

In contrast with the panegyrical tendencies of most liturgical texts that were written in honour of the Virgin Mary in the preceding centuries,

---

53 For an overview of this material, see Cunningham 2021.
54 Gador-Whyte 2013; Peltomaa 2015; Arentzen 2017.
55 Allen, Külzer, and Peltomaa 2015; Cunningham 2021, esp. chaps. 1–2.
56 On the introduction of Marian feast days into the Constantinopolitan liturgical calendar, see Cunningham 2008, 19–28; Krausmüller 2011, 219–23; Panou 2018, 41–48.
57 For a comprehensive overview of surviving menologia and panegyrical collections, see Ehrhard 1936–52.
58 See below, 29.

Epiphanios the Monk adopts a narrative approach to his subject. He avoids typological, metaphorical, and even discursive theological language when describing the conduct of the Virgin, stressing instead her genealogical background, education, and ascetic way of life. As I have suggested in previous studies of this text, the hagiographer aims both to present Mary as a human figure and to establish the 'facts' about aspects of her life that panegyrists tended to omit.[59] Spotting a gap in biblical and patristic coverage of the Virgin's life, Epiphanios sets out his intentions in his prologue, as follows: 'There have been many panegyrists of [the Theotokos] from among the holy Fathers, but not one among them elaborated her life and times truly and accurately, from her upbringing to her death.'[60] The hagiographer then proceeds to reconstruct the life and character of the Virgin Mary for his monastic audience. He describes her daily activities, physical appearance, and relationship with the early followers of Christ, finishing with a short account of her death and burial. This narrative, unlike those which followed in the tenth century (including the *Lives of the Virgin* by Symeon the Metaphrast, John Geometres, and Euthymios the Athonite),[61] mostly avoids poetic or theological praise. It is perhaps this aspect of the *LVM*, along with its simple literary style, which led Antoine Wenger to dismiss it as 'mediocre' in comparison with those that followed; the same qualities may account for its relative neglect in recent scholarship.[62]

The *Life* that Epiphanios produced was nevertheless – according to both the author's and my knowledge – the first full-length biography to appear in the Greek language, although it is possible that similar attempts had been made in Syriac from as early as the fifth or sixth century.[63] Such an innovation (at least in Greek) itself renders the *Life* worthy of study. It means that Epiphanios laid the foundations for, and possibly inspired, the three tenth-century *Lives of the Virgin*, which (especially in the case

---

59 Cunningham 2016, 156–58; eadem 2019b, 319–22.

60 Epiphanios the Monk, *LVM*, ed. Dressel 1843, 13; PG 120, 185B; see Chap. 1, 1.

61 Symeon the Metaphrast, *Life of the Virgin*, ed. Latyshev 1912; John Geometres, *Life of the Virgin*, ed. Constas and Simelidis 2023; Euthymios the Athonite, *Georgian Life of the Virgin*, ed. van Esbroeck 1986; Shoemaker 2012. For analysis of all four Marian *Lives*, see Mimouni 2011.

62 *The Life of the Virgin* by John Geometres 'est incomparablement supérieure à la Vie si médiocre du moine Épiphane...'; Wenger 1955, 188.

63 In Syriac, these take the form of independent narratives (e.g. the *Protevangelion of James*, the *Infancy Gospel of Thomas*, and accounts of Mary's dormition) being placed together in manuscript collections; see Naffah 2009.

of the *Lives* by John Geometres and Euthymios the Athonite) achieve an extraordinary synthesis of narrative, praise, and theological reflection in their retelling of Mary's story.[64] Owing to recent controversy concerning its date and attribution, it is worth taking time to discuss the Georgian *Life of the Virgin* (most recently assigned to Euthymios the Athonite) and to dismiss the possibility that its Greek prototype was composed in the early seventh century by Maximos the Confessor.[65] When the eminent Belgian and American scholars, Michel van Esbroeck and Stephen Shoemaker, separately made this important Georgian text available to French- and English-speaking readers, they both argued strongly for an early seventh-century date and, in the case of van Esbroeck, its status as an authentic work of the great Byzantine theologian, Maximos the Confessor.[66] Both scholars offered numerous arguments in favour of Late Antique Constantinopolitan provenance for the text, including the dates and nature of the sources that it employs, its treatment of Marian relics, and others. Some patristic scholars, however, were slow to accept the attribution of the *Life* (that is, the Greek prototype of the tenth-century Georgian translation) to Maximos on the grounds that it bears little resemblance to this author's other surviving works and that it is not cited either by him or by other early Byzantine writers such as the ninth-century patriarch Photios.[67] Phil Booth provided the first systematic refutation of van Esbroeck's and Shoemaker's case, arguing against both the attribution of the text to Maximos and its composition in the early seventh century.[68] He suggested instead that the Greek prototype for the Georgian *Life of the Virgin* belonged at the earliest to the tenth century and that it reveals influence from the late ninth-century Marian panegyrist, George of Nikomedia. This article, which received a response from Shoemaker a year later,[69] has now been followed by an even

---

64 For detailed study of the *Lives* by John Geometres and Euthymios the Athonite, see Simelidis 2020.
65 See also Cunningham 2021, 191–94, for further discussion of the question.
66 Euthymios the Athonite, *Georgian Life of the Virgin*, ed. van Esbroeck 1986, vol. 2, v–xiii; ed. and trans. Shoemaker 2012, 14–22.
67 An early critic of the attribution of the Georgian *Life* (or its Greek prototype) to Maximos the Confessor was Toniolo 1991. Shoemaker complains, however, of the 'silence' of most patristic scholars in response to van Esbroeck's and his attempts to date the text to the early seventh century (or in van Esbroeck's case, to attribute it to Maximos); see Shoemaker 2005, 442–44.
68 Booth 2015.
69 Shoemaker 2016b.

INTRODUCTION					15

more conclusive study by Christos Simelidis, who has collaborated with Fr Maximos Constas on a text and translation of the late tenth-century *Life of the Virgin* by John Geometres.[70] Simelidis proves beyond doubt that the Georgian *Life* represents an original composition by the late tenth-century Athonite abbot and translator known as Euthymios; the latter based his work closely on John Geometres' *Life*, adapting it for a Georgian monastic audience whose literary expectations differed slightly from those of Geometres. I am convinced by this conclusion but would add that the level of literary and theological sophistication of both texts supports a middle, rather than early, Byzantine date. It is likely that John Geometres was aware of the simpler *LVM* by Epiphanios the Monk and used it to create a high-flown set of orations (usually described by modern scholars as a *Life*) in honour of the Theotokos.[71] He used the narrative that his ninth-century predecessor supplied but combined it with the kind of panegyrical praise and theological reflection that had developed especially in festal sermons of the eighth and ninth centuries. Euthymios the Athonite then simplified some of the more elaborate sections of Geometres' composition in his Georgian version of the text but retained its basic structure, which is based around the Marian festal year, and unique combination of narrative and praise.

If we accept, then, that Epiphanios the Monk's *LVM* represents the first Greek example of a full-length account of her terrestrial life, it is interesting to note how creatively he interprets both canonical and apocryphal sources. As I have already noted in two previous studies, the ninth-century hagiographer departs from the narrative that had come to be accepted in the Byzantine liturgical tradition at a number of key moments in Mary's story.[72] These include his account of the entrance of the Virgin into the Jewish Temple at the age of seven, rather than three;[73] her experience of an annunciation just outside its inner sanctuary when she was twelve;[74] the

---

70 Simelidis 2020; for the edition and translation of the text, see Constas and Simelidis 2023. Shoemaker has replied to Simelidis 2020 in his recent article without, in my view, engaging in detail with the arguments of the latter; see Shoemaker 2023.

71 Fr Maximos Constas, one of the editors of John Geometres' *Life of the Virgin*, has confirmed this tendency in private correspondence with me. He cites, for example, John's elaboration of Epiphanios's ekphrasis of the northern end of the lake of Gennesaret, also known as the Sea of Galilee; see Chap. 1, 21.

72 Cunningham 2016, 152–56; Cunningham 2019b, 313–19.

73 Epiphanios the Monk, *LVM*, ed. Dressel 1843, 17; PG 120, 192B; see Chap. 1, 4.

74 Ibid., ed. Dressel 1843, 19; PG 120, 193C–196A; see Chap. 1, 8.

betrothal to Joseph at the age of fourteen;[75] her adoption of female disciples beginning with Joseph's daughters from a previous marriage and including Peter's mother-in-law and wife and finally Mary Magdalen;[76] and Christ's appearance to his mother after his resurrection – in the house on Mt Sion and before he manifested himself to Mary Magdalen or the other disciples.[77] Some, but not all, of these episodes are repeated in the tenth-century *Lives of the Virgin*; however, the authors of these texts elaborated some details and adapted others in line with their own literary or theological preoccupations. As far as Epiphanios the Monk is concerned, it is worth repeating how freely he was prepared to change not only accepted apocryphal sources such as the *Protevangelion of James*, but even the Gospel narratives. Adopting the silence of the canonical sources with regard to so many aspects of Mary's life and conduct as his excuse, Epiphanios perhaps decided that creative interpretation was allowable as long as it enhanced the reputation of the Mother of God. It is also possible that he had access to a lost source which transmitted an alternative narrative; however, in the absence of any other evidence for such a text, it is safer to assume that Epiphanios diverged from his biblical and apocryphal sources for his own literary reasons.

A few other aspects of Epiphanios the Monk's *LVM* are worthy of note. First, the hagiographer provides the Virgin Mary with a detailed genealogy, which begins with Nathan, the son of David, and finishes with Joachim, the Virgin Mary's father. A separate, and shorter, genealogy follows in which the priestly ancestry of Mary's mother, Anna, is traced.[78] The latter also explains the relationship between Mary and her cousin Elizabeth, mother of John the Baptist, on the grounds that their mothers were two of three sisters. Epiphanios borrows Joachim's genealogy almost verbatim from John of Damascus's *Exposition of the Orthodox Faith*, written during the first half of the eighth century,[79] which must have been available in one of the patriarchal or monastic libraries in Constantinople by the time that he was writing. However, the purpose of including such a genealogy in this hagiographical text requires explanation. Christian writers had struggled

---

75 Ibid., ed. Dressel 1843, 19–20; PG 120, 196B–D; see Chap. 1, 8–9.
76 Ibid., ed. Dressel 1843, 20, 32, 34–35; PG 120, 196D, 205D, 208C–D; see Chap. 1, 10, 20, 23.
77 Ibid., ed. Dressel 1843, 37; PG 120, 209D; see Chap. 1, 26.
78 Ibid., ed. Dressel 1843, 15–16; PG 120, 189A–C; see Chap. 1, 3.
79 John of Damascus, *Exposition of Faith* IV.14, ed. Kotter 1973, 199.32–200.44; trans. Chase 1953, 363; trans. Russell 2022, 255 (87). See also Chap. 1, 2–3, n. 16.

with the question of Jesus Christ's lineage since at least the second half of the first century.[80] Above all, they sought to prove that Christ was descended from David: he was the royal descendant whom the prophets had foretold as the Messiah. Although the Evangelists Matthew and Luke provided slightly different genealogies for Jesus in their Gospels, the problem remained that these traced the descent of Joseph, who was believed *not* to be the biological father of the Messiah, rather than that of Mary. A tacit belief that Mary belonged to the same tribe as Joseph since the Jews tended to intermarry seems to have satisfied most commentators; however some, including Eusebios of Caesarea and Andrew of Crete (who were active in the early fourth and early eighth centuries, respectively), raised the question and solved it explicitly in this way.[81] The provision of a separate genealogy for the Virgin Mary appears first in polemical texts, especially treatises directed against the Jews, before being taken up by John of Damascus.[82] One of the features of this tradition was the attestation of priestly, as well as royal, lineages for the Virgin Mary (through her mother's and father's lines, respectively). This probably reflects a desire, which is attested in a few other early Christian texts, to support Christ's priestly, as well as kingly, role in the Church.[83] The move may also have been prompted by polemical concerns since, according to writers as early as Origen (ca. 185–ca. 254 CE), both Jews and pagans questioned not only the background, but also the moral reputation, of Jesus's mother Mary.[84]

A second interesting feature of Epiphanios's *LVM* is his attention to the physical descriptions of his main protagonists, Mary and her son, Jesus Christ. Towards the beginning of the *Life*, in the course of his account of the young Virgin's sojourn in the Temple, Epiphanios provides a detailed description of her appearance. He says that she had a fair complexion with blond hair, black brows, light-coloured eyes, a prominent nose, a narrow

---

80 For background on this question, see Brown 1993, 94–95; Brock 2006; Adler 2016.
81 Eusebios relies on the early third-century Roman historian, Julius Sextus Africanus, who proved that Mary belonged to the same tribe as her husband Joseph; see Eusebios of Caesarea, *Ecclesiastical History* I.7.14, ed. Schwartz, Mommsen, and Winkelmann 1999, 60; trans. G.A. Williamson (Harmondsworth: Penguin, 1965), 56. Andrew of Crete may be aware of this background when preaching at the feast of the Nativity of the Virgin; see Andrew of Crete, *Homilies II and III on the Nativity*, PG 97, 833C–D, 856A–857C.
82 See, for example, *Doctrina Jacobi nuper baptizati* 42, dated to the seventh century, ed. Déroche 1991, 132–35.
83 Adler 2016; Mimouni 2017.
84 Vuong 2013, 52–57; Shoemaker 2016a, 54.

face, and long hands and fingers.[85] An ekphrasis of Christ follows later in the text, in the context of his visit to the Temple at the age of twelve (Lk 2: 41–51), in which he is portrayed with 'well-shaped eyes, a prominent nose, a tawny beard, and long hair'.[86] Although this passage may be based on a description of David (1 Kgs 17: 42 LXX; 1 Sam 17: 42), it corresponds in physical terms with the earlier account of Mary's appearance. Epiphanios seems to prefer fair skin and hair as a sign of outward beauty and traces a family resemblance between the two holy personages.[87] Whereas most theological and liturgical texts that deal with Christ and the Theotokos avoid physical descriptions, some works such as histories and chronicles use ekphrasis in different contexts. The sixth-century chronicler Malalas, for example, often provides short but vivid portraits of Greek or Roman heroes, kings, and emperors, probably as a way of delineating their characters according to the ancient science of physiognomy.[88] The device seems to have been applied to Christian biblical figures, including Christ and his mother, especially during the period of Iconoclasm when iconophiles sought not only to emphasise the humanity of these personages, but also to provide icon painters with reliable literary models.[89] The inclusion of these passages in Epiphanios the Monk's *LVM* may reflect this theological background; however, it also ties in with his stated purpose of providing a realistic and 'historical' account of her, as well as her son's, terrestrial life.

A third aspect of the *LVM* that is worth highlighting is its treatment of the death and burial of the Virgin Mary. This feature has long interested Roman Catholic scholars, including Martin Jugie, Antoine Wenger, and Michel van Esbroeck.[90] During the years that led up to the definition known as the 'Munificentissimus Deus' of Pope Pius XII,

---

85 Epiphanios the Monk, *LVM*, ed. Dressel 1843, 18; PG 120, 193A–B; see Chap. 1, 6.

86 Ibid., ed. Dressel 1843, 29; PG 120, 204C; see Chap. 1, 18. It is surprising, as noted in the commentary to the text below, that Epiphanios describes Christ's appearance in the context of his meeting with the Temple priests at the age of twelve. The growth of a beard at this age is unlikely, if not impossible; see Chap. 1, n. 105.

87 On concepts of physical beauty in Byzantium, see Hatzaki 2010.

88 John Malalas, *Chronicle*, Bks 2–11 (many examples); ed. Dindorf 1831, 23–282. On ancient and early Christian theories of physiognomy, see Callon 2019; Johnson and Stavru 2020.

89 See, for example, the description of Christ in the probably ninth-century text known as *The Letter of the Three Patriarchs* 7.d, ed. Munitiz, Chrysostomides, Harvalia-Crook, and Dendrinos 1997, 31.14–19.

90 Jugie 1944; Wenger 1955; van Esbroeck 1995.

which was published on 1 November 1950, Jugie investigated the patristic, Byzantine, and Western medieval background for the legend of Mary's assumption.[91] Simon Mimouni and Stephen Shoemaker followed this work with important monographs on the subject.[92] Epiphanios bases his account of Mary's death on two well-known sources in early Byzantine treatment of this subject: the late fifth- or early sixth-century passage in (ps-) Dionysios the Areopagite's *Divine Names*,[93] which was accepted by Byzantine theologians as an apostolic witness to the event, and an early seventh-century homily by John of Thessalonike.[94] Our hagiographer describes how, after receiving a message about her approaching death from the archangel Gabriel, the Virgin 'sent out [messengers] and summoned all of the apostles'. Omitting to mention the miraculous aspect of their arrival on clouds, which earlier apocryphal and liturgical sources (including the homily by John of Thessalonike) describe, Epiphanios states that Mary delivered a speech not only to the apostles, but also to her female disciples and other friends and relatives, after which Christ appeared at her bedside. As angels and apostles sang hymns, 'she delivered her spirit to her Son and God'.[95] The hagiographer then briefly describes the burial of Mary's body in a tomb at Gethsemane, adding that 'after a short time when they were all present and watching, her holy and all-holy body was taken away from before their eyes'.[96] It is possible that Epiphanios borrows this description of the immediate disappearance of Mary's body from a homily on the Dormition by the Constantinopolitan patriarch Germanos I.[97] Most other apocryphal and liturgical writers, including John of Thessalonike, suggested that the apostles only discovered the disappearance of Mary's

---

91 The Apostolic Constitution concerning the assumption of the Virgin Mary is translated in Boss 2007, 281–831. This was preceded by Jugie's monumental study of the question in idem 1944.
92 Mimouni 1995; Shoemaker 2002.
93 (ps-) Dionysios the Areopagite, *The Divine Names*, ed. Suchla 1990; trans. Luibheid 1987, 4–131.
94 John of Thessalonike, *Homily on the Dormition*, ed. Jugie 1925 (1990); trans. Daley 1998, 47–80.
95 Epiphanios the Monk, *LVM*, ed. Dressel 1843, 43; PG 120, 213D; see Chap. 1, 30.
96 Ibid., ed. Dressel 1843, 43; PG 120, 216A; see Chap. 1, 30.
97 Germanos writes about Mary's assumption as follows: 'And it was from their hands, as all looked on, that the Virgin's pure body was taken away…'; Germanos of Constantinople, *Homily II on the Dormition*, PG 98, 369C; trans. Daley 1998, 177 (9). Daley reorganises the numbering of Germanos's three homilies in his translation; it appears as *Homily III* in Combefis's edition of the text, as reproduced in PG 98, 360–72.

body after it had rested in the tomb for three days. It is also noteworthy that Epiphanios makes no mention of her assumption into heaven or possible resurrection in his *Life*. Mimouni describes the text as 'dormitionist', as opposed to 'assumptionist', classifying it with certain other early texts that avoid exploration of the afterlife of the Virgin Mary in heaven.[98]

Turning to the didactic purpose of Epiphanios the Monk's *LVM*, we may start with his stated objective in the prologue of the text, which is to provide a full and accurate account of the life of the Virgin from birth to death.[99] As I noted earlier, Epiphanios suggests here that such a biography does not yet exist, in spite of the fact that earlier apostolic and patristic writers wrote about aspects of her story. This suggests a straightforward narrative aim on the part of our hagiographer. Epiphanios is keen to present his readers or auditors with details of Mary's life which are not covered anywhere else in scripture, apocryphal writings, or liturgical orations. However, it soon becomes clear that Epiphanios has an additional agenda for this project, which is to present the Virgin Mary as a model of ascetic and spiritual endeavour.[100]

This aspect of the *Life*, which must have been intended to motivate monks and nuns in their monastic vocations, is visible especially in the sections that deal with Mary's upbringing in the Jewish Temple, conduct in Joseph's home after her engagement to him, and way of life after Christ's resurrection and ascension into heaven. It revives a tradition which had first emerged in the fourth century (especially as expressed in the letters of the Alexandrian bishop Athanasios to communities of virgins) but had then been superseded by more Christological and intercessory preoccupations on the part of Greek liturgical writers.[101] Epiphanios describes the Virgin Mary as a model of virtue and piety during her sojourn in the Temple: '...she was serious with regard to everything and spoke little; she was quick to obey, well-spoken, reserved in speech towards every person, solemn, calm, without anger, full of reverence, respectful, paying every person respect and veneration, so that they all marvelled at her intelligence and speech.'[102] Later, when Mary has

---

98 Mimouni 2011, 92. Cf. Jugie 1944, 258–59.

99 Epiphanios the Monk, *LVM*, ed. Dressel 1843, 13; PG 120, 185A–B; see Chap. 1, 1.

100 For discussion of this aspect of Epiphanios's *LVM*, see also Cunningham 2016, 152–56; Cunningham 2019b, 319–22.

101 See, for example, Athanasios of Alexandria, *First Letter to the Virgins*, ed. Lefort 1955; trans. Brakke 1998, esp. 277–79. On the more Christological preoccupations of Byzantine liturgical writers, see Cunningham 2021, passim.

102 Epiphanios the Monk, *LVM*, ed. Dressel 1843, 18; PG 120, 192C–193A; see Chap. 1, 6.

been betrothed to Joseph and left the Temple precincts, she lives quietly at his house, guiding Joseph's daughters, fasting, and praying. Epiphanios stresses the fact that the young woman is modest and discreet; she tells no one about Gabriel's life-changing message to her – that is, until years later when Christ has ascended into heaven.[103] And it is especially during that late period of her life that Mary blossoms with ascetic and spiritual virtues. Epiphanios describes how, while living in the house that the Evangelist John had purchased on Mt Sion in Jerusalem, the Theotokos 'devoted herself even more to asceticism and genuflexion'.[104] Not only did she pray, but she also guided her female followers, healed the sick, and helped the poor.[105] Later writers, including John Geometres and Euthymios the Athonite, would elaborate this theme further, suggesting that Mary also instructed the apostles and sent them out on their missions throughout the inhabited world.[106] The image of Mary as a strong and dedicated female monastic leader thus gained impetus in the Byzantine liturgical tradition with the help of Epiphanios the Monk's imaginative approach to the subject.

It is also worth asking whether the iconophile leanings of our hagiographer, which I noted earlier in relation to his *LAA*, are visible in the *LVM*. This is a question which is more difficult to answer since the latter text avoids any mention of icons or other issues that might be contentious during this period of religious debate and cultural change. Epiphanios the Monk's effort to describe the terrestrial life of the holy Theotokos may be seen as revealing his devotion not only to her theological importance, but also to her intercessory power and personal dignity. Further, his interest in the conduct and appearance of the Virgin Mary, as well as of Christ, may reflect

---

103 'And no one from her household knew what had happened, nor did she report this to anyone – not even to Joseph himself – until that time when she saw her Son ascending into heaven'; ibid., ed. Dressel 1843, 21; PG 120, 197A; see Chap. 1, 10. It is interesting to note, however, that Epiphanios contradicts this statement later in his narrative when he describes Mary's visit to Elizabeth after the annunciation; see ibid., ed. Dressel 1843, 23; PG 120, 200B–C; see Chap. 1, 12: 'And on entering and greeting her, she told her about the vision of the angel and his words – that there was a male child in her womb...' However, he goes on to say, 'And they contained the mysteries in themselves and reported to no one the things that they had spoken about.' It appears that, according to Epiphanios, secrets shared between two women are not the same as disclosure to a wider audience.
104 Epiphanios the Monk, *LVM*, ed. Dressel 1843, 38; PG 120, 209D–212A; see Chap. 1, 27.
105 Ibid., ed. Dressel 1843, 38–39; PG 120, 212A–B; see Chap. 1, 27.
106 John Geometres, *Life of the Virgin* 99, ed. and trans. Constas and Simelidis 2023, 288–89; Euthymios the Athonite, *Georgian Life of the Virgin* 99, ed. and trans. Shoemaker 2012, 125–26.

iconophile emphasis on the humanity of these holy personages.[107] Another contemporary text, namely, the anonymous *Letter of the Three Patriarchs*, also makes a point of describing the appearance of Christ, perhaps in order to emphasise his physical nature and to justify the painting of images in his honour.[108] Nevertheless, as Mimouni has pointed out, Epiphanios plays down the miraculous aspects of Mary's life and conduct; he also, as we saw above, fails to elaborate on her position in heaven after the dormition.[109] Such an approach could, according to one method for distinguishing between iconophile and iconoclast *Lives* of saints,[110] indicate a tendency towards iconoclasm in our hagiographer. On weighing up the arguments on both sides of this question, I would suggest that a nuanced approach to the positions of iconoclasts and iconophiles should be adopted in relation to hagiographical texts of the period. It is likely that, so long as the controversy continued, some Christian writers remained circumspect with regard to the cult of the Virgin Mary, saints and their relics, and even icons. Although Epiphanios sought historical confirmation, both textual and material, for his beliefs and stressed realistic, as opposed to miraculous, signs of holiness, he could also have venerated relics and icons in the face of official opposition. In other words, I suggest that we should approach his works without preconceptions and avoid assigning them to categories that may initially have been more fluid than later historians (either Byzantine or modern) have claimed.

Literary sources for the *LVM*

Epiphanios the Monk cites some of the sources that he employed in the prologue of the *LVM*; however, he also used others that helped to inspire the burgeoning cult of the Mother of God. The most obvious, and authoritative, source for any Byzantine hagiographer was the canonical New

---

107 See above, n. 89.
108 *The Letter of the Three Patriarchs* 7.d, ed. Munitiz, Chrysostomides, Harvalia-Crook, and Dendrinos 1997, 31.14–19; for discussion, see ibid., xxiii. The editors also cite a fragment that is attributed to the eighth-century preacher Andrew of Crete (possibly not authentic and contained only in a fourteenth-century manuscript), which describes Christ as σύνοφρυς, εὐόφθαλμος, μακροπρόσωπος, ἐπίκυφος, εὐῆλιξ ('with eyebrows that met, well-shaped eyes, a long face, slightly bent over [in posture], of good stature'); see Tomadakis 1965, vol. 2, 192.
109 See Mimouni 2011, 90–91.
110 Ševčenko 1977; Auzépy 1992.

Testament, including especially the four Gospels.[111] However, both apostolic and patristic writers were aware of the relative silence of the Evangelists with regard to Mary – especially as interest in her history and personality increased from about the fifth century onward.[112] Although Luke focuses especially on the Virgin Mary in the first two chapters of his Gospel, emphasising her reactions to the miraculous events that unfolded after the annunciation, the other three Evangelists relegated her largely to the background of their narratives.[113] John describes Christ's words to his mother and the 'beloved disciple' (who has been understood in Christian tradition to be the Evangelist himself) when he was hanging on the cross (Jn 19: 25–27); his entrusting of each to the other's care formed the basis of the later legend concerning the Virgin Mary's sojourn at John's house on Mt Sion during the rest of her life.[114] These passages are brief, however, in the overall context of Gospels that were concerned especially with the birth, ministry, death, and resurrection of Christ. Nor do the Evangelists associate Mary explicitly with the myrrh-bearing women who came to the tomb or with the first appearances of the Lord to people (such as Mary Magdalen) in that location.[115] It was later commentators, beginning in about the fourth century, who began to place the Virgin Mary at the scene of the resurrection, sometimes even substituting her for the Magdalen and asserting that she was the first person to see the resurrected Christ.[116] As

---

111 Cameron 1991, 89–119; Krueger 2004, 15–32; Krueger 2016.

112 The earliest and most famous reference to the 'mystery' surrounding the Virgin Mary occurs in Ignatius of Antioch, *Epistle to the Ephesians* XIX.1, ed. Lake 1912, 192–93: 'And the virginity of Mary, and her giving birth, were hidden from the Prince of this world, as was also the death of the Lord...' Andrew of Crete (referring to Ignatius) also mentions the lack of information in the Gospels concerning the first thirty years of Christ's life, along with the nature of Mary's virginity and birth-giving; see Andrew of Crete, *Homily III on the Nativity of the Virgin*, PG 97, 853C–856A.

113 Brown, Donfried, Fitzmyer, and Reumann 1978; Maunder 2008; Maunder 2019b.

114 See Chap. 1, n. 137.

115 Mt 28: 1–10 (Mary Magdalen and the other Mary); Mk 16: 1–8 (Mary Magdalen, Mary the mother of James, and Salome); Lk 24: 1–10 (Mary Magdalen, Joanna, Mary the mother of James, and the other women); Jn 20: 11–18 (Mary Magdalen). Christian commentators have differed in their opinions concerning the identity of the various 'Marys', with some accepting that 'Mary the mother of James' is the same person as Christ's mother. However, this view is not accepted in Western tradition; see Maunder 2019b, 33–35.

116 The shift to believing that it was the Virgin Mary, as opposed to Mary Magdalen, who was the first to see the resurrected Christ at the tomb seems to have occurred at an early date especially in Syria; see Murray 1975/2004, 329–35; Shoemaker 2016a, 84–87.

we saw above, Epiphanios the Monk departs even from that tradition in his narrative: unlike any earlier author that I have been able to find, he describes Christ appearing first to his mother, Mary – not at the tomb, but rather in an inner room in John's house.[117]

With regard to the elements of Mary's legendary story that do not appear in the canonical Gospels, Epiphanios cites the second-century *Protevangelion of James*,[118] the early seventh-century homily on the Dormition by John of Thessalonike,[119] and another account of Mary's death and burial known as the *Transitus*, which is falsely attributed to John the Evangelist.[120] These sources, along with many others, circulated widely in the Greek-speaking Roman world.[121] The *Protevangelion of James* provides background concerning Mary's conception and birth from the elderly, barren couple, Joachim and Anna, her dedication to the Jewish Temple at the age of three, and her betrothal to Joseph, before moving on to describe the nativity of Christ in Bethlehem, the arrival of the three Magi, the massacre of the innocents, and the death of the priest Zacharias (John the Baptist's father) at the hands of Herod. John of Thessalonike's homily meanwhile celebrates the end of the Virgin's life, relating how she received a message from 'the great angel' about her forthcoming death; following this, the apostles were miraculously transported to her house on clouds from their various missions in the inhabited world. The preacher then describes the arrival of Christ from heaven and his reception of Mary's soul as it is separated from her body. The apostles process with Mary's body to Gethsemane and, despite an unsuccessful attempt by a Jew named Jephonias to overturn the bier, place it safely in the tomb. Three days later, on opening the sarcophagus, they discover only the graveclothes; Mary's body, the author implies, has been transported to heaven where she continues to work on behalf of all who pray to her. The *Transitus*, attributed to (ps-) John the Evangelist, diverges in some respects from this narrative, but offers essentially the same story. A profusion of festal homilies, most of which were composed from the beginning of the eighth century onward,

---

117 Epiphanios the Monk, *LVM*, ed. Dressel 1843, 37; PG 120, 209D; see Chap. 1, 25.
118 *Protevangelion of James*, ed. de Strycker 1961; Tischendorf 1876 (1987); trans. Elliott and Rumsey 2022.
119 John of Thessalonike, *Homily on the Dormition*, ed. Jugie 1925 (1990); trans. Daley 1998, 47–70.
120 (ps-) John the Evangelist, *Transitus*, ed. Tischendorf 1866; trans. Elliott 1993, 701–8.
121 Shoemaker 2002, 32–57.

bears witness to the popularity of these apocryphal texts throughout the Byzantine world.[122] It is thus not surprising that Epiphanios employs these sources – as well as some of the homilies – in his hagiographical project. What is puzzling, as noted above, is his tendency to alter certain details in these well-known narratives, such as the years at which the Virgin entered and departed from the Temple or her exact location at the time of Christ's resurrection. It is possible either that the hagiographer used a lost source which contained these variations or that he deliberately changed the narrative – possibly to make it more believable for contemporary audiences. On the basis that (at least to my knowledge) no other surviving liturgical or theological texts offer the readings, the second explanation seems more likely. It reveals a dynamic, or creative, streak in Epiphanios's literary response to a well-known subject: he is not afraid to adjust the legends surrounding his holy subjects in order to enhance the impact, or persuasiveness, of his own narrative.

The ninth-century hagiographer also relies on Roman or Late Antique historians, including Flavius Josephus and Eusebios of Caesarea.[123] The latter quoted earlier writers such as the second-century Christian historians, Hegesippus and Julius Africanus; Epiphanios does not refer to these sources by name but is obviously aware of their contributions to Eusebios's *Ecclesiastical History*.[124] He relies on Josephus especially in his account of the Jewish king Herod's misdeeds. Following his slaughter of male children under the age of two in his effort to destroy the Messiah, Herod is said to have murdered his wife and two sons, Alexander and Aristoboulos – as well as another son by another woman.[125] Epiphanios's account, which is transmitted in different versions according to Dressel's and Mingarelli's editions, condenses – but also misinterprets – aspects of Josephus's narratives concerning Herod.[126] This reveals once again the freedom with which our hagiographer treats his literary sources. Epiphanios uses Eusebios of Caesarea's chronicle not only for background on Herod, but also for information concerning early apostles and bishops

---

[122] An excellent English translation of many of the homilies is available in Daley 1998.
[123] Josephus, *Jewish Antiquities*; idem, *The Jewish War*; Eusebios of Caesarea, *Ecclesiastical History*.
[124] Eusebios of Caesarea, *Ecclesiastical History* II. 23, III. 11–20, 32, IV. 21–22 (Hegesippus); ibid., I.7 (Julius Africanus).
[125] See Epiphanios the Monk, *LVM*, ed. Dressel 1843, 26; PG 120, 201C; see Chap. 1, n. 82.
[126] See Chap. 1, nn. 81–82.

such as James and Symeon.¹²⁷ He also relies on the *Ecclesiastical History* when tracing the descendants of Joseph (Mary's betrothed husband) and describing the activities of the apostles after Pentecost.¹²⁸

In addition to these historical sources, Epiphanios refers briefly to several other texts that circulated during his lifetime, as we see in the following passage from his *LVM*:

> However, even those who attempted this and spoke of certain periods [in her life] did not expound them correctly but instead disagreed with each other, as in the case of James the Hebrew and Aphrodisian the Persian, along with some others who, having mentioned only her birth, at once became silent.¹²⁹

By 'James the Hebrew', Epiphanios may mean the author of the early seventh-century polemical text known as the *Doctrina Jacobi nuper baptizati*, which deals with the genealogy of the Virgin Mary – although it is also possible that he simply refers to the purported apostolic author of the second-century *Protevangelion of James*.¹³⁰ As for 'Aphrodisian the Persian', Epiphanios probably refers to a composite text that is transmitted in various versions, a section of which is described in modern scholarship as the *Legend of Aphroditianus*.¹³¹ The text is based on the story of the adoration of the Magi in Matthew 2: 1–12.¹³² After describing how the star that announced the birth of the Messiah appeared first over a statue of Hera at a temple in the Persian empire, it states that the king sent three Magi to Judea, bearing gifts. The text goes on to describe the meeting between the Magi and the Virgin Mary (with the two-year-old Jesus); here we find a description of Mary's appearance.¹³³ It is followed by the news that the

---

127 Epiphanios the Monk, *LVM*, ed. Dressel 1843, 27–28; PG 120, 204A–B; see Chap. 1, n. 91.

128 Ibid., ed. Dressel 1843, 27–28; PG 120, 204B; see Chap. 1, n. 94.

129 Ibid., ed. Dressel 1843, 14; PG 120, 185B–188A; see Chap. 1, 1.

130 The editor of *Doctrina Jacobi nuper baptizati*, Vincent Déroche, suggests the former possibility at idem 1991, 49; on the *Protevangelion of James*, see above, n. 25; see Chap. 1, n. 5.

131 *The Legend of Aphroditianus*; ed. Vasiliev 1893, 73–125; ed. Bratke 1899, 1–45; ed. and trans. Bringel 2007; trans. Heyden 2016. A version of the text is falsely ascribed to the second-century Roman historian, Julius Africanus, in PG 10, 97–108.

132 Ibid., Heyden 2016, Introduction, 3.

133 The author of the *Legend of Aphroditianus* and Epiphanios the Monk both provide descriptions of the Virgin Mary. Although these share some elements (such as the reference to 'wheat-coloured' skin and hair), they differ in other respects. One version of the *Legend of Aphroditianus* states, 'For she was small in stature even when she stood upright, and had

Magi brought back an image of the mother and child to Persia, which they placed in the temple where the star originally appeared.[134] According to Heyden, 'the oldest written version of the *Legend of Aphroditianus* is found in an anonymous Greek work called *De gestis in Perside (Pers.)*, a fifth- or sixth-century fictional religious dispute between pagans, Christians, Jews, and a Persian magus at the court of the Sasanian Empire, in which *Leg. Aphr.* plays an important part'.[135] Later Greek manuscripts, which transmit different versions of the text, attribute it variously to the sixth-century bishop, Anastasios I of Antioch, or to the seventh-century abbot and theologian, Anastasios of Sinai.[136] The early eighth-century preacher and theologian, John of Damascus, quotes a version of the legend in his *Homily on the Nativity of Christ*, including the appearance of the star over the statue of Hera in Persia and the subsequent encounter between the three Magi and the Virgin and Child.[137] It is possible that John's endorsement of the *Legend of Aphroditianus* enhanced its popularity not only in eighth- and ninth-century Byzantium, but also in neighbouring orthodox regions during subsequent centuries.[138]

Another text that informed Epiphanios was the seventh- or eighth-century *Chronicle* by Hippolytos of Thebes.[139] The hagiographer refers to this chronicler by name towards the end of his *LVM*, when he disputes the latter's statement that Mary lived to the age of fifty-nine years on the

---

a delicate body, wheat-coloured; and she had her hair bound with a simple, very beautiful hairstyle', adding first that the child (who was two years old) had 'in part the likeness of her who bore him'. See *Legend of Aphroditianus*, trans. Heyden 2016, 17. For Epiphanios's description of the Virgin, see Chap. 1, 6; cf. Vasiliev 1893, 92; Bratke 1899, 17. 19–23.

134 Ibid., trans. Heyden 2016, 17.
135 Ibid., Heyden 2016, 4.
136 Bratke 1899, 61–127.
137 John of Damascus, *Homily on the Nativity of Christ* 8–11, ed. Kotter 1988, 335. 1–342. 35; for discussion, see Heyden 2009, 94–115.
138 Heyden investigates the continuing use and popularity of *The Legend of Aphroditianus* (as a Christmas reading for liturgical settings) in Slavic-speaking regions during the medieval and early modern periods – as testified by ninety-two surviving Slavonic manuscripts; see *The Legend of Aphroditianus*, trans. Heyden 2016, Introduction, 4–6; Heyden 2009. For a summary of Heyden's discoveries concerning the later transmission of the text, especially in Slavic regions, see the review of Heyden 2009 in Lourié 2010.
139 Hippolytos of Thebes, *Chronicle*, ed. Diekamp 1898. The text survives only in fragments, which are presented separately in Diekamp's edition. For discussion of this relatively unknown chronicler and his work, see also Jugie 1944, 224–26.

grounds that Andrew of Crete stated that she reached 'extreme old age'.[140] Epiphanios calculates instead that the Virgin lived to be seventy-two years old – a number which is obtained on the basis of his own narrative concerning her legendary life.[141] Hippolytos receives scant mention in modern accounts of Byzantine chronological writing; according to Alexander Kazhdan, his work deals primarily with 'the chronology of biblical events and genealogy of biblical personages'.[142] As Kazhdan also notes, Hippolytos devotes considerable attention to the Virgin Mary in the surviving fragments of his *Chronicle*. In addition to calculating how many years she lived, the chronicler discusses her stepsons (children of her betrothed husband Joseph by a previous marriage) and her relationship with the Evangelist John (who was also called her 'son'; cf. Jn 19: 26–27).[143] Epiphanios the Monk follows Hippolytos of Thebes in his account of the Virgin Mary's genealogy, especially with regard to her mother Anna, and in his list of Joseph's sons and daughters.[144] Both authors share a literal approach to Mary's legendary life, which perhaps reflects general trends in chronography after the end of the sixth century.[145]

More liturgical, or theological, sources for Epiphanios's *Life* include (ps-) Dionysios the Areopagite's *Divine Names*, which contains a description of the Virgin Mary's dormition, and the homilies by Andrew of Crete on the same subject.[146] None of these works is dated later than the eighth century, which supports the view that Epiphanios was active at the beginning of the ninth. His explicit citation of these various sources has led Mimouni to call the *LVM* a 'compilation' rather than an

---

140 Epiphanios the Monk, *LVM*, ed. Dressel 1843, 39–40; PG 120, 212C; see Chap. 1, 28. Epiphanios refers here to Hippolytos of Thebes, *Chronicle* III, ed. Diekamp 1898, 4, 12, 16, 19; Andrew of Crete, *Homily II on the Dormition*, PG 97, 1060B (according to Daley 1998, 135, n. 1, this is the second homily in the series, not the first, as published by J.-P. Migne in PG); see Chap. 1, nn. 162–63.

141 Epiphanios the Monk, *LVM*, ed. Dressel 1843, 43–44; PG 120, 216A–B; see Chap. 1, 30.

142 Kazhdan 1999, 20; however, note the absence of this chronographer from the *ODB*, *DHGE*, *DS*, and other dictionaries that deal with the Byzantine period.

143 Kazhdan 1999, 147–48.

144 Epiphanios the Monk, *LVM*, ed. Dressel 1843, 16; PG 120, 189C; see Chap. 1, n. 21.

145 Scott 1990, esp. 38–41 (however, there is no mention of Hippolytos of Thebes in this chapter).

146 (ps-) Dionysios the Areopagite, *The Divine Names* III.2, ed. Suchla 1990, 141; trans. Luibheid 1987, 70; Andrew of Crete, *Homilies I–III on the Dormition of the Virgin*, PG 97, 1045–1109, trans. Daley 1990, 103–52.

original composition.¹⁴⁷ Nevertheless, this method of redaction, which based itself on a variety of earlier works and which did not avoid direct copying in some instances, was standard among hagiographers during the Byzantine period.¹⁴⁸ Such works gained authority and influence by openly demonstrating their reliance on earlier literary sources – whether these were canonical, apocryphal, or patristic in nature.

The dissemination and reception of the *LVM*

Epiphanios the Monk's *LVM* survives in at least forty manuscripts, according to the *Pinakes* database held by the Institut de Recherche et d'Histoire des Textes in Paris.¹⁴⁹ The earliest manuscripts are dated to the eleventh century; these are mostly collections of homilies and saints' *Lives* that are arranged around the liturgical year, according to the categories (such as 'panegyrikon' or 'menologion') which Albert Ehrhard defined in his monumental study of Greek liturgical manuscripts.¹⁵⁰ The *LVM* is assigned as a reading for the feasts either of the Nativity of the Virgin (8 September) or of her Dormition (15 August).¹⁵¹ It is thus likely that the text was read out annually in churches and monasteries, probably during the morning office of *Orthros*, although it might also have been used for refectory or private reading.¹⁵² Epiphanios's *LVM* thus enjoyed a wider dissemination than did the late tenth-century *Life of the Virgin* by John Geometres, which is transmitted only in four manuscripts.¹⁵³ The *Life* by Symeon the Metaphrast proved even more popular than that of Epiphanios, taking the place of the latter in numerous metaphrastic *menologia* and

---

147 Mimouni 2011, 89.
148 Hinterberger 2014b, 40; Høgel 2014.
149 https://pinakes.irht.cnrs.fr/ (consulted 17 June 2024) lists forty-one manuscripts. However, the text contained in Cod. Vat. gr. 824, ff. 105ᵛ–128 (11ᵗʰ c.) is the *LAA*, not the *LVM* (as indicated in *Pinakes*). This brings the number of surviving manuscripts down to forty.
150 Ehrhard 1936–52.
151 See, for example, ibid., vol. 2, 75, n. 5, 336 (Paris. Gr. 1521, 12ᵗʰ c.); vol. 3, 776–77, n. 1 (Paris. Gr. 1538, 10ᵗʰ c.).
152 On the reading of homilies and saints' lives during the morning office (*Orthros*), see Cunningham 2011a; on the reading of Euthymios the Athonite's *Georgian Life of the Virgin* in Georgian monasteries, see Shoemaker 2012, 2–3, 161–64.
153 Wenger 1955, 186–89; Constas 2019, 326–31.

other compilations.[154] We may thus conclude that the three Greek *Lives of the Virgin Mary*, which were composed between the early ninth and late tenth centuries, became liturgical readings that appealed to somewhat different audiences. Whereas the *Lives* by Epiphanios and Symeon the Metaphrast were widely disseminated in liturgical collections, with the former perhaps being appreciated especially in monastic settings, the *Life of the Virgin Mary* by John Geometres circulated less widely, perhaps being used especially in private, devotional settings.[155]

In the twelfth century, Paschal the Roman, a priest and scholar who spent time at the court of Manual I Komnenos, translated the *LVM* by Epiphanios the Monk into Latin.[156] This caused the narrative to circulate in the West where it contributed to a developing cult of Marian devotion and festal celebration. In addition to Paschal's translation, at least two Latin epitomes of the *Life* were composed.[157] One of the Latin versions of Epiphanios's *Life* must have influenced Jacob of Voragine's *Golden Legend*, a compendium of hagiography and doctrinal instruction that was compiled in the 1260s from a variety of sources. In Chapter 54, on 'The Resurrection of the Lord', Jacob lists the separate apparitions of the risen Jesus Christ to Mary Magdalen, the myrrh-bearing women, and various disciples, in accordance with the different Gospel accounts. However, he then states that three other apparitions occurred, which are not mentioned in scripture. The third of these (following one to James of Alpheus and one to Joseph of Arimathea) was to the Virgin Mary:

> The third apparition was to the Virgin Mary and is believed to have taken place before all the others, although the Evangelists say nothing about it. The church at Rome seems to approve this belief, since it celebrates a station at the church

---

154 The Pinakes database lists ninety-seven manuscripts for this text: https://pinakes.irht.cnrs.fr/ (consulted 17 June 2024). For their placement in menologia and panegyrika, see Ehrhard 1936–52, passim. For a recent study of this text and its relationship with John Geometres' *Life of the Virgin*, see Simelidis 2023.

155 On the probable context in which John Geometres' *Life of the Virgin* was delivered, see Magdalino 2018; Simelidis 2020, 133–4.

156 Paschal Romanus, *Historia beate virginis Mariae*; ed. Franceschini 1938 (from one manuscript). According to S. Mimouni, this translation survives in four Latin manuscripts, which date from the twelfth to the fourteenth centuries; for details, see Mimouni 2011, 93, n. 66. The Italian database, *Mirabile*, provides a list of Paschal's other works, along with the manuscripts in which they appear; see http://mirabileweb.it/.

157 These texts are transmitted in three manuscripts and remain unedited; see Mimouni 2011, 93, nn. 71–72.

of Saint Mary on Easter Sunday. Indeed, if this is not to be believed, on the ground that no Evangelist testifies to it, we would have to conclude that Jesus never appeared to Mary after his resurrection because no gospel tells us where or when this happened. But perish the thought that such a son would fail to honour such a mother by being so negligent![158]

This passage, which explicitly departs from the canonical Gospels, may have been directly inspired by a Latin version of Epiphanios's *LVM* with its unique account of Christ's apparition to Mary in the upper room at Sion immediately after the resurrection. The ninth-century *Life* thus circulated more widely perhaps than it deserved, considering its unpretentious and occasionally imaginative rendition of the Marian legend. Nevertheless, it is also noteworthy that Epiphanios's version of the story does not seem to have influenced most middle and late Byzantine iconographical cycles of the infancy and later life of the Virgin.[159] These continued to reflect a more traditional narrative that was woven together from both the *Protevangelion of James* and the canonical Gospels. Such conservatism on the part of artists and their patrons contrasts with the creative liberties that hagiographers, including not only Epiphanios the Monk, but also John Geometres and Euthymios the Athonite, took with the literary building blocks of Mary's story.

Texts and variant readings

As stated above, at least forty manuscripts contain versions of Epiphanios the Monk's *LVM*. Two separate editions of the text have been produced so far, which are based on different manuscripts.[160] G.L. Mingarelli produced his edition of the *LVM* in 1783, employing a manuscript in the Naniana collection that was later transferred to the Marciana Library in Venice. According to his description of the manuscript,[161] this was probably Cod.

---

[158] Jacob of Voragine, *The Golden Legend* 54, trans. Ryan 2012, 221. The scene is also described by various other Latin authors, beginning in the thirteenth century, and it became a common image in Western medieval and Renaissance art; for examples and illustrations, see Breckenridge 1957. It did not proliferate in Byzantine monumental art, as far as I am aware, but it does appear in some ninth-century Byzantine psalters; see Chap. 1, n. 151.

[159] Lafontaine-Dosogne 1964; Lafontaine-Dosogne 1975.

[160] Epiphanios the Monk, *LVM*, ed. Mingarelli with Amaduzzi and Bianconi 1783, repr. PG 120, 185–216; ed. Dressel 1843, 13–44.

[161] PG 120, 184B–C.

Marc. gr. II. 42 (coll. 1123), ff. 237–250, which is dated to the thirteenth or fourteenth century (hereafter N).[162] Sixty years later, in 1843, Albert Dressel prepared another edition of the *LVM* using two manuscripts, Cod. Vat. gr. 442, ff. 330–349 (11th c.) (hereafter V1) and Cod. Vat. gr. 634, ff. 162v–173v (13th–14th c.) (V2).[163] I refer to the two editions in the translation and commentary that follow in Chapter One as 'M' and 'D'. It is immediately noticeable, on comparing the two editions, that their texts differ in separate sections of the *LVM*. These variations are presented for comparative purposes in Appendix A. For the sake of the present translation and commentary (since I lack the resources to produce a critical edition of the text), I have decided to use Dressel's edition while noting major divergences in that of Mingarelli in the commentary. I also examined a selection of tenth- to twelfth-century manuscripts in order to determine which version of the text circulated more widely. It is impossible at this stage to decide which of the two versions of the *LVM* can be attributed to Epiphanios the Monk; this must await a systematic study of the manuscript tradition and ultimately a critical edition of the *LVM*. It should be emphasised here, however, that both versions are important since they reflect the changing preoccupations and literary purposes of the scribes who transmitted the text to posterity.

The main differences between M and D lie in their treatment of eleven passages that occur towards the middle or end of the *LVM*. The first of these sections, which recounts the arrival of the three Magi from Persia at the time of Christ's birth in Bethlehem, describes the position of the star that led the travellers on their way.[164] Whereas D provides a longer description of the star (which 'appeared to be close to the earth and unusual compared with those that manifest themselves normally or under some particular circumstance'), M abbreviates this passage, stating merely that the star was 'near the ground'. A similar tendency to abridge longer passages in D appears in the corresponding sections of M. In a description of Herod's murder of the high priest Zacharias, for example, D provides a paragraph of explanation (attributing Herod's anger to the fact that Zacharias had allowed the Virgin Mary to enter the Holy of Holies in the Jewish Temple), whereas M

---

162 For a description of the manuscript, which contains homilies and *Lives* of saints, see Mioni 1967, series VI, vol. 1, pt. 1, 141–44.
163 Epiphanios the Monk, *LVM*, ed. Dressel 1843, x.
164 See Appendix A (a), which corresponds to *LVM*, ed. Dressel 1843, 25. 2–12; ed. Mingarelli, PG 120, 201B.

simply states, 'And the soldiers killed Zacharias while he was performing the liturgy within the sanctuary.'[165] The lengthy description of Christ's appearance, which occurs somewhat later in both texts, is also elaborate in D and shorter in M.[166] It is possible to conclude on the basis of these examples, as well as in other instances of variation within both texts, that D offers a longer and more literary version of the same narrative. It could be argued that this must be the authentic text, as conceived and written by Epiphanios the Monk, which was later abridged by a redactor or scribe who found the text too wordy. However, an alternative view might be that the ninth-century monk's original text received literary elaboration from a later scribe at some point before the eleventh century.[167] It is impossible to reach a definitive conclusion on this question, as I suggested above, until a systematic study of the manuscript tradition has been undertaken.

It is nevertheless worth presenting here some preliminary findings on the basis of a few early manuscripts which I have been able to examine. I have looked at six manuscripts, which are as follows:

- Jerusalem, Greek Patriarchal Library, Hag. Sab. gr. 60, ff. 18–31^v (12th c.) = J

- Oxford, Bodleian Library, Auct. E.5.12 (Misc. 77), ff. 235–250 (12th c.) = O

- Paris, Bibliothèque nationale, Coislin. gr. 296, ff. 1^r–1^v, 13^v–22^v, 23–25^v (12th c.) = C

- Bibliothèque nationale, Paris. gr. 1521, ff. 79^v–91^v (12th c.) = P2

- Bibliothèque nationale, Paris. gr. 1538, ff. 2–7 (fragment) (10th c.) = P3

- Rome, Vat. gr. 442, ff. 330–349 (11th c.) = V1[168]

With one exception, namely J, the manuscripts that are listed above all transmit a version of the *LVM* that is closer to M than to D. This suggests

---

165 Appendix A (b), which corresponds to *LVM*, ed. Dressel 1843, 26. 6–29; ed. Mingarelli, PG 120, 201C–D.

166 Appendix A (c), corresponding to *LVM*, ed. Dressel 1843, 29. 3–24; ed. Mingarelli, PG 120, 204C.

167 On metaphrastic practices in hagiography of the middle Byzantine period, see Høgel 2002; Flusin 2011; Høgel 2014.

168 This is one of the manuscripts which Dressel used for his edition of the *LVM* (1843).

that the shorter version of the text, as edited by Mingarelli from his Venetian manuscript (N), was in circulation at least as early as the tenth century. P3, which is the earliest witness that I have examined, contains the abridged sections of the text that appear in M – at least in those sections of this fragmentary manuscript that survive.[169] V1, however, on which Dressel based his edited text, represents a fairly early witness to the longer version of the *LVM*. It is also worth noting that, apart from the major divergences of the two versions of the text that appear in M and D, some manuscripts display even greater variation in their readings. O, for example, contains numerous readings of its own throughout the text, even while adhering for the most part to the version of M.[170] It is joined in some of these readings by P3, but such correspondence is by no means consistent. After collating the numerous alternative readings in these manuscripts, I am uncertain how a future edition of the *LVM* might present this rich tradition. Individual scribes adopt a free and creative approach to the text which allows them to change its style and content in numerous instances. To choose just one version of the text for publication would diminish readers' perception of its evolution during subsequent centuries.

The *Life and Acts of Andrew* (*LAA*): content and message

This hagiographical work differs in many ways from Epiphanios the Monk's *LVM*. The first half of the text describes the apostle Andrew's mission to the northern Black Sea coast of Asia Minor, as well as his travels in the Caucasus, southern Russia, and the Crimea, south-western parts of Asia Minor, and the Peloponnese. Epiphanios employs a combination of literary, material, and oral evidence in narrating Andrew's travels; he also juxtaposes his own tour of the area, in the company of another monk named James,[171] with his historical account. The second half of the *LAA* turns to the arrival of the apostle in the Peloponnese (now in modern Greece) and his arrest and martyrdom by the local ruler ('anthypatos' or 'proconsul') Aigeates in Patrai (or Patras) on the western coast. This section, as mentioned above,

---

169 The text begins at PG 120, 204D (ὅτι ὁ Χριστός ἐστιν...) and continues to the end.
170 See, for example, ff. 241ʳ–242; see Appendix A (b); f. 243, Appendix A (c), etc.
171 Epiphanios the Monk, *LAA*, ed. Vinogradov 2005, 239. 24–240. 7; see Chap. 2, 9. On Epiphanios's travels with the monk James, see ibid., 238. 3–4, Chap. 1, 6: Ἐν αὐτῇ δὲ γενόμενοι, ἐγώ τε καί, Ἐπιφάνιος μοναχὸς καὶ πρεσβύτερος, καὶ Ἰάκωβος μοναχὸς...

has a novelistic aspect: it focuses especially on Aigeates' wife, Maximilla, who is converted to Christianity and abandons her husband in order to lead an ascetic life.[172] The final section of the *LAA* is based on an earlier, probably second- or third-century, hagiographical work, the *Acta Andreae* (*AA*), which no longer survives in its entirety.[173] An analysis of this literary relationship appears below, but for now it is worth focusing on Epiphanios the Monk's composition as a literary work in its own right. As in the case of his *LVM*, I will highlight certain aspects of the narrative before turning to an analysis of its didactic purpose and theological message.

First, however, it is important to note that the *LAA* survives in two versions that differ in more significant ways than those which we have observed in the manuscript tradition for the *LVM*.[174] I accept Andrey Vinogradov's conclusion that both versions of the *LAA* were produced by Epiphanios the Monk himself. The first version (*BHG* 94d, 95b, and 95d) omits any form of prologue and begins after the visit of the apostles Andrew and Matthias to the Black Sea city of Sinope – perhaps because the author intended the story as a sequel to the earlier *AAMt*.[175] This account also includes longer versions of a few of the sermons that Andrew is said to have delivered at various stages during his missionary travels. The second version of the *LAA* (*BHG* 102) provides a prologue in which Epiphanios cites his literary and historical sources for the composition. The above-mentioned sermons are abbreviated in four cases.[176] Vinogradov argues that Epiphanios edited his own work within a twenty-year period after producing his first edition of the *Life* before or soon after 820 (that is, between 820 and 843). The Russian scholar also cites more minor details which Epiphanios introduced into the text, including references to clerics of the Nicene church of St Sophia who informed him of the customs of the people who currently lived in that city.[177] For the purposes of the present discussion, as well as of the translation that follows, I have decided to use

---

172 On the novelistic aspect not only of Epiphanios the Monk's *LAA*, but also of its third-century prototype, the *AA*, see Pervo 1987, esp. 122–31; Kazhdan 1999, 307; Bovon 2003, 170.
173 *AA*, ed. Prieur 1989; ed. MacDonald 1990.
174 See below, n. 303.
175 Vinogradov 2005, 30. 46–47; cf. Kahl 1989, 63–67.
176 For the longer versions of these four sermons (which appear in Version A of the *LAA*), see Appendix B (a–d).
177 Vinogradov 2005, 43. The references occur in Chapter 27 of the *LAA*.

the second version of the text (including its prologue) on the grounds that it represents Epiphanios's considered and final redaction.[178]

As stated above, Epiphanios begins his second version of the *LAA* by citing, as he did for the *LVM*, some of the literary sources that he has employed, and by providing background on the 'first-called' apostle, Andrew.[179] He then summarises briefly what is known about the apostle Andrew according to the canonical Gospels. Andrew, along with his brother Simon (later renamed Peter), was born of humble parents and became a fisherman on the west side of the Sea of Tiberias (or Galilee). It was here that he met first John the Baptist and later Jesus Christ, becoming a disciple of both holy personages in turn.[180] Epiphanios goes on to describe how, after Christ ascended into heaven (Acts 1: 9) and Pentecost took place (Acts 2: 1–4), Andrew, his brother Peter, Matthias, and some other disciples travelled to Asia Minor. Following visits to the cities of Tyana and Ankyra, they reached Sinope, on the southern coast of the Black Sea, where Matthias was arrested, and, following his miraculous escape with the help of Andrew, most of the town was converted to Christianity.[181]

Further travels follow around the coasts of the Black Sea, the Bosphoros, and the Sea of Marmara. It is interesting to note, as we saw above, that Epiphanios intersperses his account of the apostle Andrew's missionary journeys with his own pilgrimage in search of oral memories and relics of saints.[182] The hagiographer's descriptions of cities and shrines in what is now northern Turkey, Georgia, and Russia are detailed enough for the modern scholar, Cyril Mango, to have retraced his footsteps and attempted to reconstruct what Epiphanios saw on his journey. Somewhat confusingly, the ninth-century hagiographer divides Andrew's tours into three parts, which do not provide a coherent geographical sequence. Vinogradov suggests that these three trips imitate the four carried out by the apostle Paul, according to the canonical Acts of the Apostles.[183] The seemingly disorganised trajectory also reflects the fact that Andrew

---

178 Vinogradov largely follows this version of the text in his Russian translation; see Vinogradov 2005, 113–52. For further discussion of the two versions of the *LAA*, see below, 70–73.
179 Epiphanios the Monk, *LAA*, Vinogradov 2005, 236.6–18; see Chap. 2, 1.
180 Ibid., ed. Vinogradov 2005, 236.19–237.13; see Chap. 2, 2–3.
181 Ibid., ed. Vinogradov 2005, 237.14–239.19; see Chap. 2, 4–8.
182 See especially ibid., ed. Vinogradov 2005, 238.3–12, 239. 24–240.25; see Chap. 2, 6, 9.
183 Mango 2002. This study was preceded by that of Kahl 1989, which Mango was not able to access. See also Vinogradov 2005, 45.

and his companions returned to Jerusalem for Easter each year, before resuming another stage of their mission in Asia Minor or elsewhere. Mango summarises the three sequences as follows:

> The first tour starts, via Antioch and Tyana, at Sinope, but then backtracks to Nicaea and thence proceeds to Trebizond and Iberia. The second takes us from Laodikeia in Phrygia Pacatiana to Nicaea once again, along the Black Sea coast to Trebizond, then (on the return journey to Jerusalem?) inland to Neocaesarea and Samosata (spelt Amousaton and absurdly described as being by the sea). The third is from Alania to Cherson and thence by ship to Byzantium. In each case the order of localities is reasonably correct, except (in tour 1) for the sequence Amastris – Dorapin (unidentified) – Karousia – Sinope, where Karousia or Karousa should have come after Sinope, and (in tour 2) for the puzzling inclusion of 'Odyssoupolis in Mysia', presumably Odessopolis in Moesia (Varna between Laodikeia and Nicaea).[184]

Although this division of Andrew's itinerary into separate phases, punctuated by regular visits to Jerusalem, is convincing, there remain a few puzzling aspects, according to Mango. In fact these reflect the latter's confusion between Epiphanios the Monk's own travels and the legendary route of Andrew. The hagiographer does not suggest that Andrew visited Dorapin or Karousia; those cities form part of his own pilgrimage (in the company of the monk James) in search of relics.[185] Thus the misalignment of these destinations with Andrew's route does not present a problem. Reconstruction of the locations has become even easier since Mango worked on this text, thanks to the ongoing geographical project of the Austrian Academy of Sciences in Vienna, the *Tabula Imperii Byzantini* (*TIB*).[186] Nevertheless, Epiphanios's descriptions of towns and cities on Andrew's route are sometimes 'fantastic' (to use Mango's expression), including cannibals, demons, and even dragons. He does mention features such as lakes and rocks, however, which can sometimes still be spotted in modern locations.

---

184 Mango 2002, 256. For a more detailed outline of Andrew's travels, see Table 1, below. It is worth noting here that Mango used Dressel's 1843 edition of the *LAA*, which differs slightly in its account of Andrew's travels from the text that is edited in Vinogradov 2005.

185 Epiphanios the Monk, *LAA*, ed. Vinogradov 240. 12–13; see Chap. 2, 9.

186 The *Tabula Imperii Byzantini* (*TIB*) is a joint project of the research group 'Historical Geography', based at the Division of Byzantine Research at the Austrian Academy of Sciences. Online resources may be found at https://tib.oeaw.ac.at/index.php?seite=digtib. Thirteen volumes on various Byzantine provinces have so far been published; five more are in preparation.

What is perhaps most interesting about this narrative is the way in which the hagiographer weaves together his own journey with that of his first-century subject.[187] The two topics are sometimes connected in a confusing or even disjointed way, which may reflect either the author's carelessness, lacunae, or scribal interpolations that are reflected in the published text. For example, after relating the story of Andrew's and Matthias's stay in Sinope, Epiphanios states that the apostles departed for the 'East' where he taught the Gospel to 'Scythians, the Sogdians, and the Gorsinoi' – in other words, to various tribes in the Caucasus who could be called by both ancient and contemporary names.[188] A sudden change of subject follows, as the hagiographer describes how he himself and his companion James '[fled] from communion with the icon-fighters' and travelled through various cities in the Caucasus and Asia Minor in search of holy relics.[189] Epiphanios the Monk's personal experience of the places and peoples that Andrew encountered, especially when he describes material objects that were associated with these, may be intended to add credence to his account of the apostle's travels and missionary activities.

The final section of the *LAA*, which is set in Patras, focuses exclusively on Andrew and the people that he encountered in that city.[190] Much of this section is based on the earlier *AA*, as we shall see later;[191] however, it contains some unique elements that seem to reflect the literary preoccupations of Epiphanios. For example, the ninth-century hagiographer offers an oblique moral commentary on the stories of Aigeates, the proconsul, and his wife Maximilla. When Andrew first encounters them, Aigeates is about to kill himself because of Maximilla's illness and the threat of her imminent death. Before the apostle attempts to heal her, he enjoins Aigeates to put his knife away and to pray to God for mercy.[192] Later, after Maximilla leaves her husband in order to adopt a celibate way of life, Aigeates carries out his suicide, throwing himself from a 'high place' (ἀπὸ ὕψους) one night.[193] Epiphanios thus portrays the moral weakness of the

---

187 On the interaction between hagiographers and their narratives, see Hinterberger 2014a.
188 Epiphanios the Monk, *LAA*, ed. Vinogradov 2005, 239. 20–22; see Chap. 2, 9.
189 Ibid., ed. Vinogradov 2005, 239. 24–240. 25; see Chap. 2, 9.
190 Ibid., ed. Vinogradov 2005, 258.23–264.12; see Chap. 2, 36–44.
191 *AA*; ed. Prieur 1989; ed. MacDonald 1990; see below, 45–49.
192 Epiphanios the Monk, *LAA*, ed. Vinogradov 2005, 259. 9–18; see Chap. 2, 37.
193 Ibid., ed. Vinogradov 2005, 263. 25–26; see Chap. 2, 44. The scene is elaborated further in the version contained in the manuscript that Dressel used in his 1843 edition (Vat. gr. 824 [V3], f. 128): '...μανεὶς νυκτὸς ἀναστάς, σιγῆς βαθείας οὔσης, διαλαθὼν πάντας, ῥίπτει

proconsul simply by letting the narrative unfold. It is clear according to this train of events that the proconsul is not only too weak to live without his wife, but also too proud to ask for God's mercy. He is not missed by his family or friends because he has failed, unlike them, to accept Andrew's Christian message.[194]

In general terms, the hagiographer's didactic purpose is similar to that which he displays in the *LVM*. This is a text that is intended to inspire contemporary Christians, both lay and monastic (but perhaps especially monastic), to understand their Christian vocation as a radical divestment of material and worldly responsibilities. Andrew and his disciples are described in one passage of the *LAA* as follows: '...they possessed only one garment and went barefoot in sandals, being fed on bread and water once a day, and they were equipped with pallets.'[195] Epiphanios implies here and elsewhere that the Jews and Greeks who encountered the apostles were impressed by their austerity to the extent that they listened to their sermons and converted to Christianity. Even more important, however, is the promotion of celibacy as the ideal way of life for followers of Jesus Christ. Emphasis on this aspect of asceticism, even for married converts such as Maximilla, featured in the original third-century *AA*, as we shall see later.[196] Indeed, this is one aspect of the latter text which caused it to circulate especially among Encratite and Manichaean communities during the Late Antique centuries and which provoked condemnation by Greek and Latin church leaders.[197] It is likely that the ninth-century monk, Epiphanios, was attracted to this aspect of Andrew's legend and chose to emphasise it for the sake of his largely monastic audience. We see the same tendency in his *LVM*, for example, in his retelling of the story of the Marriage of Cana (Jn 2: 1–11) in which he has the bridegroom leave his new wife in order to become a celibate disciple of Christ.[198] For Epiphanios, the ideal Christian

---

ἑαυτὸν ἀπὸ ὕψους μεγάλου τοῦ ἑαυτοῦ πραιτωρίου· ('...he got up in a frenzy one night when there was a deep silence and, escaping the notice of everyone, threw himself off his own praetorium from a great height'). Ed. Dressel 1843, 81. 15–18. Alexander Kazhdan comments on the literary power of this scene; Kazhdan 1999, 308. It should be noted, however, that this manuscript copies its epilogue verbatim from the text of the anonymous *Narratio* 36, ed. Vinogradov 2005, 196. 7–10; for discussion, see ibid., 79.

194 Epiphanios the Monk, *LAA*, ed. Vinogradov 2005, 263.25–264.12; see Chap. 2, 44.
195 Epiphanios the Monk, *LAA*, ed. Vinogradov 2005, 243. 1–2; see Chap. 2, 13.
196 *AA*, ed. Prieur 1989; ed. MacDonald 1990; for discussion, see below, 67–68.
197 *AA*, ed. Prieur 1989; *Actes*, trans. Prieur 1995, Introduction, 26; Prieur 1992, 101–3.
198 Epiphanios the Monk, *LVM*, ed. Dressel 1843, 31–32; PG 120, 205C; see Chap. 1, 20.

life, as carried out by the Virgin Mary and the apostle Andrew, consists in ascetic practices such as kneeling, all-night vigils, constant prayer, and celibacy. This is a form of spiritual and physical endeavour which, by the ninth century, could be achieved best in monastic settings, but which could also (at least in moderation) represent a goal for laypeople too.

Another possible literary goal for Epiphanios, which has been explored especially by Francis Dvornik, is the promotion of a legend concerning the apostolic foundation of Constantinople.[199] It is worth remembering here that the relics of the apostle Andrew, along with those of Luke and Timothy, had been translated to the church of the Holy Apostles in Constantinople during either the reign of Constantine I (324–37 CE) or that of his son, Constantios (337–61).[200] As Dvornik demonstrates, however, it is difficult to find explicit mention of these relics in texts that belong to the centuries that followed their deposition in the imperial city. John Chrysostom, for example, expresses doubt concerning the authenticity of Andrew's relics when he writes that 'the tombs of Peter, Paul, John and Thomas are known; [the tombs] of the others who are so many have never become known'.[201] Even more important, for our purpose, is the fact that neither Chrysostom nor any other Constantinopolitan preachers or historians made any attempt to connect Andrew's relics with a legend concerning the apostolic foundation of the imperial city. Other surviving Greek sources that provide this story are anonymous and difficult to date: they include an account of the apostle's travels known as a *Narratio* (or *Martyrion*) and two catalogues, or lists, of the apostles which are falsely attributed to Epiphanios of Cyprus and a shadowy figure known as Dorotheos of Tyre.[202]

This detail is picked up in the tenth-century *Lives of the Virgin* by John Geometres and Euthymios the Athonite, with the further addition that the wife becomes one of Mary's disciples; see Cunningham 2019b, 316.

199 Dvornik 1958, esp. 225–26. See now also Lequeux 2019 on this legend.

200 Dvornik 1958, 138–48. Dvornik's thesis that the relics of the apostles were placed in the church during the reign of Constantios (337–61) is contested in S.F. Johnson 2020, 95–97. The latter argues, on the basis of Eusebios of Caesarea's statement that Constantine hoped to share in the honour that belonged to the relics of the apostles, that they must have been in place in the Apostoleion from at least as early as 337; see Eusebios of Caesarea, *Life of Constantine* IV. 60, ed. Winkelmann 1991, 144–45; trans. Cameron and Hall 1999, 176–77.

201 John Chrysostom, *Homily on Hebrews* 26, ed. Field 1862, 291B; quoted in Dvornik 1958, 146.

202 Anon., *Narratio* 8, ed. Vinogradov 2005, 182. 11–21; (ps-) Epiphanios of Cyprus, *Index apostolorum* 20, ed. Schermann 1907, 120; (ps-) Dorotheos of Tyre, *Index apostolorum*, ed. Schermann 1907, 137, 146–47.

These texts describe how Andrew, after carrying out his missionary travels in Asia Minor and the Caucasus, returned to Thrace and, in a suburb of the city called Argyropolis, ordained Stachys as the first bishop of Byzantion.[203] We shall return later to the relationship of these sources with Epiphanios's *LAA*; for now, it is simply worth noting that, by including this episode, the ninth-century hagiographer draws attention to the fact that Andrew, the first-century apostle, was responsible for founding the episcopal see of Constantinople. The story was of course legendary, as the lack of references noted by Dvornik has shown; however, its appearance in our text, as well as in the earlier sources, reveals that it was beginning to be regarded as important between about the sixth and ninth centuries. From this period onward, the patriarchate of Constantinople began to claim its apostolic legitimacy in relation to that of Rome – and presumably to value its stewardship of the relics of St Andrew more highly. In short, Epiphanios the Monk's composition of the *LAA* may not only reflect an important stage in the development of the legend concerning the apostolic foundation of Constantinople, but may also have contributed to its dissemination.[204]

The inclusion of sermons, some of which are lengthy, in the *LAA* reflects both the influence of the *AA* and the didactic purpose of Epiphanios the Monk.[205] The apostle delivers the homilies to communities that he meets during his travels, both before and after they have been converted to Christianity. The homilies usually express basic tenets of the faith, such as the existence of one all-powerful God whose Son, Jesus Christ, became incarnate from the Virgin Mary and the Holy Spirit, suffered on the Cross, was buried, and rose again after three days. Andrew also stresses the importance of baptism whereby human beings, including Jews, Greeks, and other peoples, are reborn into a new life. They must thereafter worship the one Trinitarian God and be guided by the commandments of Moses in the Old Testament and those of Jesus in the New. In addition to such standard teaching, however, which Epiphanios describes as the 'word' or 'message' (*logos*) of Christ, it is worth noting several interesting features

---

203 Dvornik 1958, 171–78.
204 Ibid., 175–76, 179–80, 225–27.
205 Epiphanios the Monk, *LAA*, ed. Vinogradov 2005, 238. 29–239.18, , 241. 7–242. 2, 242. 8–24, 243. 9–244. 18, 247. 13–22, 249. 19–252. 30, 253. 1–254. 24; see Chaps. 2, 8, 11, 12, 14, 20, 24, 25. Prieur devotes a section of his Introduction to the literary role of the apostle's sermons in the original *AA*; see ibid., ed. Prieur 1989, 166–285. There are strong echoes in the content and style of Andrew's preaching from apostolic texts such as Clement of Rome's first letter to the Corinthians; see ibid., trans. Holmes 2007.

that recur in Andrew's sermons. First, he enjoins his audiences repeatedly to reject the pagan gods and idols, which he calls 'demons', that they have been worshipping. This message reveals the hagiographer's awareness that the first-century apostle worked within a largely pagan world – although he also suggests that Judaism was widespread in Asia Minor and the Caucasus. Second, we may note Andrew's frequent references to the doctrine that one God created all things out of nothing. He reminds his audiences of the harmony of creation, which reflects the orderly method of the all-powerful and good God. There is recognition here of the disruptive power of other gods, or demons, which Christians must confront and defeat as they seek to live peacefully in this fallen world. Frequent references in the text to the forces of evil, which manifest themselves especially in demons or dragons, may reflect a dualist tendency in Epiphanios's main literary source, the lost *AA*, to which we shall return below.

Finally, it is worth remarking on the discussion of the seven sins and seven punishments of Cain, which appears in one of Andrew's sermons to the people of Nicaea.[206] This occurs in the context of a narrative beginning with Adam, who was given immortality in the Garden of Eden, but chose to disobey God. One of the consequences of the fall was the birth of a 'son of disobedience' to Adam and Eve, namely, Cain 'who bore the stamp of the devil' (cf. Gen 4: 15). It is possible that Epiphanios borrowed the idea of Cain receiving seven punishments for his seven sins either from a letter of Basil of Caesarea or from one of John Chrysostom's homilies on Genesis.[207] However, his list of sins diverges slightly from that of Chrysostom.[208] For Epiphanios, they include greed, envy, deceit, hatred, disobedience, trickery, and falsehood. It is interesting that the murder of Abel is not included among these; nevertheless, many of Cain's misdeeds played a part in that dreadful act – and all revealed the moral failings that led up to, or attempted to conceal, the crime. The seven punishments that God imposed on Cain caused him to live unhappily for the rest of his life. The purpose

---

206 Epiphanios the Monk, *LAA*, ed. Vinogradov 2005, 249. 19–252. 30; see Chap. 2, 24.

207 Basil of Caesarea, *Letter 260 to the bishop Optimos*, ed. Courtonne 1966, 107. 28–108. 37; John Chrysostom, *Homily 19 on Genesis*, PG 53, 158–66; trans. Hill 1990 (18), 21–34, esp. 32.

208 Chrysostom lists seven sins: 1) that Cain envied someone (his brother) for having grace and favour from God; 2) that he envied his *brother*; 3) that he devised a plot against him; 4) that he committed murder; 5) that it was his brother that he killed; 6) that he was the first human being to commit murder; 7) that he lied to God. Chrysostom also says that whoever kills Cain will receive a sevenfold punishment; trans. Hill 1990 (17), 31.

of Andrew's elaboration of the Genesis story in this sermon is to persuade the newly converted Christians to live righteous lives according to the commandments of Moses and Christ. The homily also provides a sweeping synthesis of Old and New Testament history, furnishing the audience with a narrative account of God's whole dispensation for human salvation.

The iconophile content of the *LAA* appears especially in the section in which Epiphanios the Monk describes his travels in search of saints and their relics.[209] We have already seen how he and his companion James reached Sinope, on the southern coast of the Black Sea, and were shown an icon of the apostle Andrew which had survived an attempt at defacement by iconoclasts during the reign of Constantine V. The elderly monastic presbyters, named Theophanes and Symeon, who showed the two Constantinopolitan monks this object also produced the seats or 'thrones' (τὰς καθέδρας), as well as the apostles' imprints (τὰς ἀνακλίσεις) on the stone (seats).[210] These material reminders of the apostles Andrew and Matthias, including especially the icon, testify to Epiphanios's reverence for physical signs of holy people in the created world. His respect for early martyrs and their relics is further revealed in the following passages of the *LAA*, in which he describes his visits to shrines in Nicaea, Nikomedia, and other cities.[211] Scholars continue to debate the extent to which iconoclasts, including especially the emperor Constantine V, discouraged the veneration of saints and their relics;[212] whatever their views may have been, our ninth-century hagiographer demonstrates his adherence to the sanctity of both relics and icons especially in the sections of his text that deal with his own travels in Asia Minor.

The *LAA* thus provides an eyewitness account of the religious landscape of late eighth- and early ninth-century Byzantium, including especially in its north-eastern provinces and the Bithynian hinterland of Constantinople. According to Mango, Epiphanios the Monk's account of various cities and shrines around the Black Sea and Sea of Marmara should be taken seriously: his text provides a rare witness to such outlying regions.[213] Further, the

---

209 Epiphanios the Monk, *LAA*, ed. Vinogradov 2005, 239. 24–240. 25; see Chap. 2, 9.
210 Ibid., ed. Vinogradov 2005, 238. 3–12; see Chap. 2, 6.
211 See above, n. 210.
212 See Gero 1973; Gero 1977; Barber 2002; Brubaker and Haldon 2011; Elsner 2012; Dell'Acqua 2020, 185–88; Humphries 2021.
213 Mango 2002, 256; cf. Kahl 1989.

monastic author offers his own, iconophile, perspective concerning the veneration of icons and relics during this period. He testifies to the attempted destruction of a marble icon of St Andrew by iconoclasts of a previous generation but suggests that the relics of various martyrs remained accessible in various cities. Epiphanios's hagiographical production also deserves attention from literary and theological perspectives. The *LAA* contains descriptive sections that evoke the landscape and people whom the apostle (or more likely, his hagiographer) encountered. It contains dramatic narrative, dialogue, and homilies that help to bring Andrew to life for Epiphanios's readers or audiences. The text may also reflect an ecclesiological move, which gathered pace especially in the eighth and ninth centuries, to provide Constantinople with an apostolic foundation.[214] As we attempt to disentangle the many strands that are woven together in this narrative, it is important to evaluate the various sources that Epiphanios employed in constructing his version of Andrew's story. Although he names some of these, there are others, such as the probably third-century *AA*,[215] which represent an important basis for his narrative but which he does not explicitly cite.

The sources of the *LAA*

As in the case of the *LVM*, Epiphanios the Monk cites in his prologue some of the literary sources that he used in order to compose the *LAA*.[216] He mentions first Clement of Rome and Evagrios of Sicily.[217] It is likely that Epiphanios the Monk refers not only to the *First Letter to the Corinthians* that is ascribed to Clement (possibly one of the first bishops of Rome), but also to an apocryphal tradition known as the *pseudo-Clementine* texts (*Homilies* and *Recognitions*), which contained legends and teachings of the apostles and circulated widely in the early Church.[218] As for Evagrios of Sicily, Epiphanios indicates the author of the *Life* of St Pankratios of

---

214 Dvornik 1958, esp. 225–27.
215 *AA*, ed. Prieur 1989; ed. MacDonald 1990.
216 Vinogradov also discusses the sources of the *LAA* in idem 2005, 44–45.
217 Epiphanios the Monk, *LAA*, ed. Vinogradov 2005, 236. 14–15; see Chap. 2, 1.
218 For Clement of Rome, *Letter to the Corinthians*, see Holmes 2007. On the pseudo-Clementine texts, see ed. Rehm and Strecker 1992 and 1994; see also Chap. 2, n. 3.

INTRODUCTION   45

Taormina, who was probably active during the eighth century.[219] Our hagiographer is aware of the latter text and mentions the legend of Pankratios (also believed to be an early apostle) later in the *LAA*.[220] He also mentions Epiphanios of Cyprus, not realising that the *Index apostolorum* which is ascribed to the fourth-century bishop was pseudonymous, having been composed sometime between the sixth and eighth centuries.[221] Other literary influences, which Epiphanios does not name, include (as in the case of the *LVM*) Roman and Late Antique historians including Josephus and Eusebios of Caesarea, as well as, of course, the canonical Gospels and Acts of the Apostles. Epiphanios provides background information on the other apostles, as well as on important figures such as Herod and John the Baptist, with the help of these reputable sources.

The most significant source for Epiphanios the Monk, which he also fails to cite in his prologue, is undoubtedly the second- or third-century apocryphal *AA* – or a later version of that text. As mentioned earlier, this text no longer survives in its original form; modern editors have reconstructed it on the basis of later sources, which include Greek, Latin, Armenian, and Coptic versions of the text, especially for the latter half which deals with Andrew's mission and martyrdom in the Greek city of Patras.[222] Epiphanios appears to have used a version of the *AA* especially when composing the final section of his *LAA* in which Andrew reaches the city of Patras, works miracles, and is eventually crucified.[223] The first half of Epiphanios's text, which deals with the apostle's travels in Asia Minor and the Caucasus, relies primarily on (ps-) Epiphanios's *Index apostolorum* – which the ninth-century hagiographer supplemented with oral traditions that he encountered in the course of his own travels around the Black Sea and western Asia Minor.[224] Owing to the influence of the *AA* especially

---

219 (ps-) Evagrios of Sicily, *Life of St Pankratios of Taormina*, ed. Stallman-Pacitti and Burke 2018. On the probable date of the *Life*, see ibid., 11–19.
220 Epiphanios the Monk, *LAA*, ed. Vinogradov 2005, 245. 24; see Chap. 2, 17.
221 (ps-) Epiphanios of Cyprus, *Index apostolorum*, ed. Schermann 1907. On the date of this text, see Vinogradov 2005, 33.
222 For a description and analysis of these sources, see especially *AA*, ed. Prieur 1989, 1–31; *Actes*, trans. Prieur 1995, 55–64. Further studies of the literary, theological, and historical importance of the *AA* can be found in Bremmer 2000.
223 Epiphanios the Monk, *LAA*, ed. Vinogradov 2005, 258. 23–264. 12; see Chap. 2, 36–44; *AA*, ed. Prieur 1989, 18–20, 442–549; ed. MacDonald 1990, 274–441.
224 (ps-) Epiphanios of Salamis, *Index apostolorum*, ed. Schermann 1907, 108–9. On the

on the last section of the *LAA*, however, it is worth summarising past and current scholarship on this early apocryphal text.

The original *AA* belonged to a group of apocryphal narratives concerning the apostles which were composed in the second and third centuries CE and circulated widely thereafter. Although these texts share many common elements, scholars now consider that they were written by separate, mostly anonymous, authors.[225] They were intended to supplement the stories about the apostles in the canonical New Testament, especially the *Acts of the Apostles*, providing details about their separate missions throughout the inhabited world. The apocryphal *Acts* share with each other a tendency to describe miracles that the apostles worked as they were preaching the Gospel. They also describe the martyrdoms of these holy figures, some of which have a historical basis while others (such as that of Andrew) are embedded in legend. The term 'apocryphal', which means 'hidden' in Greek, reflects the fact that these texts were never officially accepted by Christian leaders even though they circulated widely in the late Roman world and were translated into many languages.[226] Suspicion of the apocryphal *Acts* was caused by their occasionally 'heretical' content: some, such as the *AA*, contained enough dualist or Encratite elements to render them unacceptable to writers including Eusebios of Caesarea, Epiphanios of Cyprus, and Philastrus of Brescia.[227] The *Gelasian Decree*, which was issued in the sixth century, also condemned many of these literary works, while approving a canon of biblical texts.[228] Nevertheless, as Averil Cameron suggests, these were the stories that people wanted to hear.[229] Building on this idea, Scott Fitzgerald Johnson states that 'this literature is "dark matter" first and foremost because it is only rarely

different versions of this text, one of which Epiphanios the Monk used for the two editions of the *LAA*, see Vinogradov 2005, 33.

225 Elliott 1993, 229–30.

226 Scholars are beginning to recognise the influence and importance of these texts, even if they were not considered 'canonical' in Church tradition. For discussion, see Shoemaker 2008b; Gregory and Tuckett 2015; S.F. Johnson 2020.

227 For general discussion, see Hartenstein 2015; Tissot 2015. For specific reference to the apostle Andrew, see *Actes*, trans. Prieur 1995, 18–23.

228 *Gelasian Decree*, ed. Dobschütz 1912, 49–52. According to the editor, this is not a Papal work, but rather a private compilation which was composed in Italy (but not Rome) in the early sixth century. Some scholars argue for an origin in Gaul; see *ODCC*, *Decretum Galesianum*, s.v., 462.

229 See Cameron's chapter, 'Stories People Want', in eadem 1991, 89–119; cf. S.F. Johnson 2020, 55.

included in literary surveys, despite the cultural and religious impact it clearly had'.[230] The wealth of copies and new redactions that were produced in subsequent centuries, in both East and West, testifies to the importance of the material and its influence on Christian hagiography, iconography, and liturgical celebration.

The *AA* has been reconstructed and published separately by two scholars, Jean-Marc Prieur and Dennis R. MacDonald.[231] According to MacDonald,[232] the two editors worked together and remained in agreement about most aspects of the text, with one exception: whereas Prieur, following Flamion, believes that there were originally two separate texts, the *Acts of Andrew and Matthias* (hereafter *AAMt*) and the *AA*,[233] MacDonald claims that the former text formed the introduction to the latter.[234] His edition of the *AA* thus begins with the narrative of the *AAMt*, which describes the visit of the apostle Matthias to a city called Myrmidonia ('city of the ants'), which was inhabited by cannibals.[235] The text then relates how Andrew was called by the Lord Jesus to travel from 'a city of Achaia' to Myrmidonia in order to rescue Matthias from imminent death. On arriving there, having travelled in a boat that was captained by Christ, Andrew released Matthias, along with other captives, from prison and proceeded to convert the cannibals and their leader to Christianity. A few parallels between this narrative and that of Epiphanios the Monk, who describes the imprisonment and rescue of Matthias in Sinope,[236] suggest that the ninth-century hagiographer was aware of a version of this text – whether or not it formed part of the original *AA*.[237] Prieur meanwhile chooses to separate the *AAMt* and the *AA* in his edition and translation, arguing that they were composed by

---

230 S.F. Johnson 2020, 55–56.
231 *AA*, ed. Prieur 1989; ed. MacDonald 1990. On the probable second- or third-century date of the *AA*, see above, n. 19.
232 *AA*, ed. MacDonald, Preface, ix.
233 *AA*, ed. Prieur 1989, 32–35; *Actes*, trans. Prieur 1995, 56; Flamion 1911, 301–9.
234 *AA*, ed. MacDonald 1990, 1–59.
235 *AA*, ed. MacDonald 1990, 70–177.
236 Epiphanios the Monk, *LAA*, ed. Vinogradov 2005, 238. 29–239. 19; see Chap. 2, 8.
237 Epiphanios the Monk assumed readers' knowledge of the *AAMt* when he wrote the first version of the *LAA*. This omits the account of Andrew's and Matthias's stay in Sinope and begins with the account of Epiphanios's own travels to eastern regions (Chap. 2, 9); Vinogradov 2005, 197. Although Epiphanios the Monk omits any mention of cannibals in his first account of the events that took place in Sinope (apart from saying that the inhabitants were called 'eaters of men'), he later describes Andrew's return to that city and the inhabitants' harsh treatment of him, which included 'biting his flesh like dogs'; see

different authors.[238] The answer to this question is not essential to our topic, although we may note again that Epiphanios was probably aware of both texts when he composed his *LAA*.

One of the most important witnesses to the lost *AA* is the long *Liber de miraculis beati Andreae apostoli* (hereafter *Epitome*) by Gregory of Tours.[239] According to MacDonald, the sixth-century author announced his discovery of a book of miracles concerning the holy apostle Andrew 'which some dub apocryphal because of its excessive verbosity'. Gregory did not read Greek, so it is likely that he found this text in a Latin translation. He undertook to rewrite 'the miracles only, disregarding whatever would breed disgust'; in other words, he produced an edited version of the text which focused on Andrew's miracles, removing sections that might be interpreted as heretical.[240] Gregory also softened the emphasis on celibacy, pacifism, and other ascetic themes which existed in the ancient *Acts*.[241] There are overarching parallels between his and Epiphanios the Monk's redactions of Andrew's story which suggest that they both used versions of the original source. However, the two texts also differ in significant ways. To some extent, such divergences reflect the separate literary intentions of each redactor. Whereas Gregory focuses especially on miracles, some of which are racy in content, and confines Andrew's travels to a more western trajectory, Epiphanios describes Andrew's extensive travels and missionary work especially around the coast of the Black Sea and in Bithynia.

Gregory's *Epitome* and Epiphanios the Monk's *LAA* thus offer contrasting accounts of Andrew's mission in eastern regions of the Roman world and beyond. It is worth comparing their narratives – especially for the part of the *LAA* that deals with the period before Andrew's arrival in Patras. However, there are other sources, including anonymous Greek texts such as the *Narratio*, as well as (ps-) Dorotheos of Tyre's and (ps-) Epiphanios

---

Epiphanios the Monk, *LAA*, ed. Vinogradov 2005, 237. 29–30, 255. 21–22; Chap. 2, 5, 29. For further discussion, see below, 61–62.

238 See above, n. 235.

239 This text, which is titled 'Liber de miraculis beati Andreae apostoli' by its editor, Bonnet, is also known as 'Epitome' (*AA*, ed. MacDonald 1990, 181) and 'Life of Andrew' (*AA*, ed. Prieur 1989, 8–12). I have chosen, for reasons of economy, to call the text 'Epitome' throughout this study. Flamion proved that Gregory of Tours' redaction of the *AA* is the most comprehensive witness to survive; see Flamion 1911, 213–63.

240 Gregory of Tours, *Epitome*, ed. Bonnet 1883, vol. 1, 826; quoted in *AA*, ed. MacDonald 1990, 1–2.

241 *AA*, ed. MacDonald 1990, 181–82.

INTRODUCTION   49

of Cyprus's lists of the apostles, which should also be considered. In the discussion that follows, I will deal with the first and second parts (that is, the narrative before and after Andrew's arrival in Patras) of the *LAA* separately, examining literary parallels and influences in each case.

1. Andrew's travels in Asia Minor and the Caucasus: literary parallels and sources

As mentioned above, the two recent editors of the third-century *AA*, Prieur and MacDonald, both believe that Gregory of Tours' *Epitome* represents the most reliable version of the lost apocryphal text – at least for the section that deals with the apostle Andrew's travels before his arrival in the Achaian city of Patras.[242] Although the two scholars accept the importance of Epiphanios the Monk's *LAA* as an imaginative reconstruction of Andrew's mission in its own right, they reject its value as a witness to the *AA*; the ninth-century Greek text seems to draw on other, less reliable, sources than did Gregory of Tours. They also rejected the historical value of the *LAA* on the grounds that it lacked a critical edition – this problem has of course now been rectified with Vinogradov's recent work on the text.[243] MacDonald suggests that Epiphanios 'gathered some of his information from local legends which may well have issued from the *AA*, but whose paternity can no longer be proved. Second, Epiphanius was not an historian but a panegyrist quite capable of fetching content from his private stock.'[244] Since they differ so radically, it is worth comparing the accounts of Gregory of Tours and Epiphanios in detail. Leaving aside the text of the *AAMt*, which only MacDonald places at the beginning of the *AA*, Table 1 sets out the main differences between the two authors' accounts of Andrew's journeys.

---

242 Prieur asserts that 'Ce récit est un document unique pour tout ce qui précède l'arrivée de l'apôtre à Patras'; see *AA*, ed. Prieur 1989, 8. MacDonald agrees with this thesis, stating that 'because no complete text of the *Acts of Andrew* now exists, Gregory's epitome, albeit tendentious and frequently garbled, provides our most inclusive overview of its narrative architecture and is the only witness to long stretches of it'; see *AA*, ed. MacDonald, 1990, 1–2. Both editors follow the earlier work of Flamion 1911, esp. 213–63, in reaching this conclusion.
243 *AA*, ed. Prieur, 18–20; ed. MacDonald 1990, 183–84. On the problem of Dressel's 1843 edition of the *LAA*, see below, 70–73. For Vinogradov's critical edition of two versions of the *LAA*, see idem 2005, 197–264.
244 *AA*, ed. MacDonald 1990, 184.

Table 1

Gregory of Tours' *Epitome*	Epiphanios the Monk's *LAA*
2–4: In **Amasia** Andrew heals a blind man, heals a boy with a fever, and deals with an incestuous mother.	4–5: After travelling to **Tyana** **(Cappadocia)** and then **Ankyra** **(Galatia)**, Andrew raises a man from the dead.
5: **Sinope**. Here Andrew exorcises a demon from a boy, also exposing the sins of his parents and converting them to Christianity.	5, 7–8: **Sinope**. Peter, Andrew, and Matthias take up residence at the furthest point of the peninsula beyond the city. Matthias is arrested by the local Jews. Andrew rescues him, along with other prisoners, and takes them to a refuge by the sea. Here he converts and baptises them.
	9: **Sebastopolis**. Andrew teaches 'Scythians, Sogdians, and Gorsinoi'. 'Iberians, Sousa, Phoustians, and Alans' also live in this city.[245]
	10–15: **Amisos**. Andrew preaches in a synagogue and again outdoors. He frees some citizens from demons. Andrew also founds churches and appoints priests. He preaches another long sermon in which he focuses on Old Testament stories such as that of Cain and Abel.

---

245 On these peoples and locations (which include legendary, e.g. 'Scythians', and contemporary names), see Kahl 1989, 81–86. This section of the narrative is disjointed, both because Epiphanios breaks off to describe his and his companion's own travels in search of relics (in section 9) and because he later states that Andrew and his disciples, accompanied by Matthias, went straight from Sinope to Amisos (section 10).

Gregory of Tours' *Epitome*	Epiphanios the Monk's *LAA*
	16–17: **Trebizond** and **Phasis** (in **Lazica**). After visiting these cities, Andrew travels back to **Jerusalem**. After Pentecost, Peter, Andrew, John (son of Zebedee), Philip, and Bartholomew return to **Antioch**. From there, Philip and Bartholomew travel to upper **Phrygia** and **Pisidia**. Andrew goes with John to **Ephesus** and then travels with his own disciples to **Laodikeia**, **Mysia**, and **Odyssoupolis**.[246]
6: **Nicaea**. Andrew expels seven demons who were living in tombs by the roadside. He then baptises the inhabitants of the city and installs Callistus as their bishop.	18–27: **Nicaea**. Andrew kills a dragon, on a rock nine miles outside the city, and then deals with eight robbers (two of whom are possessed by demons). On the way back to Nicaea, Andrew destroys an idol of Artemis which had been inhabited by demons and sets up a cross in its place. He also expels a dragon and demons from a copse near that site. He expels demons from people on a mountain to the east of the city, which caused them to eat their own flesh. He preaches to them, providing the narrative of God's dispensation from creation through to the resurrection and ascension of Christ. Andrew then baptises many people and ordains presbyters, deacons, and a bishop, Drakontios.

---

246 Mango suggests that 'Odessopolis' may be the city in Moesia that was located between Laodikeia and Nicaea; see Mango 2002, 256. For further discussion of these locations, see Kahl 1989, 96–98.

Gregory of Tours' *Epitome*	Epiphanios the Monk's *LAA*
7: **Nikomedia**. Andrew revives a boy who has been killed by seven dogs (in fact the seven demons which were expelled from Nicaea). The boy becomes a disciple.	28: In **Nikomedia**, Andrew revives a certain Kallistos who had been killed by a demon. Travelling on to **Chalcedon**, he ordains Tychikos as bishop. He moves on from there to **Herakleia** (on the Black Sea), **Amastris**, and then **Sinope**.
	29: **Sinope**. The inhabitants attack Andrew, biting his flesh like dogs and expelling him from the city. Christ appears and heals him, restoring a finger which has been bitten off. Andrew re-enters the city and preaches. He heals the sick and raises a man from the dead. Andrew ordains presbyters and deacons.
	30: Andrew travels on to **Zalichos**, then **Trebizond**, and finally **Neokaisareia**.
	31: Andrew then goes to **Samosata** (in Parthia), which contains many philosophers. From there he returns to **Jerusalem**.
	32: After Pentecost, Andrew and other apostles visit **Edessa** (city of Abgar). They then move on into **Iberia** as far as **Phasis** and **Sousania**. Simon and Andrew then go to **Phousta** (Alania) and **Abasgia**. They then visit **Sebastopolis**. Andrew goes on with his disciples to **Zekchia** (Zichia) and **Sougdaia**.
	33–34: Andrew travels on to **Bosporos** and from there to **Theudesia** and **Cherson** (on the Crimean peninsula). He then sails from **Bosporos** back to **Sinope**.
8: **Byzantium**. After a boat trip across the Hellespont during which Andrew quells a storm, he arrives in Byzantium. No account of his activities here is provided.	35: From **Sinope**, Andrew goes to **Byzantion**. Here he appoints Stachys as bishop of Argyropolis and consecrates a sanctuary to the Theotokos on the acropolis of Byzantion. After this he travels to **Herakleia** in Thrace.

Gregory of Tours' *Epitome*	Epiphanios the Monk's *LAA*
9: **Thrace**. Andrew subdues (with the help of an angel and by making the sign of the cross) an attack by armed men. They then 'throw away their swords and adore him'.	
10: **Perinthus** (a Thracian coastal town). Andrew finds a boat about to leave for Macedonia. On board he converts a sailor 'and all who were with him'.	
11–12: **Philippi**. Andrew prevents two wealthy brothers from having their children marry each other, on the grounds of incest. The apostle is followed by a rich and noble young man from **Thessalonike** who defends the apostle from his enraged parents. When the latter eventually return home and die, the young man inherits their wealth and distributes it to the poor.	35: **Macedonia**. Andrew travels around the cities of Macedonia, teaching, healing, founding churches, and appointing clergy before concluding his travels in **Patras** in the Peloponnese (Achaia).
13–14: **Thessalonike**. Andrew heals one boy and raises another (who has been killed by a demon) from the dead.	
15–17: **Philippi**. Andrew heals the crippled son of a man named Medias but demands that the latter release prisoners whom he was mistreating. The apostle also converts a wealthy citizen named Nicolaus and heals his daughter from an illness. Andrew also expels a demon from a young man.	

Gregory of Tours' *Epitome*	Epiphanios the Monk's *LAA*
18: **Thessalonike**. The proconsul, Varianus (or Virinus), hears about Andrew's activities and sends for him. However, on finding him in Philippi, the soldiers are frightened at the sight of his shining face. The proconsul then comes himself but is unable to see Andrew. The apostle opens his eyes and then revives a dead soldier. The proconsul is unconvinced, calling Andrew a sorcerer, and orders that he be thrown into the arena with a wild boar. The boar circles the apostle three times and fails to harm him. The boar is followed by a bull and then a leopard – the last of which leaps onto the proconsul's throne and kills his son. The proconsul loses his sanity and remembers nothing. Andrew revives the son, but Varianus goes back to the praetorium in a confused state.	
19: **Thessalonike**. A woman asks Andrew to come to her estate and deal with a large serpent. He complies and kills the snake. He also revives a boy who was killed by the snake, thereby converting his parents.	
20: **Thessalonike** (?). Andrew has a vision in which he is standing with the apostles Peter and John, looking at an unearthly mountain. John raises Peter and Andrew to the top of the mountain, then reveals the meaning of this sign. It symbolises the crucifixion which they will both experience later. Andrew then preaches and prays with his followers.	
21: The trip from **Macedonia to Patras**. A storm builds, sweeping someone from the boat into the sea. When the apostle prays, the man is saved. After twelve days, they land at Patras, a city in Achaia.	

It is evident that Gregory of Tours and Epiphanios the Monk employed quite different sources for their separate accounts of the apostle Andrew's travels and missionary activities before he arrived in Patras. Gregory describes an itinerary that begins in Pontic cities including Amasia and Sinope, on the southern shore of the Black Sea, before moving on to Bithynia (with focus on the cities of Nicaea and Nikomedia), Byzantion (Constantinople), Thrace, and finally 'Macedonia' (with Thessalonike and Philippi receiving most attention). Epiphanios meanwhile has the apostle follow three tours, each beginning in Jerusalem, which encompass the northern coast of the Black Sea as far as Trebizond, cities in Bithynia (including Nicaea, Nikomedia, and Chalcedon), Iberia, the Crimea, and finally Byzantion and Thrace. The decision of the two editors of the third-century *AA* to accept Gregory of Tours' narrative as a basis for its reconstruction rules out not only Epiphanios, but also earlier Greek sources which show affinities with his account, including the so-called *Martyrium prius*,[247] the two works which are both known as *Index apostolorum* by (ps-) Dorotheos of Tyre and (ps-) Epiphanios of Salamis,[248] and the anonymous *Narratio*.[249] All of these texts belong to the early Byzantine period. Since there is no reason to engage in the debate concerning the closest witnesses to the *AA* in the context of this study – or to attempt an alternative reconstruction of the second- or third-century *Acts* – it is enough merely to assess the Greek textual tradition concerning the apostle Andrew in relation to Epiphanios the Monk's *LAA* and its possible sources.

The *Index apostolorum*, which is ascribed falsely to Epiphanios of Cyprus, belongs to a group of texts that are best described as catalogues: it lists the missions of the apostles with their seventy disciples, as well as the first bishops whom they were believed to have ordained. Most scholars, beginning with its editor Theodore Schermann, have dated the text to between the sixth and eighth centuries.[250] Another catalogue of the apostles, which is falsely ascribed to Dorotheos of Tyre, reveals similarities and differences with that of (ps-) Epiphanios. Lequeux dates this source to the first half of

---

247 Anon., *Mart. pr.*, ed. Bonnet 1898; ed. Prieur 1989.

248 (ps-) Epiphanios of Salamis, *Index apostolorum* and (ps-) Dorotheos of Tyre, *Index apostolorum*, ed. Schermann 1907, 107–63. On the deficiencies of Schermann's edition of these texts, see Dolbeau 2012, 173–80, 243.

249 Anon., *Narratio*, ed. Vinogradov 2005, 178–96.

250 (ps-) Epiphanios of Salamis, *Index apostolorum*, ed. Schermann 1907, 1–25, 107–31; on the genre and possible date of the text, see Dvornik 1958, 173–78; cf. Vinogradov 2005, 33.

the sixth century.²⁵¹ Epiphanios the Monk appears to have been ignorant of (ps-) Dorotheos's *Index* since he does not follow its trajectory for Andrew's missionary travels.²⁵² Instead he follows the account that is provided in the earlier *Index apostolorum* by (ps-) Epiphanios of Salamis. Whereas (ps-) Dorotheos describes the apostle travelling clockwise around the Black Sea (beginning in Bithynia and travelling through 'Scythia' to 'Sebastopolis the Great'), (ps-) Epiphanios charts a counter-clockwise journey.

The anonymous *Martyrium prius*, which Flamion (followed by Prieur) dates to the eighth century, begins with an account of the dispersion of the apostles which may have been inspired by the original *AA*.²⁵³ It has little to say about Andrew's travels before he reached Patras, however: the bulk of this text deals with his activities and martyrdom in that city.²⁵⁴ The anonymous *Narratio*, which also provides an account of the apostle Andrew's mission, acts, and martyrdom, may date roughly to between the sixth and eighth century.²⁵⁵ This text does provide an account of Andrew's travels before he reached Patras, describing a route that encompasses Bithynia, Thrace, 'Scythia', and Sebastopolis (in Georgia where, according to the author, 'Ethiopians' lived). Prieur, following Flamion, suggests that this itinerary is inspired by the *Index apostolorum* of (ps-) Dorotheos of Tyre; this is certainly possible if Lequeux is correct in dating the latter text to the first half of the

---

251 (ps-) Dorotheos of Tyre, *Index apostolorum*, ed. Schermann 1907. Scholars differ in their dating of this text. Most recently, X. Lequeux dates the text to between 525 and 551 CE; see idem 2019, 248–52 (I am grateful to Marc Lauxtermann for alerting me to this article). Prior to this study, Francis Dvornik believed that the text was compiled after the composition of Theophanes' *Chronicle* (which ends in 813 since the chronicler appears to be unaware of this specific text (although he does know of a spurious 'Dorotheos')); see Theophanes, *Chronographia*, ed. de Boor 1883–85, 24; for commentary, see ibid., trans. Mango and Scott 1997, 38–41, n. 30. I am convinced by Lequeux's redating of (ps-) Dorotheos's *Index*; however, our Epiphanios does not follow its narrative.
252 Vinogradov also reaches this conclusion in idem 2005, 34.
253 Flamion 1911, 61–62; *AA*, ed. Prieur 1989, 14, 38–40; cf. Vinogradov 2005, 29.
254 Discussion of this text therefore appears in the next section of this chapter, which deals with the narrative after Andrew's arrival in Patras.
255 Anon., *Narratio*, ed. Vinogradov 2005. On the dating of this text, Dvornik argues that the use of the phrase 'western parts' (τοῖς δυτικοῖς μέρεσιν) to describe Thessaly, Hellas, and Achaia in one section indicates that the author was unaware of the reappropriation of these territories under the iconoclast emperor Leo III, either in 733 or between 752 and 757; see Dvornik 1958, 171–73. Vinogradov rejects Dvornik's argument as 'tenuous', however; he suggests on the basis of the *Narratio*'s content and style that it may belong to the sixth or seventh century; see Vinogradov 2005, 37–39.

INTRODUCTION 57

sixth century.[256] Table 2 provides a synoptic summary of Andrew's travels before his arrival in Patras, according to (ps-) Epiphanios of Cyprus's *Index apostolorum*, the anonymous *Narratio*, and Epiphanios the Monk's *LAA*.

Table 2

(ps-) Epiphanios of Salamis, *Index apostolorum*	Anonymous, *Narratio*	Epiphanios the Monk, *LAA*
	4: Having departed on his missionary journey from Jerusalem, Andrew goes first to **Nicaea**. From there he travels to 'Scythia', reaching **Sebastopolis**.	4–5: After travelling to **Tyana (Cappadocia)** and then **Ankyra (Galatia)**, Andrew raises a man from the dead.
	5–7: After leaving the Pontic Black Sea (τὸν Εὔξεινον πόντον), Andrew goes to **Sinope** where savage, blood-sucking people live. They seize the apostle Matthias and threaten to kill him. However, Andrew rescues him along with the other prisoners. The citizens of Sinope then arrest Andrew and drag him through the streets before throwing him into prison. He prays for them to be converted. After a miracle involving a statue, the people repent.	5, 7–8: **Sinope**. Peter, Andrew, and Matthias take up residence at the furthest point of the peninsula beyond the city. Matthias is arrested by the local Jews. Andrew rescues him, along with other prisoners, and takes them to a refuge by the sea. Here he converts and baptises them.

---

256 *AA*, ed. Prieur 1989, 17; cf. Flamion 1911, 68–69. See also above, n. 251.

(ps-) Epiphanios of Salamis, *Index apostolorum*	Anonymous, *Narratio*	Epiphanios the Monk, *LAA*
		10–15: **Amisos**. Andrew preaches in a synagogue and again outdoors. He frees some citizens from demons. Andrew also founds churches and appoints priests. He preaches another long sermon in which he focuses on Old Testament stories such as that of Cain and Abel.
		16–17: **Trebizond and Phasis (in Lazica)**. After visiting these cities, Andrew travels back to **Jerusalem**. After Pentecost, Peter, Andrew, John (son of Zebedee), Philip, and Bartholomew return to **Antioch**. From there, Philip and Bartholomew travel to upper **Phrygia** and **Pisidia**. Andrew goes with John to **Ephesus** and then travels with his own disciples to **Laodikeia**, **Mysia**, and **Odyssoupolis**.

INTRODUCTION 59

(ps-) Epiphanios of Salamis, *Index apostolorum*	Anonymous, *Narratio*	Epiphanios the Monk, *LAA*
	4: **Nicaea (Bithynia)**. Andrew preaches, performs miracles, and then expels demons from a place outside the eastern gate of the city.	18–27: **Nicaea**. Andrew kills a dragon, on a rock nine miles outside the city, and then deals with eight robbers (two of whom are possessed by demons). On the way back to Nicaea, Andrew destroys an idol of Artemis which had been inhabited by demons and sets up a cross in its place. He also expels a dragon and demons from a copse near that site. He expels demons from people on a mountain to the east of the city, which caused them to eat their own flesh. He preaches to them, providing the narrative of God's dispensation from creation through to the resurrection and ascension of Christ. Andrew then baptises many people and ordains presbyters, deacons, and a bishop, Drakontios.
		28: In **Nikomedia**, Andrew revives a certain Kallistos who had been killed by a demon. Travelling on to **Chalcedon**, he ordains Tychikos as bishop. He moves on from there to **Herakleia** (on the Black Sea), **Amastris**, and then **Sinope**.

(ps-) Epiphanios of Salamis, *Index apostolorum*	Anonymous, *Narratio*	Epiphanios the Monk, *LAA*
		29: **Sinope**. The inhabitants attack Andrew, biting his flesh like dogs and expelling him from the city. Christ appears and heals him, restoring a finger which has been bitten off. Andrew re-enters the city and preaches. He heals the sick and raises a man from the dead. Andrew ordains presbyters and deacons.
		30: Andrew travels on to **Zalichos**, then **Trebizond**, and finally **Neokaisareia**.
		31: Andrew then goes to **Samosata** (in Parthia), which contains many philosophers. From there he returns to Jerusalem.
2: **Sebastopolis**. Andrew 'preached to Scythians and Sogdians and Gorsinians (ἐκήρυξε Σκύθαις καὶ Σογιανοῖς καὶ Γορσίνοις) and in **Sebastopolis the Great**, where are the encampment of Apsaros and the bay of Hyssos and the river Phasis, beyond which live the Ethiopians...'[257]	4: **Thrace**, then **Scythia**. After leaving Nicaea, Andrew goes to Thrace, then Scythia 'to **Sebastopolis the Great**, in which are the encampment of Apsaros and the rivers (sic) Phasis, and where the Ethiopians live in the interior...'	32: After Pentecost, Andrew and other apostles visit **Edessa** (city of Abgar). They then move on into **Iberia** as far as **Phasis** and **Sousania**. Simon and Andrew then go to **Phousta** (Alania) and **Abasgia**. They then visit **Sebastopolis**. Andrew goes on with his disciples to **Zekchia** (Zichia) and **Sougdaia**.[258]

---

257 (ps-) Epiphanios of Salamis, *Index apostolorum*, ed. Schermann 1907, 108–9; trans. Dvornik 1958, 174. (Ps-) Dorotheos of Tyre provides an alternative account: ['Andreas travelled to Sebastopolis the Great where are the encampment of Apsaros and the river Phasis, beyond which (in the interior) live the Ethiopians...']; ed. Schermann 1907, 153 (my translation).
258 On this itinerary, see above, n. 247.

INTRODUCTION 61

(ps-) Epiphanios of Salamis, *Index apostolorum*	Anonymous, *Narratio*	Epiphanios the Monk, *LAA*
		33–34: Andrew travels on to **Bosporos** and from there to **Theudesia** and **Cherson** (on the Crimean peninsula). He then sails from **Bosporos** back to **Sinope**.
20: **Byzantion**. Andrew ordains Stachys the first bishop, in Argyropolis, a suburb of Constantinople.[259]	8. **Byzantion**. Andrew reaches this city from the Black Sea. He ordains Stachys the first bishop, in Argyropolis, Thrace. The Roman tyrant Zeuxippos is in power. Andrew departs 'to the western parts' as he continues his mission.	35: From **Sinope**, Andrew goes to **Byzantion**. Here he appoints Stachys as bishop of Argyropolis and consecrates a sanctuary to the Theotokos on the acropolis of Byzantion. After this he travels to **Herakleia** in Thrace.
	9: **Thessaly, Greece,** and the cities that form part of **Achaia**, leading finally to **Patras**.	35: **Macedonia**. Andrew travels around the cities of Macedonia, teaching, healing, founding churches, and appointing clergy before concluding his travels in **Patras** in the Peloponnese (Achaea).

This synoptic table, which summarises the places or regions in which Andrew carried out his mission, shows that the three texts differ considerably in their presentation of a shared legend. The anonymous *Narratio*, for example, mentions Andrew's stay in Sinope, but places the events that took place there *after* his visits to both Nicaea and Sebastopolis. The tale of the arrests of Matthias and Andrew himself in Sinope depends more closely on the earlier *AAMt* than does the narrative of Epiphanios the Monk.[260] Here we have the cannibalistic and 'blood-sucking' inhabitants abusing and imprisoning both apostles before Andrew succeeds in converting them by calling on Christ to enact a dramatic miracle. However, Epiphanios

---

259 (ps-) Epiphanios of Salamis, *Index apostolorum*, ed. Schermann 1907, 120.
260 *AAMt*, ed. Bonnet 1898; ed. MacDonald 1990.

alludes to the cannibalistic behaviour of some of the subjects of Andrew's mission in other sections of his *LAA*. When he returns to Sinope later in his mission, for example, the inhabitants beat the apostle, drag him through the city, and bite his flesh 'like dogs' – to the extent that he loses a finger.[261] It appears that our hagiographer, having become acquainted with the story of the cannibals either from the original *AAMt* or a later version, modified the story but still associated it with the Pontic city of Sinope.

Other passages show even closer resemblances in their content or literary expression. The almost identical wording of the passage concerning Sebastopolis in all three sources suggests either mutual influence or a common source; in the case of Epiphanios the Monk, this appears to be a direct borrowing from (ps-) Epiphanios of Salamis since he cites the latter before quoting the passage.[262] Once again, however, the passage appears out of sequence in Epiphanios's narrative. The placement of the first sentence in section nine of the *LAA* makes no sense, especially since the apostle's journey to the Crimea resumes in section thirty-two – at a more logical point in the narrative. Epiphanios's narrative is marked throughout by such lapses in compositional structure and clarity. It is possible that this reflects his use of random notes that he made in the course of his journey around the Black Sea.

2. The activities and martyrdom of Andrew in Patras

Turning to the final section of the *LAA*, in which Andrew arrives and is martyred in Patras, we find closer parallels between Epiphanios the Monk's composition and the reconstructed text of the *AA*, as well as the later Greek sources. Even so, features such as Andrew's speech to the cross, an example of the rhetorical device of prosopopoeia, appear in all these sources – but not in Epiphanios's *LAA*.[263] Our hagiographer provides a shorter ending than that which appears in earlier sources such as the *AA* and the *Narratio*. The main obstacle to tracing parallels between the *LAA* and the original *AA* for this section of the narrative remains the fragmentary nature of the latter. Because Epiphanios follows the *AA* fairly closely in this section of the *LAA*

---

261 Epiphanios the Monk, *LAA*, ed. Vinogradov 2005, 255. 21–22; Chap. 2, 29.
262 Ibid., ed. Vinogradov 2005, 239. 20–24; see Chap. 2, 9.
263 For examples of the apostle's speech to the cross, see *AA* 54 (4), ed. Prieur 1989, 515–17; *Narratio* 27, ed. Vinogradov 2005, 190. 18–191. 7.

INTRODUCTION   63

(apart from, as we have just seen, its more rhetorical closing sections), it is worth recalling the literary evidence which the modern editors have used to reconstruct the *AA*. According to Prieur,[264] there are five significant sources or groups of sources, which are as follows: 1) the *Epitome* of Gregory of Tours;[265] 2) a Coptic translation of an extract of the *AA*;[266] 3) the final section, or *Passion*, of the *AA*, which survives in five Greek recensions;[267] 4) an Armenian *Passion*, dated to the sixth century, which provides a complete version of the final section of the *AA*;[268] 5) extracts of the text which are preserved in various later redactions, including that of Epiphanios the Monk.[269] The last mention of the *AA*, which occurred soon after Epiphanios composed his version of the narrative, appears in the *Bibliotheca* of the ninth-century Constantinopolitan patriarch, Photios. In Codex 114, the latter states that he has read the *AA*, along with the *Acts* of Peter, John, Thomas, and Paul, in a book that is ascribed to an author named Leucius Charinus. He condemns the heretical tendencies of these books, also commenting that the style is foolish and contradictory.[270] After Photios, the full text of the early *AA* is no longer mentioned in Byzantine sources, although the early *Acts* of other apostles continued to be disseminated in Eastern and Western Christendom.

In view of the wealth of surviving versions of the apostle Andrew's sojourn and martyrdom in Patras, I have chosen for reasons of economy to compare the narratives of four witnesses belonging to the Greek textual tradition: 1) Prieur's reconstruction of the *AA*;[271] 2) the anonymous

---

264 The following list is provided in *Actes*, trans. Prieur 1995, 55–64.
265 See above, n. 239.
266 Coptic Papyrus Utrecht 1; ed. R. van den Broek in *AA*, ed. Prieur 1989, 656–71.
267 See *AA*, ed. Prieur 1989, 442–549; for further discussion of the manuscripts, see *Actes*, trans. Prieur 1995, 59–61. An edition based on two witnesses, Sinai gr. 526 (10th c.) and Jerus. Sab. 103 (12th c.) appears in Détorakis 1981–82. Extracts of the *Passion* that appear in three other witnesses are edited in Bonnet 1898, 38–45, 58–64.
268 This text is incorporated into the *AA* of both modern editors: MacDonald 1990, 322; Prieur 1989, 436 ('...nous avons constamment éclairé [l'édition] par la Passion arménienne').
269 For details of these extracts, see *Actes*, trans. Prieur 1995, 62–64.
270 Photios, *Bibliotheca*, Codex 114, ed. Henry 1960, vol. 2, 84–86; for discussion, see *AA*, ed. Prieur 1989, 122–23.
271 *AA*, ed. Prieur 1989, 442–549. Prieur uses five manuscripts, along with several other Greek sources, to reconstruct the text; see ibid., 423–39. Although he cites the *Martyrium prius* and the *Narratio* occasionally in his apparatus, he does not use these sources for his edition of the *AA*; see ibid., 430–31.

Martyrium prius; 3) the anonymous *Narratio*; and 4) Epiphanios the Monk's *LAA*. Owing to the complexities of the various narratives, it is easier to summarise their similarities and differences than to attempt a synoptic table (as in the case of Andrew's travels before his arrival in Patras).[272]

One element of the story, which appears only in the *Martyrium prius*, is the conversion of the proconsul who preceded Aigeates in Patras, named Lesbios. Although this governor is at first alarmed by stories of Andrew's miracles and growing fame in the Achaian city, he is visited by an angel and is converted. When the apostle is summoned, Lesbios falls at his feet and asks for mercy. He then resigns from his governorship and is replaced by Aigeates.[273] The reconstructed *AA*, *Narratio*, and Epiphanios the Monk's *LAA* all omit the story of Lesbios's conversion. These texts do begin the story of Andrew's sojourn in Patras, however, with accounts of his miracles. According to Epiphanios, the apostle first met a man named Sosios whom he cured of a mortal illness. He was then approached by Ephidama, the servant of Aigeates' wife Maximilla, since the latter had already heard of the stranger's wisdom and healing powers.[274] The *AA* and *Narratio* are silent about this phase of Andrew's ministry, although Gregory of Tours mentions the role of Sosios in bringing about a meeting between the apostle and Maximilla.[275]

The story of Maximilla's illness, which causes her to summon Andrew to her bedside, is emphasised in Epiphanios the Monk's *LAA*. According to the ninth-century hagiographer, her husband, Aigeates, is so grief-stricken that he is about to kill himself with a knife. Andrew first persuades him to put down the knife and then banishes Maximilla's fever. He refuses payment from Aigeates and returns to his work in the city, healing the ill

---

272 See above, Tables 1 and 2.

273 Anon., *Mart. pr.* 3–6; *AA*, ed. Prieur 1989, 685–90. Vinogradov suggests that this text represents a full reworking of the *AA* and that it may have shared a common source with Niketas David's *Laudatio*. The latter text also contains the story of Lesbios's conversion. See Vinogradov 2005, 29.

274 Epiphanios the Monk, *LAA*, ed. Vinogradov 258. 27–259. 2; see Chap. 2, 36. Note that the name 'Ephidama' appears in various forms in different texts in the Andrew tradition. She is sometimes called 'Ephidamia' or 'Iphidama', for example.

275 Gregory of Tours, *Epitome* 30, *AA*, ed. Prieur 1989, 642–43; MacDonald 1990, 306–9. On comparing Gregory of Tours' *Epitome* with the *LAA*, Prieur suggests that Epiphanios invents an extra miracle involving a paralytic at this point in the text; see *AA*, ed. Prieur 1989, 46–47.

and expelling demons.[276] The next important episode to appear in both the *AA* and the *LAA* is the miracle involving a servant of Aigeates' brother, Stratokles. Soon after Stratokles arrives in Patras from Athens (where he had been studying), his beloved servant Alkmanas is possessed by a demon. Andrew is summoned and expels the impure spirit, after which Stratokles is converted to Christianity.[277] Stratokles goes on to play an important role in all the surviving versions of the *AA*. He stands by the apostle Andrew during his subsequent imprisonment and execution, supports his sister-in-law Maximilla, and tries to influence the behaviour of his jealous brother, Aigeates.

The four narratives all describe Andrew's mission in Patras as he performs more miracles and attracts a growing number of disciples. Whereas the *Martyrium prius* provides scant detail after the story involving the previous proconsul, Lesbios, the *AA*, *Narratio*, and *LAA* all offer detailed accounts of Andrew's activities in Patras, Maximilla's growing attachment to the apostle – to the extent that she rejects her husband Aigeates – and the apostle's eventual arrest at the command of the proconsul. One element that appears only in the *AA* is the story of Maximilla's plot to escape the unwanted attentions of Aigeates. According to this tradition, the proconsul's wife instructs one of her servants (named Euklia), who is young, beautiful, and promiscuous, to disguise herself as her mistress and sleep with Aigeates. This manoeuvre succeeds for eight months, but Euklia begins first to blackmail Maximilla for greater rewards and then to boast about her wealth to her fellow servants. They eventually betray Euklia to Aigeates, who cuts out her tongue and expels her from the household. The unfortunate woman is subsequently devoured by wild dogs while the three servants who exposed her are crucified.[278] It is possible that the dubious morality of this story led Epiphanios the Monk to omit it from his narrative. However, like other compilers or redactors of the legend, the ninth-century hagiographer stresses Maximilla's growing determination to live a life of chastity and to abandon her powerful husband. The apostle Andrew encourages her in this endeavour while Aigeates grows increasingly jealous and miserable.

The *AA* also provides colourful detail in its description of the proconsul's subsequent dealings with his errant wife and Andrew. After arresting the

---

276 Epiphanios the Monk, *LAA*, ed. Vinogradov 2005, 259. 23–260. 29; see Chap. 2, 38–39.
277 *AA*, *Actes* 4–5, ed. Prieur 1989, 446–49; Epiphanios the Monk, *LAA*, ed. Vinogradov 2005, 261. 3–15; see Chap. 2, 40.
278 *AA*, *Actes* 17–22, ed. Prieur 1989, 462–69.

apostle and imprisoning him, Aigeates goes into Maximilla's chamber where she is eating bread and olives ('because it was that time of day') with her servant Ephidama (here called Iphidama). He tells her that Andrew will die if Maximilla does not renounce his friendship.[279] Maximilla and Iphidama, however, are only encouraged to visit the apostle more often and to listen throughout the night to his teaching. The *Narratio* and *LAA* also describe this phase of Andrew's mission, including the sermons that he delivers to his followers.[280] Eventually, after delivering an ultimatum to Maximilla which she rejects, Aigeates condemns Andrew to death by crucifixion, according to all the surviving narratives.[281]

As stated above, the anonymous *Narratio* provides an elaborate conclusion to the story of Andrew's martyrdom in Patras; this ending appears in one manuscript (V3) of the *LAA* and thus in Dressel's earlier edition of the text.[282] According to this account, the progress to the place of execution, which is said to be 'on the edge of the sand by the sea' outside the city, is interrupted by Stratokles' angry attempts (by hitting them and tearing their clothes) to stop the executioners from proceeding on their way.[283] When they return to Aigeates in order to complain of this treatment, however, the proconsul orders them to put on new clothes and carry out his orders. Stratokles meanwhile leads Andrew gently to the cross where the latter proceeds to address it directly in glowing terms.[284] Rather than attempt to escape, the apostle willingly mounts the cross and allows the executioners to tie him, rather than nail him, to the wood. According to all the sources, Aigeates has commanded that he be crucified in this manner so that he will survive long enough to be devoured by wild dogs. In fact

---

279 *AA, Actes* 27, ed. Prieur 1989, 474–77.
280 Anon., *Narratio* 12–13, ed. Vinogradov 2005, 183. 29–184. 26; Epiphanios the Monk, *LAA*, ed. Vinogradov 2005, 262. 20–263. 3; see Chap. 2, 42.
281 *AA, Actes* 51, ed. Prieur 1989, 508–9; *Mart. pr.* 13, ed. Prieur 1989, 697; Anon., *Narratio* 22, ed. Vinogradov 2005, 188. 22–189. 3; Epiphanios the Monk, *LAA*, ed. Vinogradov 2005, 263. 5–6; see Chap. 2, 43.
282 Anon. *Narratio* 23–38, ed. Vinogradov 2005, 189. 4–196. 24; Epiphanios the Monk, *LAA*, ed. Dressel 1843, 74. 9 (Διεδόθη)–82. 7 (Ἀμήν).
283 *AA, Actes* 52, ed. Prieur 1989, 508–11; Anon., *Narratio* 23, ed. Vinogradov 2005, 189. 4–18; Epiphanios the Monk, *LAA*, ed. Dressel 1843, 74; PG 120, 249D–252A; see Chap. 2, 36.
284 *AA, Actes* 54 (4), ed. Prieur 1989, 514–17; *Mart. pr.* 14, ed. Prieur 1989, 698–99; Anon., *Narratio* 27, ed. Vinogradov 2005, 190. 18–191. 7.

Andrew uses the extra time to deliver another sermon to his followers, before he finally expires.[285]

The *Narratio* offers a vivid description of the subsequent suicide of Aigeates (who has not succeeded in regaining the affections of Maximilla), stating that it occurred in 'deep silence' at the dead of night.[286] The *AA*, *Martyrium prius*, and *LAA* leave out this descriptive phrase, as well as the statement that Aigeates threw himself off the roof of his own government building (praetorium), stating merely that 'escaping everyone's notice, he threw himself from a great height'.[287] Aigeates' suicide is followed in all four strands of the tradition by the statement that Stratokles rejected his brother's inheritance and that Maximilla dedicated herself to a life of prayer, remaining close to the site of Andrew's crucifixion (and presumably the shrine containing his relics).[288] The *Narratio* and *LAA* also state that Andrew's death occurred on 30 November, a date that is corroborated in middle Byzantine liturgical calendars.[289]

In summary, the four Greek narratives which that we have compared in this section reveal common access to a shared tradition – or in some cases even a literary source – in relation to the narrative of Andrew's mission and martyrdom in Patras. This half of the *LAA* (as well as other sources that treat the story both before and after his arrival in the Peloponnesian city) displays a novelistic, or fanciful, aspect that is lacking earlier in the narrative. The story of Maximilla and Aigeates, which explores the tension between marriage and a dedicated Christian life, must have featured in the earliest version of the *AA*. It was presumably picked up by later redactors and hagiographers because of its appeal to themes of passion, loyalty, and abandonment. Epiphanios the Monk omits some elements in the story, such as Maximilla's deception of her husband, but includes others that demonstrate her commitment to Christian

---

285 *AA*, *Actes* 63 (9), ed. Prieur 1989, 542–43; *Mart. pr.* 16, ed. Prieur 1989, 700–1; Anon., *Narratio* 30, ed. Vinogradov 2005, 192. 3–20; Epiphanios the Monk, *LAA*, ed. Vinogradov 2005, 263. 8–10; see Chap. 2, 43.

286 Anon., *Narratio* 36, ed. Vinogradov 2005, 196. 7–10: Ὡς δὲ οὐκ ἴσχυσεν αὐτὴν ὁ ἀνθύπατος πειθήνιον αὐτῷ καταστῆσαι, μανείς, νυκτὸς ἀναστὰς σιγῆς βαθείας οὔσης, διαλαθὼν πάντας ῥίπτει ἑαυτὸν ἀπὸ ὕψους μεγάλου τοῦ ἑαυτοῦ πραιτωρίου....

287 *AA*, *Actes* 64 (10), ed. Prieur 1989, 544–47; *Mart. pr.* 18, ed. Prieur 1989, 702–3; Epiphanios the Monk, *LAA*, ed. Vinogradov 2005, 263. 25–26, see Chap. 2, 44.

288 *AA*, *Actes* 64 (10), ed. Prieur 1989, 546–47; *Mart. pr.* 18, ed. Prieur 1989, 702–3; Anon., *Narratio* 36–37, ed. Vinogradov 2005, 195. 23–196. 20; Epiphanios the Monk, *LAA*, ed. Vinogradov 2005, 264. 1–12; PG 120, 258D–260B; see Chap. 2, 44.

289 *SynaxCP*, 265–68.

faith, chastity, and loyalty to the apostle Andrew. Although these values may have offended some patristic readers of the *AA*, they continued to appeal to the monastic Byzantine hagiographer. For this reason, he revived the story (having judiciously edited it) and passed it on to later redactors, as we shall see in the following section.

Epiphanios the Monk's version of the *Acts* of Andrew stands out especially for its innovative (and perhaps original) treatment of the apostle's travels in Asia Minor, the Caucasus, and the Crimea, as opposed to the concluding section that is set in Patras, which closely resembles other surviving narratives. The first section of the *LAA* is especially interesting because Epiphanios juxtaposes his own journey around the Black Sea with that of Andrew, thereby adding a dimension of personal and physical witness to the story. The second half, which deals with the apostle's activities in Patras, is less original since it is based more or less on the account that appears in early versions of the *AA*. Thanks to Vinogradov's critical edition of the *LAA*, we now know that the two authentic versions (excluding the text that appears in V3) provide shorter, less rhetorical conclusions to the story of Andrew's martyrdom in Patras than that which appears in earlier texts such as the anonymous *Narratio*.[290] Nevertheless, this text represents an important early contribution to the full-fledged Byzantine hagiographical tradition that followed it.

Dissemination and influence of the *LAA*

Judging by the number of surviving manuscripts,[291] Epiphanios the Monk's oration on the apostle Andrew was less popular that his work on the Virgin Mary. One reason why Epiphanios's text may not have reached a wider audience is that it was quickly superseded by new works that were composed in honour of the apostle Andrew during the ninth and tenth centuries. Epiphanios the Monk's *LAA* inspired a panegyrical piece which is usually called a *Laudatio* but which appears in some manuscripts under the title, 'Acts and travels of the holy and illustrious apostle Andrew, recorded in the form of a homily.'[292] Scholars including Prieur and Vinogradov have

---

290 For discussion of the peculiarities of V3, see Vinogradov 2005, 79.
291 On the manuscript tradition of the *LAA*, see below, n. 301.
292 Niketas David the Paphlagonian, *Laudatio*, according to the edition that appears in Bonnet 1894, 309–52; ed. idem 1895, 2–44. Vinogradov's critical edition of the text provides

INTRODUCTION   69

identified this text as a work of the late ninth- and early tenth-century writer, Niketas David of Paphlagon.[293] A student of Arethas of Caesarea, Niketas was involved in numerous ecclesiastical and political controversies of the period, including those concerning the patriarch Photios and the emperor Leo VI's four marriages.[294] In addition to this, he produced at least fifty enkomia of saints, along with theological treatises, commentaries, and other works.[295] Niketas borrowed material from Epiphanios the Monk's *LAA*, expanding his account of Andrew's ordination of the first bishop of Constantinople, Stachys, and of the apostle's foundation of a church in honour of the Theotokos on the acropolis of the imperial city.[296] Eighth- and ninth-century literary interest in the apostle Andrew, including the anonymous *Narratio*, Epiphanios the Monk's *LAA*, and Niketas David's *Laudatio*, may reflect official efforts to provide an apostolic foundation for Constantinople in response to the growing power of the papacy in Rome. The trend may also reflect increasing emphasis on the cults of saints and their relics, following attempts to discourage such devotion especially during the reign of the iconoclast emperor, Constantine V.[297]

The celebration of Andrew in literary and liturgical texts continued in the tenth century. The prolific hagiographer Symeon the Metaphrast produced another version of the life and passion of the apostle, basing his work on that of Epiphanios the Monk. According to Symeon, Andrew's mission included 'all the land of Bithynia, the Pontus Euxeinus, both sides of the Propontis, as far as the Gulf of Astacos, and the passage to the sea there. Added to this were far-famed Chalcedon and Byzantium, and the nations inhabiting Thrace and Macedonia, and extending from there as far as the Danube; also Thessaly and Hellas, and the lands extending from there to Achaia.'[298] The extensive scope of Andrew's travels, according to Symeon,

---

a different title: see idem, ed., 2005, 265–307. Dvornik, who did not associate this text with the late ninth-century writer, believed that its anonymous author belonged to the same monastery as Epiphanios; see Dvornik 1958, 226–27.
293   *AA*, ed. Prieur 1989, 15, n. 2.
294   For background and bibliography on this writer, see *ODB*, vol. 3, 1480.
295   Antonopoulou 1998, 330–36; Kazhdan 2006, 91–102; Efthymiadis 2011b, 116. Niketas David the Paphlagonian produced another *Enkomion of St Andrew*, PG 105, 53–80.
296   Dvornik 1958, 234.
297   Dvornik presents this theory in idem 1958, 168–71.
298   Symeon the Metaphrast, *Commemoration of St Andrew*, ed. *Menaia Novembris* 1843, 235, ff.; translated in Dvornik 1958, 257. This passage can now be consulted in the new edition of the text in Vinogradov 2005, 311. 35–312. 4.

may reflect the expanding horizons of the Byzantine empire during this period, thanks to both military campaigns and missions to the Slavs. The tenth-century *Synaxarion* of Constantinople also includes an account of Andrew's mission and passion, which was celebrated annually on his feast day, 30 November. The compiler includes details that derive from various earlier sources including (ps-) Dorotheos of Tyre's *Index apostolorum*, which states that 'Ethiopians' lived in the region of the Phasis river in the Caucasus.[299] A version of Andrew's legend also appears in the *Menologion* of Basil II, which is dated to the beginning of the eleventh century.[300]

In conclusion, narratives about the apostle Andrew, whether in the form of narrative *Acts* or panegyrical enkomia, began to circulate widely in Constantinople from about the middle of the ninth century onward. Focus on the apostle reflected a developing need to establish an apostolic foundation for the see of Constantinople, in response to the increasing power of the Roman papacy, as well as renewed interest in the relics of important saints. Epiphanios the Monk's *LAA* thus joined several other early Byzantine literary attempts to celebrate Andrew's mission and passion; in the West, the Latin traditions had culminated in the late sixth-century *Epitome* by Gregory of Tours. Epiphanios the Monk's work directly inspired two other panegyrical texts in honour of Andrew during the ninth century, as well as a new redaction by Symeon the Metaphrast in the tenth. It is likely, however, that his hagiographical effort was superseded by those of his successors – all of which represented more sophisticated works from both theological and rhetorical points of view. The relative paucity of surviving manuscripts that contain Epiphanios's *LAA* probably reflects a limited circulation of the text in subsequent centuries.

The text and its variations

According to the *Pinakes* database, the *LAA* survives in two versions, with the first (A) being transmitted in nine witnesses and the second (B) in five.[301] Albert Dressel employed a single manuscript, Cod. Vat. gr. 824 (11th c.) (V3), when he produced his edition of the *LAA*. According to *Pinakes*,

---

299 *SynaxCP*, 266–68; cf. (ps-) Dorotheos of Tyre, *Index apostolorum*, ed. Schermann 1907, 153–54.
300 *Menologion of Basil II*, PG 117, 185; Cod. Vat. 1613, fol. 215; Paschalidis 2011, 145.
301 See https://pinakes.irht.cnrs.fr/. According to this database, the tradition includes

INTRODUCTION 71

this manuscript belongs to version B. More recently, Andrey Vinogradov has examined the differences between the two versions (as well as the discrepancies that are found only in V3) in the introduction to his critical edition of the *LAA* and presented convincing reasons for their ascription to Epiphanios himself.[302] Vinogradov argues that Epiphanios the Monk conceived his first version of the text (A) as a continuation of the *AAMt*. For this reason, it begins after the episode in Sinope and finishes with the martyrdom of the apostle Andrew in Patras. It is possible that Epiphanios composed his first version of the text in a monastery on Mt Olympos. A connection with the Studite monks is indicated by his citation at the beginning of version A of letters by Theodore the Studite.[303] Version B of the *LAA*, on the other hand, is more difficult to place. Vinogradov suggests that Epiphanios the Monk decided to revise his earlier version in order to create a proper hagiographical *Life* of the apostle Andrew. He therefore added a prologue in which, following the conventions of the genre, he defended the need to celebrate the life and conduct of this saint and cited some of his literary sources. A few details in the apostle's itinerary were changed and some of the longer sermons that he had composed for him were abbreviated. Nevertheless, as Vinogradov has also argued, the style of the text, along with allusions to the previous version (A), testify to the authorial hand in both.[304]

When preparing my original translation and commentary of the *LAA*, I (like Prieur, MacDonald, Flamion, and others) quickly became aware of the large discrepancies between Dressel's edition of the text and the versions that appeared in various manuscripts belonging to recension A. Lacking the resources or time to prepare a critical edition myself, I resorted to transcribing and translating two manuscripts that contained the latter text, namely, Cod. Esc. y-II-6 (E) and Cod. Paris. gr. 1510 (P1).[305] The

---

two 10th-c., two 12th-c., and five post-14th-c. manuscripts for version A; one 11th-c. and three post-14th-c. manuscripts for version B.

302 Vinogradov 2005, 46–48. Various scholars had previously called for such a study, and especially for a critical edition of the *LAA*: see *AA*, ed. Prieur 1989, 20; ed. MacDonald 1990, 184; cf. Flamion 1911, 70, n. 3.

303 This citation appears in section 9, that is, the beginning, of Epiphanios the Monk's *LAA* (A), ed. Vinogradov 2005, 197. 9–12; cf. ibid., 47–48; Chap. 2, n. 33 below.

304 Vinogradov 2005, 47.

305 I would like to thank again the librarians at the Escorial Library, Spain, for providing me with digital photographs of ff. 226^v–246^r in E. I consulted P1, ff. 1–19^v online at https://gallica.bnf.fr/ark:/12148/btv1b10723747p.

variations, which consist mainly in six extended sermons, are included in Appendix B of my 2023 edition of the present book.[306] On learning about Vinogradov's critical edition of both versions of the text shortly after the publication of that book, I set about revising my translation, introduction, and commentary of the *LAA*.[307] Whereas Vinogradov chooses to translate (into Russian) an amalgamation of versions A and B of the *LAA*, I have decided to focus on B.[308] This, if Vinogradov is correct in his conclusions, is the version that Epiphanios himself prepared, taking into account his earlier notes (from both literary and oral sources) about Andrew's travels and mission, editing the sermons that he had already composed for the apostle, and using a version of the original *AA* for the end of the narrative that is set in Patras. Readers should consult Vinogradov's critical edition of the first version of the text (A) if they wish to understand that stage of its development.[309]

One of the most striking differences between the two versions of the *LAA* (A and B) and the manuscript that Dressel used for his edition (V3) is that the latter provides a different ending for Epiphanios the Monk's *LAA*.[310] The section that appears only in this manuscript is in fact copied verbatim from the anonymous text known as the *Narratio*.[311] In all of the other manuscripts that contain either version of Epiphanios's *LAA*, a much shorter conclusion is used. This omits the *Narratio*'s account of Stratokles' interference with Andrew's progress through Patras to the cross, the apostle's address to this instrument of torture, and his speeches to the spectators once he is hanging on the cross. Epiphanios's *LAA*, in both versions, offers a much simpler account of Andrew's martyrdom. It is likely that a later scribe, on comparing the *Narratio* and the *LAA*, simply decided that he preferred the former. The change might have been made to

---

306 Epiphanios the Monk, *LVM* and *LAA*, trans. Cunningham 2023, 155–68.
307 I would like to express again my gratitude to Clare Litt and Liverpool University Press for allowing me to undertake this revised version of the 2023 publication. Judith Herrin, Elizabeth Jeffreys, and Judith Ryder also supported my decision to embark on this work. I am also grateful to Andrey Vinogradov for his gracious acknowledgment of my error and for helpful advice that he offered in the course of my revisions.
308 For Vinogradov's Russian translation of the *LAA*, see idem 2005, 113–52.
309 Vinogradov 2005, 197–235.
310 This was noticed first by Flamion 1911, 70, n. 3. It is also discussed in the introductory section of the *AA*, ed. Prieur 1989, 20.
311 The variation from *LAA*, ed. Dressel 1843, begins at 74. 9 after the word αὐτῷ. For its source, see Anon., *Narratio* 23–38, ed. Vinogradov 2005, 189. 4–196. 24.

V3 itself or to an earlier prototype. In any case, Vinogradov has correctly provided the original ending in his editions of both versions of the *LAA*.

In conclusion, the *LAA* is a complex work due not only to its various literary influences, but also to its transmission in two separate versions (as well as the third that is contained only in V3 and Dressel's edition). Vinogradov has succeeded in elucidating many aspects of this rich tradition, and I am indebted to his work in the present revised version of my original translation. Epiphanios the Monk's *LAA* deserves to be studied for its own merits as well as for its important place in the Greek hagiographical tradition that developed in relation to the apostle Andrew. This was the first attempt to reconstruct an itinerary for the apostle that almost circumnavigated the Black Sea while also taking in western Asia Minor, Thrace, and mainland Greece. The hagiographer's efforts to retrace the steps of the apostle and to gather both oral and material evidence in support of his narrative was a remarkable achievement. Although neither version of his work circulated widely in subsequent centuries, they did inspire other hagiographers and encomiasts to build on this narrative. And, as a work of the period of second Iconoclasm that was composed during the first decades of the ninth century, the *LAA* provides valuable information concerning the cult of St Andrew in Constantinople, as well as that in outlying territories both within and outside the borders of the empire.

1

[D 13] [M 185] BY EPIPHANIOS, MONK AND PRESBYTER, CONCERNING THE CONDUCT OF THE SUPREMELY HOLY THEOTOKOS AND THE YEARS OF HER LIFE[1]

1) Many of the teachers of ancient times have provided narratives about Mary, who is properly and truly [called] Theotokos and Ever-Virgin. Some of these were the prophets,[2] who foretold things about her and about Christ our true God who was inexplicably born from her, by means of diverse prophetic forms and names;[3] others were the holy apostles, who took pains [to write] about the incarnation of the Word of God from her. [The latter] focused on [Christ's] actions but passed quickly over matters relating to [Mary], saying just a few things that the Spirit ordained. They all say that she is descended from David.[4] There have been many panegyrists of [the Theotokos] from among the holy Fathers, but not one among them elaborated her life and times truly and accurately, from her upbringing to her death [D 14]. However, even those who attempted this and spoke of certain periods [in her life] did not expound them correctly, but instead disagreed with each other, as in the case of James the Hebrew and Aphrodisian the

---

1 I am following the edition by Dressel 1843 (D [in text]), with references to that by Mingarelli 1774 (M [in text] = PG 120, 185–216). The Mingarelli version includes the title 'Bless, Master, Oration 41'; see PG 120, 185A.

2 The noun προφῆται is replaced by an adjective, προφητικοῖς, in the Mingarelli edition, which would translate as 'Some of these, by means of diverse prophetic forms and names…'; however, the noun balances οἱ ἅγιοι ἀπόστολοι (in the following clause) better; cf. PG 120, 185A.

3 It is likely that Epiphanios means not only prophetic utterances, such as 'Behold, the virgin shall be with child and bear a son, and you shall name him Emmanuel' (Is 7: 14), but also Old Testament types, such as the burning bush, Jacob's ladder, and others, which were understood to foreshadow Mary's virginal motherhood of Christ. On Marian typology in the Byzantine and modern Orthodox liturgical traditions, see Ledit 1976, 64–97; Ladouceur 2006.

4 Many patristic and Byzantine writers asserted both royal and priestly lineage for the Virgin Mary. See Introduction, 16–17.

Persian, along with some others who, having mentioned only her birth, at once [M 188] became silent.[5] And whereas John of Thessalonike composed a famous oration on her 'falling asleep', he kept himself hidden,[6] while another John, who styled himself 'Theologian', attracted to himself the charge of falsehood.[7] Meanwhile, Andrew, the bishop of Crete who was from Jerusalem, having said a few things and taught them correctly, arranged the narrative into the form of an enkomion.[8] And after evaluating the majority and having collected those elements that are trustworthy, sure, and true, both from the *Ecclesiastical History* of Eusebios (who took the name of Pamphilos) and from the other historians and teachers,[9] we will provide something in simple language for those who long for the [facts] about her. And we will indicate in the margin[10] the name of each [writer]

---

5 It is possible that Epiphanios refers here to the author of the polemical text known as the *Doctrina Jacobi nuper baptizati*, which deals with the genealogy of the Virgin Mary; see Déroche 1991, 49; however, he may also mean the apostle James who was the purported author of the second-century text, the *Protevangelion of James*. By 'Aphrodisian the Persian', Epiphanios means a version of the *Legend of Aphroditianus*, which was also known to the early eighth-century preacher John of Damascus, and circulated widely in the Eastern Christian world. For editions and discussion of the text, see Introduction, 26–27, and n. 131.

6 John of Thessalonike, *Homily on the Dormition*, ed. Jugie 1925/1990. It is unclear what Epiphanios means when he says that this preacher 'kept himself hidden'; he may refer to John's failure to name himself when delivering the sermon – a common topos of humility among Byzantine preachers.

7 Epiphanios is referring here to a popular text on the Dormition of the Virgin, known as the *Transitus*, that was attributed falsely to John the Evangelist or 'Theologian' (*CANT* 101, *BHG* 1055–56); see also Shoemaker 2002, 51. Epiphanios reveals his awareness that this text, in spite of its popularity (it survives in over 100 Greek manuscripts and in various other versions), is pseudonymous.

8 Andrew of Crete, *Homilies on the Nativity and Dormition of the Virgin Mary*, PG 97, 805–81, 1045–1109. Epiphanios's belief in the authenticity and reliability of Andrew's orations on the Virgin reflects the popularity that this early eighth-century preacher enjoyed throughout the Byzantine centuries.

9 Pamphilos was a disciple of the early third-century Christian teacher Origen, and later directed a theological school at Caesarea in Palestine. It is possible that Epiphanios refers here to Eusebios of Caesarea's use of Pamphilos's work, along with his library, to the extent that he assumed the latter's name (ὁ τοῦ Παμφίλου); see Livingstone 1997, 1213.

10 The phrase ἐπὶ τοῦ μετωπαίου, which appears in Dressel's edition, refers to the margin of a book where glosses or notes may be added; see LS 1123: μέτωπον, II. 2 (I am grateful to Fr Maximos Constas for pointing out this meaning to me). The remark suggests that Epiphanios (or his scribe) wrote notes indicating the authors that he was citing in the margins of his manuscript. Such glosses do not however appear in any of the manuscripts that I have been able to consult.

LIFE OF MARY, THE THEOTOKOS 77

from whom we have taken anything, so that no one may accuse us of adding or leaving out anything that is peculiar. And even if we should take something from apocryphal or heretical [texts], let no one find fault with us.[11] 'For the testimonies from enemies are worthy of greater trust', as the great Basil says.[12] Even the marvellous Cyril, bishop of Alexandria, did this same thing [D 15] [when he established] the genealogy of Joseph, the betrothed husband of the all-holy and God-bearing Mary, from Abraham to David;[13] and, for the rest of it, since both Joseph and the Theotokos were born from relatives,[14] having showed that the two Evangelists were in harmony – although Matthew went downward and Luke [M 189] worked his way up[15] – [Cyril] began with Nathan who was David's son. There is thus proof for the words [that follow].

2. From the line of Nathan, the son of David, Levi was born. And Levi bore Melchi and Panther. Melchi took a wife and died without offspring. But Panther bore Barpanther. Barpanther bore Joachim, the father of Mary, the Theotokos. And Matthan was born of the line of Solomon, the son of David. He bore James, the father of Joseph, and then died. Melchi, Panther's brother, took his wife, the mother of James, and bore Eli. So James was from the tribe of Solomon while Eli was from that of Nathan. Eli took a wife and died without offspring. And his brother, James, who shared the same mother, took his wife and bore Joseph. Thus Joseph was by nature

---

11 This is an interesting statement, since it suggests the author's distrust of so-called 'apocryphal' texts, many of which were associated with heresy during the middle Byzantine period. Although Epiphanios does not explicitly reject the *Protevangelion of James*, he may be referring to ancient traditions concerning the Dormition of the Virgin that contained Angel Christology, Docetism, Gnosticism, and other heterodox elements; see Shoemaker 2002, 212–56. On the association of some apocryphal texts (such as the *AA*) with heretical groups, see Introduction, 46–47.

12 The quotation, ...[Αἱ γὰρ] παρὰ τῶν ἐχθρῶν μαρτυρίαι ἀξιοπιστότεραί εἰσιν, is taken verbatim from Basil of Caesarea's *Homily on the Nativity of Christ*, PG 31, 1469C.

13 It is possible that Epiphanios refers here to Cyril of Alexandria's *Commentary on Twelve Minor Prophets*, ed. Pusey 1868, vol. 2, 127. 24: ...ἔστι γοῦν ἀκοῦσαι σαφῶς τοῦ μὲν μακαρίου Λουκᾶ τὸν τῆς γενεαλογίας ἐκλογισμὸν ἀναφέροντος ἐξ Ἰωσὴφ ἐπὶ τὸν Ἀδάμ, Ματθαίου γενὴν ἐκ Δαυίδ τε καὶ Ἀβραὰμ κατακομίζοντος πάλιν στοιχηδόν, ὡς ἔφην, ἐπὶ τὸν Ἰωσήφ.

14 Epiphanios uses the word ἀδελφῶν here, which should more literally be translated as 'brothers'. However, he follows normal patristic exegesis of this term in interpreting it more broadly; see Lampe, 30: ἀδελφός, 5.

15 Mt 1: 1–17; Lk 3: 23–38.

the son of James, but by law the son of Eli.[16] And they dwelt in Galilee.[17] The two brothers [thus] took the same wife (since the law commands this if one of them should die without issue), in order that one brother might take the wife of the other and thereby resurrect his brother's seed.[18] Joachim and Eli were brothers from [D 16] their [grand-] father Panther, while Eli and James were brothers from their father Matthan. Joachim bore Mary the Theotokos, while Eli bore Joseph according to the law, so that Joseph and Mary were children of brothers.[19] And Joseph was by profession a carpenter. And he had a brother who was born from the same mother and from James, namely, Klopas or even Kleopas.

3. With regard to her mother, the [lineage of the] Theotokos was as follows: Matthan,[20] the priest from Bethlehem, had three daughters, Mary, Sobe, and Anna. And Mary gave birth to the midwife Salome, while Sobe bore the mother of John the Baptist.[21] But Anna took Joachim, the brother of

---

16 The first part of this genealogy is borrowed almost (but not completely) verbatim from John of Damascus's *Exposition of the Orthodox Faith*; see idem, *Exposition of Faith* IV.14, ed. Kotter 1973, 199.32–200.44; trans. Chase 1953, 363; trans. Russell 2022, 255. In the following paragraph (beginning 'With regard to her mother [Anna]'), however, he may be following Hippolytos of Thebes (see below, n. 21). I am grateful to Andrey Vinogradov for sending me a transcription of Cod. Petropol. RNB gr. 96 (11th c.), ff. 98–99[v], which also contains a short discourse on the genealogy of the Virgin Mary. This text diverges from John of Damascus's *Exposition of Faith* in some details; it also covers the Virgin's dedication to the Temple and includes a description of her physical appearance.

17 Epiphanios uses the preposition εἰς with the accusative, rather than ἐν with dative, here and elsewhere in his texts. This was a common substitution in medieval Greek texts that adopted the koine style.

18 I have paraphrased the Greek slightly here in order to provide the sense of the passage in English.

19 This highly confusing genealogy depends on a rather loose usage of words such as ἀδελφός and πατήρ, which can mean either 'brother/sister' or 'cousin' and 'father' or 'grandfather', respectively; see also above, n. 14. Although Epiphanios seems for the most part to follow the genealogy that John of Damascus provides (see above, n. 16), there are other earlier sources that may have provided inspiration. For a full discussion of these sources, including Syriac ones, see Introduction, 16–17; Brock 2006.

20 Both Mingarelli and Dressel spell this name as Μάτθαμ in Greek; however, most sources spell it with a final ν. See, for example, Hippolytos of Thebe's *Chronicle* 6, ed. Diekamp 1898, 9. 1.

21 The information about three sisters, Mary, Sobe, and Anna, corresponds with that provided in Hippolytos of Thebe's fragmentary *Chronicle* 6, ed. Diekamp 1898, 9. 4–6, 14. 16–19, 23, 1–6, 31. 16–20, 50. 23–26. See also Andrew of Crete, *Kanon on the Nativity of the Virgin*, Stichos after Ode Six, PG 97, 1325B.

Joseph's father. Anna went down as a bride into the city of Nazareth in Galilee and lived with Joachim for fifty years, and they did not produce a child. And it came to pass that they went up into Jerusalem for the feast of the Dedication [of the Temple]. And while Joachim was praying in the Temple, it happened that he heard a voice from heaven saying to him, 'You will have a child and you will be glorified through it.'[22] Then his wife Anna conceived in her old age [M 192] and bore a female child. And she gave her the name of Mary, on account of her sister. And all their relatives and friends rejoiced with them.

4. When the infant Mary was three years old, her parents led her up into Jerusalem and presented her to the Lord with gifts. And the priest Judah,[23] who was also Barachias, the father of Zacharias, received her along with her gifts. And all [D 17] the priests were rejoicing and, having prayed, they blessed Joachim and Anna and the child Mary. And they went down to Nazareth.[24] And when she was seven years old, her parents again led her up into Jerusalem and entrusted her to the Lord as a consecrated offering for all the days of her life.[25] Having accomplished this, her father Joachim, so they say, died a little later at the age of eighty. But Mary did not leave the Temple by night or by day. And Anna, having left Nazareth, went to Jerusalem and remained there with her daughter Mary. And she, after living for two more years, died, having reached the age of seventy-nine.[26]

---

22 It is noteworthy that Epiphanios, along with other middle Byzantine hagiographers who wrote about the Virgin Mary, transfers Joachim's vision from the wilderness to the Temple. It occurs during his forty-day sojourn in the desert, according to the *Protevangelion of James* 1, trans. Elliott and Rumsey, 69. On the vision that took place in the Temple, according to middle Byzantine *Lives* of the Virgin, see Cunningham 2019b, 314–15.

23 The Greek name given here is Ἰωδαέ. This personage is not mentioned in the *Protevangelion of James* – or indeed in any other apocryphal or liturgical texts of which I am aware.

24 Mingarelli's text substitutes 'departed' (ἀπῆλθον) for 'went down' (κατῆλθον) here; see PG 120, 192A–B. I have retained Dressel's version here because it correlates with his (incorrect) statement later in the text that Nazareth lay at a lower altitude than Jerusalem and Bethlehem; see below, n. 63.

25 Epiphanios once again deviates from the narrative that is provided in the *Protevangelion of James*, which states that Mary was dedicated to the Temple at the age of three. See *Protevangelion of James 7*, trans. Elliott and Rumsey 2022, 73–75. It is possible either that Epiphanios drew on a different narrative tradition or that he emended this detail in order to make the story more realistic for contemporary auditors or readers.

26 The tenth-century *Synaxarion of Constantinople* provides a short biography of Anna, the mother of the Virgin Mary (feast day 25 July), which reflects apocryphal and

5. Mary, having been entirely orphaned, became a recluse, not departing from the Temple of the Lord. And if she ever needed anyone, she would simply go to Elizabeth – for she lived nearby. She [had] learned her Hebrew letters while her father Joachim was still alive. And she was learned and a lover of learning; and although she was solitary, she laboured and devoted herself to the divine scriptures. She was admired for her work [spinning] wool, flax, silk, and linen;[27] with regard to wisdom and intelligence, she exceeded all of the young girls in that generation. Thus her forefather Solomon [might have] said about her (for how truly he said this concerning her), 'Who will find a manly wife?', along with everything in the rest [of that passage].[28]

6. There was a place in the Temple of the Lord, near the left-hand[29] part of the sanctuary, which was set apart; [D 18] only the virgins would stand within this space.[30] And all the other virgins departed to their families after the synaxis and the dismissal. But Mary applied herself to guarding the sanctuary and the nave, also serving the priests in this way. Her character was as follows: she was serious with respect to everything and [M 193] spoke little; she was quick to obey, well spoken, reserved in speech towards every person, solemn, calm, without anger, full of reverence, respectful, paying every person respect and veneration, so that they all marvelled at her intelligence and speech. She was of medium stature, although some say

---

hagiographical traditions concerning this holy figure; see *SynaxCP*, 841–42. Various eighth- and ninth-century preachers composed enkomia in honour of St Anna, but none of these mention her age at the time of death; see *BHG*, vol. 1, 44–45, nos. 131–134d. For further background on Anna, see Panou 2018.

27 The Greek word βύσσος means 'fine flax' and the linen that is made from it. See LS, 334.

28 Cf. *Septuagint*, Prov 31: 10: Γυναῖκα ἀνδρείαν τίς εὑρήσει; Brenton translates this as 'Who shall find a virtuous woman?' in idem 1851, 818. Compare this with the more recent translation, 'Who can find a courageous wife?', in Pietersma and Wright 2007, 647. Neither of these translations conveys the gendered nuances of the adjective ἀνδρείαν.

29 Mingarelli gives the reading ἐμβόλου in place of εὐωνύμου here at PG 120, 192C. This translates as '...near the colonnaded part of the sanctuary...'.

30 Epiphanios visualises the Jewish Temple in Jerusalem as a Christian church. He suggests here that women (described as 'virgins') stood in the nave near the left side of the sanctuary. On the disposition of women in Byzantine churches through the first millennium, see Taft 1998 (2001), I. On the rare instances of women being allowed into the sanctuary, see ibid, 72 (St Nonna, d. ca. 373); Holum 1982, 145 (Pulcheria, d. 453). However, if Epiphanios is imagining a monastic church that is largely occupied by women, their arrangement in the nave – and possibly also the sanctuary – would be different.

LIFE OF MARY, THE THEOTOKOS 81

that she was taller than this. She was fair in colouring,[31] with blond hair, light-coloured eyes that were well shaped,[32] black-browed, with a prominent nose, long hands, long fingered, and with a narrow face,[33] filled with divine grace and beauty, without pride, unpretentious,[34] active, and in possession of surpassing humility. For this reason, God looked upon her as she spoke and magnified the Lord. She preferred and wore undyed[35] clothing, and her holy maphorion bears witness to this.[36] She spun the [threads] for the holy things, that is, those that belonged to the Temple of the Lord, and was nourished from the Temple, devoting herself to prayers, reading, fasting, handiwork, and every virtue – to the extent that the entirely holy Mary became a teacher of all women by means both of the diversity of her works and her demeanour.[37]

7. When she reached the age of twelve, when [Mary] was praying one night

---

31 On the Virgin Mary's fair skin (literally, 'like ripe wheat'), see the *Legend of Aphroditianus*, ed. Bratke 1899, 17. 22; trans. Heyden 2016, 17.

32 The juxtaposition of the adjectives ξανθόμματος and εὐόφθαλμος here is puzzling. It is possible that the latter means 'with good eyesight'; however, this does not fit with the other adjectives in the sentence, which describe Mary's appearance. I am inclined to translate εὐόφθαλμος as 'well shaped' since it is likely that in addition to describing the colour of the Virgin's eyes, Epiphanios wishes to convey their beauty.

33 This characteristic contrasts with the statement that Mary's face was 'round' (στρογγυλοπρόσωπος) in some versions of the *Legend of Aphroditianus*; see, for example, (ps-) Julius Africanus, *Spuria, De rebus Persicis post Christum natum*, PG 10, 108A.

34 Although this word, ἀσχημάτιστος, normally means 'without form' or 'indescribable', according to Platonic philosophy, Lampe gives this meaning at 253: 3; cf. John Chrysostom, *On the Priesthood* 6.3.7, ed. Nairn 1906, 143. 21.

35 According to LS, 284, αὐτόχροος means 'with its own, natural colour'. Epiphanios views this aspect of Mary's dress as a form of asceticism.

36 On the relic of the robe or mantle (here called 'maphorion'), which was housed in a dedicated shrine at the church of the Blachernai in Constantinople, see Cameron 1979; Shoemaker 2008a; Weyl Carr 2001.

37 Such descriptions of the Virgin Mary appear in other *Lives* that were composed in her honour. See, for example, Euthymios the Athonite, *Georgian Life of the Virgin*, which states: 'She was blessed by all and was full of all grace, and I will say even further that she was supremely worthy of every grace, intelligent with respect to images and words, a scrutinizer of divine visions, completely removed from restlessness, wrath, and gossip, beautiful in soul and body and ordinary in measure of stature, full of every goodness and every good deed. Nevertheless, she was in this way holy by nature and truly a virgin to the point that not even the slightest desire of any passion that would be corrupting of spiritual holiness ever came upon her'; ibid., 13, ed. Shoemaker 2012, 44. On the authorship of the Georgian *Life*, see Simelidis 2020. There is an equivalent passage in John Geometres' *Life of the Virgin* (also in the context of Mary's sojourn in the temple); see Constas and Simelidis, ed. and trans. 2023,

by the doors of the sanctuary, it came to pass at midnight that a light that was brighter than the sun shone out and a voice came out of the sanctuary towards her, saying, 'You will bear [D 19] my Son.'[38] But she kept this quiet, telling no one of the mystery, until the time when Christ was taken up [into heaven].

8. The high priest Abijah bore Jodae, whom they called Barachias.[39] And he bore Aggaios and Zacharias – and they were also priests. And Zacharias took Elizabeth, Mary's cousin, and they lived in Bethlehem. And he begot John the Baptist. Meanwhile Aggaios, Zacharias's brother, bore a daughter named Salome. And Joseph, [M 196] the carpenter, son of Eli and James,[40] who was Mary's cousin, took [Salome] and bore six children from her: James, Simon, Judas, Joses, Sobe, Martha, and Mary.[41] And his wife Salome died. And Joseph continued as a widower and in chastity.[42] When he was about seventy years old, poor with regard to his wealth and at the height of his power as carpenter, he went down into the city of Nazareth in Galilee. And meanwhile, Mary was in Jerusalem, in the house of the Lord. And when she had reached the age of fourteen, and when the weakness of her female nature was showing,[43] the priests considered her as one of

---

40–43 (11). Byzantine hagiographers stressed Mary's ascetic qualities in such descriptions, presenting her as a model for monastic readers to imitate.

38 The story of Mary's vision in the Temple at the age of twelve first appears (in much greater detail) in *The Questions (or Gospel) of Bartholomew* II.15, an apocryphal text that was compiled between the second and sixth centuries; see Schneemelcher 1991, 544–45; Kaestli and Cherix 1993, 111–12. The vision is also described in the three other middle Byzantine *Lives* of the Virgin; for discussion, see Cunningham 2019b, 315–16.

39 Cf. Mt 23: 35. On the relationship of Salome, the first wife of Joseph the carpenter, to the priests of the Jewish Temple, sf. Hippolytos of Thebes, *Chronicle* 6, ed. Diekamp 1898, 8. 1–7, 14. 8–13, 22. 14–21, 30. 16–20, 31. 7–13.

40 See above, section 2.

41 The list of Joseph's children (four sons and two daughters from his previous marriage) also appears in Hippolytos of Thebes, *Chronicle* 6, ed. Diekamp 1898, 7. 5–9, 14. 5–8, 22, 30. 14–16, 31. 5–6; cf. Epiphanios of Salamis, *Panarion* 28.7.6 (who gives slightly different numbers and names to Joseph's children), ed. Bergermann, Collatz, and Holl 2013, 319–20; trans. Williams 2009, 121.

42 Σωφροσύνη can also mean 'prudence', 'moderation', or 'discretion'. In this context, 'chastity' fits best.

43 Epiphanios refers here to the time of puberty when Mary began to menstruate. She would henceforth be considered impure and therefore unable to remain in the holy spaces of the Temple; for this reason, the priests needed to find a husband or guardian for her.

the many – for the mysteries about her were not yet clear – and, having convened a council, they engaged in prayer concerning her.

9. But the high priest Zacharias, the father of John the Baptist, took twelve rods from the priests who were relatives of the Virgin and placed them around the sanctuary, saying, 'The Lord God will reveal a sign, [showing] whose [responsibility] the Virgin will be.' As they were praying, the rod of Joseph the carpenter sprouted [D 20].[44] And consequently, by God's decision, they betrothed the Virgin Mary to him – not for marriage, but for the protection and preservation of [her] blameless virginity. And this is clear on the basis of the holy Virgin's words themselves, which came to pass [in conversation][45] with the angel Gabriel. For when the latter was saying to her after his greeting, 'And behold, you shall conceive a son and you will name him Jesus, and the Lord God will give him the throne of his ancestor David', and the rest, the Virgin answered him, [saying,] 'How will this happen to me, since I do not know a man?'[46] For if Joseph was betrothed to her according to the law of partnership and marriage, she would not have answered in this way but would instead have said, 'Shall I conceive from the man to whom I was betrothed, that is, to whom I was entirely promised?' However, since she knew clearly that he had taken her not for marriage, but rather for protection and preservation, she uttered that speech which was full of the whole truth. 'How will this happen to me, since I do not know a man?' – that is to say, 'I was not entrusted to a man for marital cohabitation, but rather so that my virginity might be continually kept both pure and intact. And this was the reason for my betrothal.'[47]

---

44 This story (which is told in the *Protevangelion of James* with the variation that a dove came out of the rod and flew onto Joseph's head) is reminiscent of that of the miraculous choice of Aaron as the first priest of the Jews in Numbers 17, when one of twelve rods sprouted within the tabernacle. Cf. *Protevangelion of James* 9, trans. Elliott and Rumsey 2022, 75.

45 Mingarelli provides τῶν λεγομένων in place of Dressel's τῶν γενομένων here; see PG 120, 196C.

46 Cf. Lk 1: 31–34.

47 Epiphanios stresses here the importance of Mary's virginity and lifelong celibacy for the benefit of his monastic audience. Her *postpartum* virginity was not explicitly affirmed in the canonical Gospels, although patristic and Byzantine commentators increasingly accepted this dogma, along with the epithet Ἀειπάρθενος ('Ever-Virgin'). See Graef 2009, 62, 120; Reynolds 2012, 91–106.

10. Joseph, on taking his cousin Mary from the hand of the Lord and all the priests who witnessed this, led her into his house and entrusted his two daughters to her so that she could give them instruction and understanding [so as to be] like herself. And she passed her life in Joseph's house with both humility [D 21] and piety. When she had spent six months there, fasting in the accustomed way until the ninth hour [M 197] of the day,[48] the archangel Gabriel, who was sent from God, revealed himself to her as she was praying. And he disclosed to her all the mysteries about the Only-Begotten Son of God that are written down in the Gospels. And no one from her household knew what had happened, nor did she report this to anyone – not even to Joseph himself – until that time when she saw her Son ascending into heaven.[49] On this account, the Evangelist Matthew says, 'And he did not know her until she had born her son, the first-born',[50] that is to say, he did not know about the mysteries of God that surrounded her or the hidden depth of the things that had been fulfilled in her. It was the first day of the week, on the twenty-fifth day of the month in the month of March, the first day of the moon. But, according to the lunar cycle, this is to say that the first month is April. This is the first among the months of the year; this is the first day on which the first-created darkness was driven out even as God said, '"Let there be light", and there was light.'[51] But it was in the sixth month that John the Baptist was conceived. For it was in the seventh month – when the Consecration of the Tabernacle was being celebrated,[52] along with the Resting of the Ark – that Zacharias consequently went, all alone, into the Holy of Holies for the censing. And the archangel Gabriel appeared to him there.[53] The months are therefore numbered from that time

---

48 Epiphanios envisions here a rigorous daily schedule with regard to fasting and eating, which is in line with monastic practices of his period. For example, monks at the Stoudios monastery in Constantinople consumed their midday meal at variable times, normally at the sixth or ninth hour, with the Divine Liturgy being celebrated three hours earlier; see *Rule of the Monastery of St John Stoudios in Constantinople* 27 in *Monastic Typika, Byzantine Monastic Foundation Documents*, ed. Thomas and Hero 2000, vol. 1, 108–9.

49 Acts 1: 9. The involvement of the Virgin Mary in this scene, which was picked up early by Christian exegetes and iconographers, is based on the statement in Acts 1: 14 according to which she, along with the eleven remaining disciples and 'certain women', devoted herself to prayer.

50 Mt 1: 25.

51 Gen 1: 3; cf. Jn 1: 5.

52 Cf. Jn 7: 2 (ἡ ἑορτὴ τῶν Ἰουδαίων ἡ σκηνοπηγία).

53 See Lk 1: 8–20.

LIFE OF MARY, THE THEOTOKOS 85

in accordance with the [D 22] lunar cycle. Later the indictions and the months were calculated in accordance with the Romans.[54]

11. But concerning the speech of the holy Virgin to the archangel, 'How will this happen to me, since I do not know a man?',[55] this has another meaning (as we have already said) that is not inconsistent with our earlier discussion, which is to say, 'I do not desire a man, nor do I possess any desire for a man, nor do I know the will of fleshly desire for a man.' For she did not have her virginity on account of self-control and struggle, as in the case of those women who are more disciplined and who care for their modesty; rather she [possessed it] by nature – in a way that was distinct from all women and foreign to human nature.[56] And this is what was spoken of by the prophet Ezekiel: 'There will be the gate, facing east, which has been closed, and no one may pass through it except for the Lord alone, the God of Israel. He alone will enter and go out through it, and the gate will remain closed.'[57] And all the prophets and apostles bear witness to the same thing. And our fathers, the lamps and teachers of the catholic and apostolic Church, also speak of the same [type] with one voice. For this reason, the great Dionysios the Areopagite says about Christ that he practised human things in a manner transcending the human.[58] And the begetting and birth-giving without pains are proof of her virginity [M 200].[59] Athanasios of Alexandria

---

54 Epiphanios refers here to the Roman civil calendar, based on consulships and indictions, which overlapped with ecclesiastical calendars that were based on lunar and solar cycles. For background, see *ODB*, vol. 1, 448–49 ('Chronology'); Grumel 1958.

55 Lk 1: 34.

56 In addition to emphasising Mary's ascetic qualities, Epiphanios suggests here that she lacked normal human passions including desire or lust. This comes close to Western ideas concerning her 'immaculate conception', which would cause controversy during the high Middle Ages and beyond. It is unlikely that our monastic author approached the topic in a systematic way; however, he built his ideas about the Virgin on a liturgical tradition that consistently stressed her purity and perpetual virginity. See Cunningham 2021.

57 Cf. Ezek 44: 1–3.

58 See, for example, (ps-) Dionysios the Areopagite, *The Celestial Hierarchy* VII. 3, ed. Heil and Ritter 1991, 30. 7–10; PG 3, 209B, trans. Luibheid 1987, 164; idem, *The Ecclesiastical Hierarchy* I. 1, ed. Heil and Ritter 1991, 63.11–64.14; PG 3, 372A–B, trans. Luibheid 1987, 195–96, etc. Fr Maximos Constas has suggested to me (in private correspondence) that ἀνθρώπων should be emended to ἄνθρωπον here. The former seems more in line with the ideas of (ps-) Dionysios, whereas the latter formulation could be translated as 'human things for the sake of humans'.

59 (ps-) Dionysios the Areopagite, *The Divine Names* II. 9; ed. Suchla 1990, 133. 5–12; PG 648A, trans. Luibheid 1987, 65: 'We have no way of understanding how, in a fashion at

and Leo of Rome [D 23] said of her that she was ignorant of desire for a man.[60] And all of the holy councils bear witness in an orthodox fashion to the same thing. Not only our own, but also some from among the Jews together bear witness to this, including James the Hebrew.[61] He, having been present then and written about her, says that the begetting was strange and different in every respect since, having been examined by the midwife, she was discovered to be a virgin – just as [she was] before the birth. And the priest Reuben, having initiated this same act, was convinced of [the result] by the midwife.[62] Certain others who heard about this miraculous event said that nature was discovered to be exceptional [in this case]; but others said that it went beyond the boundaries of nature.

12. As soon as the vision of the angel had taken place, the holy Virgin went at once to Bethlehem in order to see Elizabeth. Judaea, in which Bethlehem is located, is on higher land than Galilee, where Nazareth is.[63] On this account, Luke says, 'Mary went with haste to the hill country,

---

variance with nature, he was formed from a virgin's blood'; idem, *Epistle* 4, PG 3, 1072B, trans. Luibheid 1987, 264: 'A proof of [the incarnation] is that a virgin supernaturally bore him...' M has a slightly different reading here: ...καὶ μαρτυρεῖ παρθενίαν γέννησιν καὶ τόκος ἄνευ ὠδίνων; PG 120, 197D–200A.

60 Epiphanios may be referring to Athanasios of Alexandria's well-known treatise, *On the Incarnation II.8.3* here, in which the author states that Christ 'takes that which is ours, and that not simply, but from a spotless and stainless virgin, ignorant of man, pure and unmixed from intercourse with men', ed. Kannengiesser 1973, 290.24–292.27. However, it is also possible that he knew of Athanasios's *First Letter to Virgins*, in which the fourth-century bishop provided a lengthy description of Mary's ascetic qualities; ed. Lefort 1955; trans. Brakke 1995, 277–79. Leo the Great's writings may have circulated in Byzantium in connection with the *Acts* of the Council of Chalcedon. Epiphanios may have been familiar, for example, with Leo's letter to Flavian, patriarch of Constantinople, which states, 'And he was born by a new birth, since inviolate virginity, without experiencing desire, provided the material of the flesh'; *Tomus ad Flavianum, Acts of the Council of Chalcedon* II. 22; trans. Price and Gaddis 2005, vol. 2, 19.

61 Epiphanios refers here to the author of the *Protevangelion of James*; see Elliott 1993 and Rumsey 2022. The account of Salome's post-natal examination of the Virgin occurs at 20; ibid., 85.

62 There is no reference to this version of the story in the *Protevangelion of James* 20: in fact the author states that 'the Lord cried, "Salome, Salome, do not report what marvels you have seen, until the child has come to Jerusalem"'; Elliott and Rumsey 2022, 85.

63 This remark reveals Epiphanios's ignorance of the Holy Land. Galilee in fact lies on higher ground than Bethlehem in Judaea. See Dräseke 1895, 351. For other primary and secondary sources on Bethlehem, see Tsafrir, Di Segni, and Green 1994, *TIB*, 83.

where she entered the house of Zachariah and greeted Elizabeth.'[64] And on entering and greeting her, she told her about the vision of the angel and his words – that there was a male child in her womb and that Zachariah had seen an angel in the Temple and had become mute on this account; for Zachariah was not speaking at all since he was unable to do so.[65] And they contained the mysteries in themselves and reported to no one the things that they had spoken about. [D 24] After three months, the holy Mary went down into Galilee, to the house of Joseph. The holy one was orderly in her speech, manner, and way of life. But when the time came and her belly was expanding, Joseph, on seeing the holy one and not knowing about the mysteries that surrounded her, was overcome with shame and wished to banish her secretly from his house. However, an angel of God prevented him, as the Evangelist Matthew relates.[66]

13. It came to pass at that time that the census occurred, according to the command of the Caesar Augustus. And Joseph went up from Galilee into Judaea, along with his whole household, in order to register in accordance with Caesar's decree.[67] And he sent his sons in advance, while he himself, taking his daughters and the holy Virgin Mary, went up along with a beast of burden. And when they did not reach Jerusalem, [M 201] they rested at a property on the outskirts of Bethlehem which belonged to Salome, a cousin of the Theotokos. And on the same night, the holy Virgin bore the Emmanuel, with Salome the midwife attending to everything; [the latter] was from Bethlehem and happened to be the cousin of the holy Virgin and Theotokos Mary according to her maternal line – just like Elizabeth, the wife of Zacharias.[68] The place in which they had rested was a cave and a home for four-footed animals. But Elizabeth, along with some other relations of theirs, brought them whatever they needed when she learned of their stopping place.[69] [D 25] And on hearing of the things that were being

64 Lk 1: 39–40.
65 Lk 1: 20–23.
66 Cf. Mt 1: 20.
67 Cf. Lk 2: 4.
68 The inclusion of Salome in the Nativity story occurs in the *Protevangelion of James* 19–20, but not in the Gospel of Luke. However, according to the apocryphal text, a different midwife attends to the birth of Christ. Salome only arrives afterwards and examines Mary in order to verify her *postpartum* virginity. There is no mention of her ownership of the 'property' (τὸ κτῆμα) in which Joseph and Mary stayed, according to Epiphanios. Cf. Elliott and Rumsey 2022, 83–85.
69 I have substituted ἐπίστασιν ('stop' or 'halt') for ἐπιστασίαν ('authority') here, since

said by the shepherds, they were astonished. After a short time the Magi from the temperate east came out of Persia,[70] having seen the star from the left-hand side of Jerusalem – for Persia lies beside Judaea in this way.[71] But the star was not from among the rest of the stars or even from the height to which the other stars are fixed; rather, it appeared to be close to the earth and unusual compared with those that manifest themselves normally or under some particular circumstance – nor had it ever appeared before,[72] as both the great Basil and John Chrysostom say.[73] [The Magi] found [the holy family] in the place in which the pure and ineffable birth of Jesus had come to pass – no longer in the cave but in a certain house.[74] Jesus was at that time [discovered to be] not like a baby but instead like a child, as the divine Evangelist Matthew himself bears witness.[75] But in any case, [Matthew testifies] that, during their deviation [from the journey], they were present there – both Joseph and the all-blameless Virgin, with the One born from her without seed – in order that they might hear from the Magi, who were of a different race and were strangers to the covenants of God, [not knowing]

the latter does not make sense in the context of this sentence. This is possibly a scribal error, although the manuscripts which I have checked, including Vat. gr. 442 (11th c.), fol. 337[v], and Hagios Sabas 60 (12th c.), fol. 2[v], also contain this reading.

70 Mingarelli substitutes 'from the Persian city of Babylon' for 'Persia' here; see PG 120, 201B.

71 Once again, Epiphanios displays rather vague knowledge of the geography of the Near East in this statement; he is trying to visualise the scene, presumably on the basis of contemporary maps. Mingarelli's text adds a phrase before 'But the star was not...', which reads, ἀλλὰ χαμηλὸς ἦν· καὶ μηδέποτε φανείς, ὥς φησιν Ἰωάννης ὁ Χρυσόστομος ('...but it was on the ground and was never visible, as John Chrysostom says...'); PG 120, 201B. The author (or scribe) may be referring to John Chrysostom's *Homily 6 on Matthew* here; see PG 57, 64. See also below, Appendix A (a).

72 I have paraphrased this sentence since the Greek is difficult to render literally into English.

73 It is possible that Epiphanios refers here to Basil of Caesarea's and John Chrysostom's *Homilies on the Nativity of Christ*, PG 31, 1472B and PG 49, 354, respectively. However, the reference is too vague for these sources to be securely identified. Mingarelli's text simplifies this passage; see below, Appendix A (a).

74 According to the *Protevangelion of James* 21, the holy family were still in the cave when the Magi arrived; see Elliott and Rumsey 2022, 85. However, Epiphanios reverts to the canonical narrative of Matthew here, which uses the word 'house' (τὴν οἰκίαν) at 2: 11.

75 It is possible that Epiphanios is referring to Matthew's choice of the word παιδίον (Mt 2: 11) here, when the latter describes the Magi's first sight of Jesus. However, he is probably also alluding to the *Legend of Aphroditianus*, which describes the miraculous reasons for the Magi's journey to Bethlehem, followed by their encounter with the Virgin Mary and the two-year-old Jesus; see Hayden 2016, 16–18; cf. Introduction, n. 131.

who he was or why he had condescended to come to humanity.[76] Not only they, but also the whole of Jerusalem, and Herod who then governed and ruled over the Jews [were ignorant about these things]. On the eighth day, they circumcised the child and named him Jesus, which means 'Saviour'.[77] And they returned to Nazareth.[78] And when the forty days were completed [D 26], they brought the child up into Jerusalem and presented him to the Lord with gifts; this is when the elder Symeon received him in his arms and blessed them.[79] It was there that Joseph was instructed to flee into Egypt.[80]

14. But Herod,[81] having been tricked by the Magi, sent out a decree and then killed all the children in Bethlehem who were two years of age or less on the basis of what he learned from the Magi. And his whole household and the nearest and dearest of his family were immediately overthrown since he slaughtered his wife, from whom he had begotten two sons, Alexander and Aristoboulos, along with the two sons themselves, and another, Antipater, whom he had begotten from another woman. And Herod himself succumbed to a divinely sent illness, enduring a putrefaction around both his genitals and his intestines; teeming with worms, he expired, as Josephus testifies in his history about him.[82]

---

76 Cf. Mt 2: 11.

77 Cf. Lk 2: 21. The Hebrew name 'Jesus' is indeed based on the root ישע, which means 'to deliver' or 'to rescue'.

78 Neither the canonical Gospels nor the *Protevangelion of James* mention a return to Nazareth at this point in the narrative; however, cf. Lk 2: 39 (after the presentation of Jesus to Symeon in the Temple).

79 Cf. Lk 2: 25–35.

80 Cf. Mt 2: 13–15.

81 There is a major discrepancy between Dressel's and Mingarelli's texts at this point in the narrative; see Appendix A (b). Both versions provide a condensed (and somewhat garbled) version of Josephus's account of Herod's sins and demise: according to Josephus, Herod's wife was named Mariamme (sometimes spelled 'Mariamne') (I) whereas Salome was the name of his sister. According to the Jewish historian, Herod killed Mariamme's grandfather, Hyrkanos, and later – in a fit of jealousy – murdered his wife and his brother-in-law (the husband of Salome) too. Sometime later, Herod ordered that his sons by Mariamme, Alexander and Aristoboulos, be strangled at Sebaste in Cappadocia; see Josephus, *The Jewish War* I. 551, trans. Thackeray 1961, 260–61.

82 On Herod's death, see Josephus, *The Jewish War* I. 655–73, trans. Thackeray 1961, 310–19; idem, *Antiquities* XVII. 168–92, trans. Marcus and Wikgren 1963 (1998), 242–55. Epiphanios may also have been influenced by Eusebios of Caesarea in his account both of Herod's crimes and gruesome death; see Eusebios of Caesarea, *Ecclesiastical History* I.8.5–16, ed. Schwartz, Mommsen, and Winkelmann 1999, 64–68; trans. Williamson 1965, 57–59.

15. The soldiers killed Zachariah when he was performing his duties between the nave and the altar.[83] The reason for his murder was double: for some say that he was destroyed because of the disappearance of his son, who was being sought by Herod; but others say that it was on account of the holy Virgin and Theotokos, since Zachariah led her into [the part of the Temple] which virgins were allowed to enter[84] – and it was in the same place that he was killed by the scribes, as one who had clearly transgressed the law since he was telling everyone of the matters relating to her,[85] that is, how she had remained a virgin and was just as she had been before giving birth.

16. [D 27] Meanwhile Elizabeth was in Bethlehem. Taking John, she departed into the wilderness and hid with the child in a cave for forty days.[86] Then she returned alone.[87] But John, having been reared there, remained in the wilderness until the time of his manifestation to Israel.[88] [M 204]

17. But Joseph, having gone down into Egypt, spent five years there, so they say, with his sons and daughters, as well as with the Theotokos and Christ.[89] And he returned again on account of a revelation, and came into

---

83 For the murder of John the Baptist's father, Zachariah, see *Protevangelion of James* 23–24, trans. Elliott and Rumsey 2022, 87–89. It is possible that this story, which is not mentioned in the canonical Gospels, was inspired by that of Zachariah, son of the priest Jehoiada, who was stoned to death in the court of the Temple (2 Chron 24: 20–22). However, the tradition that Zachariah, the father of John the Baptist, was killed by the Jews because he allowed Mary (after the birth of Christ) to enter the sanctuary along with other virgins, also appears in Origen's *Commentary on Matthew 23:35*; see ibid., trans. Heine 2018 vol. 2, Series 9–28, 574–76.

84 On Epiphanios's idea of the Jewish Temple as a Christian church, see above, n. 30.

85 There is an inconsistency here in that Epiphanios previously said that Zachariah was killed by soldiers. The latter's transgression of the law must refer to the high priest's decision to admit the child, Mary, to the Holy of Holies in the Temple; see above, n. 83.

86 *Protevangelion of James* 22, trans. Elliott and Rumsey 2022, 87.

87 For the phrase Ἔπειτα ἐπανῆλθε μόνη ('Then she returned alone'), Mingarelli substitutes Ὁ δὲ Ἡρώδης μετὰ τὴν βρεφοκτονίαν, ἑαυτὸν ἀνεῖλε μαχαίρᾳ, ὢν ἐτῶν ο΄ ('But, following the slaughter of the infants, Herod killed himself with a knife at the age of seventy'); see PG 120, 201D.

88 Cf. Mt 3: 1–2; Mk 1: 4; Lk 3: 3; Jn 1: 6–7.

89 Various apocryphal 'Infancy Gospels' deal with the sojourn of the holy family in Egypt. It is likely that Epiphanios made this statement on the basis of a Greek equivalent of one of the various versions of this narrative that survive. See, for example, the *Infancy Gospel of Thomas* (Latin version), *Gospel of Ps-Matthew*, and the *Arabic Infancy Gospel*, which are translated in Elliott 1993, 68–110.

LIFE OF MARY, THE THEOTOKOS 91

Nazareth in Galilee, as the Gospel bears witness.[90] His brother Klopas (who had the same father, that is, James, who was Joseph's natural father) took his daughter Mary as his wife. And he bore Symeon, who was also called Kleopas, from her. This Symeon became bishop of Jerusalem after James, the brother of the Lord, and was later crucified, after many torments, under the emperor Domitian of Rome, having reached the very old age of about one hundred and twenty [years].[91] It was this Kleopas who, along with his fellow traveller Nathaniel, beheld Christ when he had been raised from the dead [D 28] after three days, near the village of Emmaus, as the marvellous Luke relates.[92] Meanwhile James, the son of Joseph, took a wife, as some say, who lived with him for two years.[93] And when she died, he did not take another. Judas, his brother, had two sons, who were given the names Zoker and James. They stood up to the emperor Domitian and, as descendants of David and of the same family as our Lord Jesus Christ, they taught about the Kingdom – that it was the Kingdom of Christ and a heavenly, rather than earthly, kingdom. And he put an end to the persecution of Christians on account of their virtue and wisdom.[94] James and Judas, who were called the 'brothers of the Lord', were numbered among the twelve apostles. But Joses and Symeon took wives for themselves. Sobe remained with the Theotokos for the whole time. But Joses had been abandoned[95] by his mother when he was still breast-feeding; however, Mary, the daughter of Salome who was also called his sister,[96] reared him.

---

90 Cf. Mt 2: 19–22.
91 On the replacement of the first bishop of Jerusalem, James, by Symeon, son of Klopas, see Eusebios of Caesarea, *Ecclesiastical History* III.11, ed. Schwartz, Mommsen, and Winkelmann 1999, 226–28, trans. Williamson 1965, 123–24. On the martyrdom of Symeon by crucifixion, see ibid., III.32.6, ed. Schwartz, Mommsen, and Winkelmann 1999, 270, trans. Williamson 1965, 142–43. Eusebios cites the second-century Church historian Hegesippus as his source, stating that Symeon 'won the prize of an end like that suffered by the Lord'; however, he places this martyrdom during the reign of Trajan, not Domitian.
92 Cf. Lk 24: 13–35.
93 I am not aware of any sources that support this statement concerning the marriage of James, 'brother of the Lord' and first bishop of Jerusalem.
94 Eusebios, quoting Hegesippus again, describes the descendants of Christ's family (that is, the half-siblings who were sons of Joseph) persuading the emperor Domitian to terminate his persecution of the Church; see Eusebios, *Ecclesiastical History* III. 20, ed. Schwartz, Mommsen, and Winkelmann 1999, 232–36, trans. Williamson 1965, 126–27.
95 The reading κατελήφθη is an iotacism: I have substituted κατελείφθη. The information seems inconsequential in the context of Epiphanios's narrative.
96 According to Mingarelli's edition, Salome was the cousin of the Virgin Mary; see PG

18. At the time of the feast of the Passover, they went up from Nazareth into Jerusalem. And Jesus was twelve years old when they departed for Jerusalem; many people recognised him and marvelled at his intelligence and wisdom. And he surprised many scribes and pharisees among those who were in Jerusalem so that they all marvelled at his [D 29] responses.[97] He was exceedingly handsome in his countenance – even as the prophet says, 'You are more beautiful in appearance than the sons of men.'[98] His age, or rather, the growth of his body had reached six full feet;[99] he had tawny hair which was not completely bushy,[100] but rather had a close-curling tendency; his eyebrows were dark and not entirely curved; his eyes were tawny and sparkling with joy – just as the story of his forefather David relates, when it says, 'And he was ruddy with beauty of eyes.'[101] And so [Christ] also had well-shaped eyes, a prominent nose,[102] a tawny beard, and long hair. For never did a razor encounter his head, nor did a human hand – apart from that of his mother when he was nursing [as a baby]. He inclined his neck slightly so that he might not entirely achieve the straight and erect stature of his body.[103] His complexion was fair;[104] he did not have a round face but one that, like his mother's, was somewhat long and was ruddy, enough to give an indication of his piety, his intelligence of character, his gentleness, and his unequivocal lack of anger; and [his face was] of the same sort as the sketch that this text, a little earlier, drew of his mother.[105] For he had things

---

120, 204B–C.
97 See Lk 2: 41–51. Mingarelli's text shortens this passage, substituting ὡς καὶ πολλοὺς ἐξέστησεν for καὶ πολλοὺς τῶν ἐν Ἰερουσαλὴμ ἐξέστησε γραμματεῖς τε καὶ φαρισαίους, ὥστε θαυμάζειν ἅπαντες ἐπὶ ταῖς ἀποκρίσεσιν αὐτοῦ; see PG 120, 204C.
98 Cf. Ps 44: 2 LXX; 45: 2.
99 Mingarelli provides an abbreviated version of this description of Christ's appearance here; see Appendix A (c).
100 The adjective ἐπίξανθος/ ον (for Christ's hair) is translated as 'inclining to yellow' or 'tawny' (with reference to hares or deer) in LS, 649. As in the case of his mother, Mary, Epiphanios sees this as a sign of beauty.
101 1 Kgs 17: 42 (LXX); 1 Sam 17: 42. This is the translation provided by Pietersma and Wright 2007, 261.
102 Cf. (ps-) John of Damascus, *Epistola ad Theophilum imperatorem*, PG 95, 349C.
103 It is possible that the description of such posture is intended to convey humility on the part of Christ.
104 Literally, 'corn-coloured' (σιτόχρους); cf. John of Damascus, *On the Two Wills of Christ*, PG 95, 136A.
105 It is odd that Epiphanios inserts this description of Christ, which portrays him as a grown man, into the section of the *Life* that deals with his appearance at the Temple of Jerusalem at the age of twelve. Many of the qualities that he describes (Christ's height, hair, beard, etc.)

LIFE OF MARY, THE THEOTOKOS 93

in common with her and resembled her in every way. When he reached the age of thirty, he was baptised by John in the Jordan river.[106]

19. As for John, the Lord's word about the baptism came to him when he was in the wilderness and had himself reached the age of thirty-one years, [since his conception occurred at] the beginning of the year – [D 30] that is to say, in the month of September.[107] And he went into Judaea and Galilee, preaching repentance and the remission of sins through baptism, as well as about the Kingdom of Heaven – although not as far as the Holy Spirit.[108] As the people saw his awe-inspiring and miraculous conversion, many followed him and became his disciples. Among them were Andrew, from Bethsaida, the city of Galilee, and John, son of Zebedee. But when the priests of the Jews heard the news about John and his teaching, some said that [M 205] he was the Christ while others maintained that he was not. And when much investigation had gone on between them concerning this report, they sent to John and questioned him. And he said to them, 'I am not the Christ, but he who is coming behind me [is the Christ]; he has stood among you.'[109] It then came to pass after [a few] days that many people and rulers went into the Jordan in the desert, confessing their sins to John and being baptised by him. When John was teaching the people in Bethabara, a village on the other side of the Jordan,[110] Jesus came and was baptised by him.[111] And on the eighth day, Jesus went out into the desert around the Jordan and spent forty days there.[112] This is when Satan assailed him and was defeated. And after he had fasted [D 31] for forty days and

---

could only apply to someone over the age of twenty. A similar (but not identical) description of Christ appears in *The Letter of the Three Patriarchs* 7.d, ed. Munitiz, Chrysostomides, Harvalia-Crook, and Dendrinos 1997, 31. 14–19.

106 Mt 3: 13–17; Mk 1: 9–11; Lk 3: 21–22; Jn 1: 29–34.

107 The conception of St John the Baptist was celebrated on 23 September in the Byzantine Church; see *Typikon of the Great Church*, ed. Mateos 1962, vol. 1, 42–43.

108 Epiphanios refers here to the Christian belief that the Holy Spirit manifested himself in creation at the time of Christ's baptism; see Mt 3: 16; Mk 1: 10; Lk 3: 22; Jn 1: 32–33.

109 Cf. Mt 3: 11; Mk 1: 7; Lk 3: 16; Jn 1: 26–27.

110 On Bethabara, see Jn 1: 28. Although most early manuscripts, including the Codices Sinaiticus, Vaticanus and Alexandrinus, locate John's preaching in 'Bethany', a few versions, supported by Origen, offer 'Bethabara'. See *The Greek New Testament*, ed. Aland et al. 2014, 308–9, apparatus. Although many modern English translations employ the former reading, the Authorised King James version chooses the latter; see ed. Norton 2005, 1659.

111 See above, n. 106.

112 Mt 4: 1–11; Mk 1: 12–13; Lk 4: 1–13.

been tempted by the devil, he returned again to John. When John saw Jesus coming towards him, he said, 'Behold, the Lamb of God who bears the sin of the world.'[113] For, in the course of baptising [Christ], he had seen the Holy Spirit coming down from heaven and remaining on him, and the voice from heaven saying, 'This is my beloved Son in whom I am well pleased.' And the people heard about him from John and were amazed. The next day, John saw Jesus walking about and said concerning him, 'Behold the Lamb of God.'

20. After hearing this, [John's] disciples, Andrew and John, left him and followed Jesus. And they came with him into the inn and stayed there with him that day. Andrew found his own brother Simon and led him to Jesus.[114] When Jesus heard that John had been delivered up [to the authorities], he went out the next day into Galilee with his three disciples. He found Philip and pulled him in, while the latter [found] Nathanael.[115] And they went into Cana of Galilee. The wedding took place there, and [Jesus] and his disciples were summoned to the wedding. And when they did not have enough wine, he turned the water into wine. The name of the bridegroom was Simon.[116] After a few days, he followed [D 32] Jesus. He was Simon the Canaanite, one of the twelve, who was also a zealot.[117] From there he went into Bethsaida, a city of Galilee, and went into the house of Peter. And since his mother-in-law was ill, Christ attended and healed her.[118] And when they had returned to Nazareth, Joseph, the betrothed and guardian of the Theotokos, died as a rather elderly man who was full of days. For they

---

113 Jn 1: 29.
114 Cf. Mt 4: 18–20; Mk 1: 16–18; Lk 5: 1–11; Jn 1: 35–42. The four Gospels tell somewhat different stories of how these disciples came to follow Jesus; Epiphanios follows John's narrative here.
115 Cf. Jn 1: 43–45.
116 Cf. Jn 2: 1–11. The Gospel does not mention the name of the bridegroom.
117 Simon the Canaanite is listed as one of Jesus's disciples, for example, in Mt 10: 4. Epiphanios appears to be the first Greek Marian hagiographer to suggest that the marriage at Cana ended with the bridegroom abandoning his wife and following Christ. The tenth-century hagiographers, John Geometres and Euthymios the Athonite, adopted the idea and expanded it further. Both suggested that not only the bridegroom, Simon, but also his bride decided to adopt an ascetic way of life. According to Euthymios, the bride became a disciple of Mary, Jesus's mother; see, for example, Euthymios the Athonite, *Georgian Life of the Virgin* 68, ed. Shoemaker 2012, 95–96. It is also striking that Epiphanios does not mention the Virgin Mary's role in this narrative, which is prominent in Jn 2: 3–5.
118 Cf. Mt 8: 14–15; Mk 1: 29–31; Lk 4: 38–41.

LIFE OF MARY, THE THEOTOKOS   95

say that he had reached about a hundred and ten years. His sons, James and Judas, followed Christ and went with him to every city and land, as he proclaimed the Kingdom and healed every illness and every weakness. Meanwhile, Peter's mother-in-law, along with her daughter who was Peter's wife, followed them and stayed with the Theotokos.[119]

21. Departing from there, they went up into a certain city of Galilee in which there is the lake that is called Gennesa, which is also Gennesaret.[120] Many kinds of trees grow in this area, but it contains especially both balsam and flax, which have been cultivated in this land. And Gennesa is also called 'Bowl' (Phiale) because it is equal on all sides and spherical.[121] And its waters are finer than the muddy thickness [of other lakes].[122] Nevertheless, it nurtures every kind of fish. And those of the trees that bear fruit differ even more from the rest; for they have very many trunks and are extremely productive. [M 208] And there is a surfeit of wine and oil.[123]

---

119 None of these details appear in the canonical Gospels. The identification of James and Judas, as sons of Mary's husband Joseph by a previous marriage, developed in Christian tradition during the first millennium; on Joseph's children, see above, n. 41. The canonical New Testament does not allude to Peter's wife (although her existence is implied in the statement that the apostle has a mother-in-law [ἡ πενθερά] in Mt 8: 14–15). She is also mentioned in the *(ps-) Clementine Homilies* 13.1, ed. Rehm and Strecker 1992, 192. 2–4; *Recognitions* 7. 25, 36, ed. Rehm and Strecker 1994, 208. 23–209. 8, 214. 14–25; cf. Flamion 1911, 75, n. 1; Eusebios of Caesarea, *Ecclesiastical History* III.30.2, ed. Schwartz, Mommsen, and Winkelmann 1999, 262. For more information on Peter's wife, see Chap. 2, n. 9.

120 The lake of Gennesaret, also known as the Sea of Galilee or the Sea of Tiberias, was the largest body of fresh water in the Holy Land.

121 On the town of Gennesaret, see Mt 14: 34–36; Mk 6: 53; Lk 5: 1. It was located at the north-western end of the lake. For early pilgrim accounts that also mention this lake and its biblical associations, see Wilkinson 1977, 63 (Theodosius), 81 (Piacenza pilgrim), 107–8 (Adomnan), and others; see also Tsafrir, Di Segni, and Green 1994, *TIB*, 132.

122 Epiphanios quotes Josephus's description of the lake in *The Jewish War* here, which offers νᾶμα ('running water' or 'stream') in place of Dressel's (or Epiphanios's) ἄμμα ('noose', 'halter', or 'knot'); see Josephus, *The Jewish War* III. 507, ed. and trans. Thackeray 1961, 718–19. I am grateful to Marc Lauxtermann for providing this reference. John Geometres, who was probably inspired by this passage, expands the description of the lake in his *Life of the Virgin*. I would also like to thank Father Maximos for alerting me to the appearance of this motif in John Geometres' hagiographical work. See John Geometres, *Life of the Virgin* 69, ed. Constas and Simelidis 2023, 184–87.

123 Mingarelli's text diverges from that of Dressel here; see Appendix A (d). According to Jn 1: 44, Bethsaida was the hometown of the apostles Peter, Andrew, and Philip. It was also located on the northern shore of the Sea of Galilee; see Tsafrir, Di Segni, and Green 1994, *TIB*, 85.

22. Jesus, on coming into the [D 33] house of Zebedee, along with his mother and his disciples, rested there with Zebedee, who had a wife, named Salome, and two sons, James and John, whom Jesus took as disciples.[124] Their mother, on hearing and believing Jesus's teaching (since he was making proclamations about the earthly kingdom),[125] begged him in order that her sons might sit in his Kingdom, one on the right side and one on his left.[126] She did this both because she loved her children and because she bore a certain family relationship with the Theotokos. On departing from there, they went into Capernaum and he healed the paralytic and many other people.[127] Wherever they went, those who were healed and who were instructed in his word offered them whatever they needed. And his disciples also taught and baptised many people. But Jesus did not baptise; rather, he only instructed and cured those who were infirm. When Zebedee died, James approached Christ and said, 'Allow me to go and bury my father.' But Jesus did not then give him permission, but later released [D 34] both James and John to go away.[128] They departed and buried their father; then they brought their mother to Christ. And she stayed with the Theotokos for the time that remained of his life.[129] After selling their property, they came to Jerusalem and bought the [house] on Sion. When the Lord came into Judaea with his mother and the disciples, they were evangelising, baptising, and serving everywhere.[130] And when they went up into Jerusalem, Salome, the wife of Chuza, the steward of Herod of Philippi,[131] had an evil spirit. She went and prayed to Christ – and

---

124 Cf. Mt 4: 21–22; Mk 1: 19–20; Lk 5: 10–11.
125 Epiphanios displays a loose approach to Greek syntax here, changing subject from the mother of James and John to Jesus in the course of one sentence.
126 Cf. Mk 10: 35–40. Although James and John ask Jesus to allow them to sit at his right and left hand 'in your glory', there is no mention of their mother in Mark's Gospel.
127 Cf. Mt 9: 1–8, Mk 2: 1–12, Lk 5: 17–26.
128 Epiphanios associates James and John here with the biblical passage in which Jesus tells a man to proclaim the Gospel rather than bury his father with the words, 'Let the dead bury their dead'; cf. Lk 9: 60.
129 The possessive pronoun αὐτοῦ ('his') must refer to Christ; however, it is possible that this is a scribal error and that the word should be αὐτῆς ('her'). Mingarelli shares the reading αὐτοῦ at PG 120, 208B.
130 I have inserted a full stop into my English translation, although the Greek, using a string of genitive absolutes, includes the story of Salome in this sentence.
131 See Lk 8: 2–3 for another version of this story. Epiphanios associates the possession by demons with another Salome (whom Luke calls Joanna) instead of with Mary Magdalene. It is possible that he seeks to clear the latter of the problematic background that Luke attributes to her.

LIFE OF MARY, THE THEOTOKOS 97

was freed from it. And she no longer distanced herself from the Lord, but instead followed him.

23. When they had spent some days there – for it was also the feast of the Tabernacles – and Christ had illumined many by means of his teaching in the Temple, and had also thrown out the money changers, the small coin changers,[132] and all of those who trade in divine things,[133] and, having healed many of those who were ill from a variety of ailments, he returned again into Galilee.[134] And when he arrived at the city of Magda, a certain woman named Mary, who was well-born and wealthy, received him into her house. And on hearing Christ's word [D 35] and seeing the miracles which he worked, she renounced her house entirely, came to Christ, and followed him.[135] And she stayed with his mother and the rest of the women. She was very intelligent and fervent in spirit, just as Peter was among the men. And she served them out of her own resources. The disciples who followed Jesus were as follows: Peter and Andrew, who were brothers from the city of Bethsaida; James and John, the sons of Zebedee; Philip and Bartholomew; James, the son of Alphaeus, and Judas, who were brothers of the Lord (for [M 209] Joseph, their father, had the surname Alphaeus); Simon from Cana in Galilee and Thomas, who was called Didymos; along with Matthew the Evangelist and Judas the Iscariot.[136]

---

132 Κολλυβιστής is a synonym of κερματιστής according to LS, 972; however, the former appears to mean a 'small' money changer, as opposed to a dealer in larger quantities of cash.
133 For the term θεοκάπηλοι, cf. Gregory Nazianzen, *Oration* 21.31, PG 35, col. 1117C. Elsewhere the term is used for simoniacal priests or false teachers; see Lampe, 626.
134 For this part of the narrative, cf. Mt 21: 12–14; Mk 11: 15–18; Lk 19: 45–46. The Evangelists place this story fairly late in the ministry of Jesus; they do not mention a return to Galilee after the expulsion of the money changers from the Temple.
135 Cf. Lk 8: 2–3. Epiphanios, like most early Christian and Byzantine exegetes, conflates Mary Magdalen with Mary, the sister of Lazarus, here. The story of his reception into the latter's house (when an altercation with her sister Martha occurs) appears in Lk 10: 38–42. Pope Gregory I also associated both Marys with the unnamed 'sinful woman' who anointed Jesus's feet in Lk 7: 36–50. This conflation of three Lukan women into one 'Mary Magdalen' persisted especially in the Christian West, according to which she is often portrayed as a repentant prostitute who nevertheless achieved a close (albeit platonic) relationship with Christ. See Gregory the Great, *Homily 33*, PL 76, 1239A; Haskins 1993, 95–97.
136 This list of the disciples' names follows that provided by the Evangelist Luke at Lk 6: 12–16. Matthew and Mark substitute the name Thaddaeus for Judas; see Mt 10: 2–4; Mk 3: 16–19. Luke differs from Epiphanios in identifying the first Judas (not Judas the Iscariot) as the son of James, not Alphaeus (nor does Luke identify Alphaeus with Joseph, as

24. John, the son of Zebedee, sold his whole property in Galilee after the death of his father. And coming into Jerusalem, he purchased Sion. This is the higher part of Jerusalem.[137]

25. But the high priests of the Jews at that time used to change each year and [D 36] they procured the priesthood by means of money.[138] For this reason, even Caiaphas did not originate from Jerusalem, but rather from a certain one of the external eparchies; he was a high priest for that year, but they say that he did not have a residence in his own house – but [stayed] instead in John's inherited property. It is on this account that the Evangelist John himself says in his Gospel that 'that disciple was known to the high priest'.[139]

Epiphanios does here); see Lk 6: 16; Acts 1: 13. Biblical scholars mostly identify this Judas with Thaddaeus, perhaps in order to distinguish this disciple from Judas Iscariot. He is also sometimes known as Jude, patron saint of desperate cases and lost causes; see Bauckham 1990; Livingstone 1997, 907, 1596. Mingarelli's version of the text changes the order of the names and adds a thirteenth – not eliding Judas 'of Jerusalem' with Thaddaeus; see Appendix A (e).

137 According to Mimouni, the tradition of the house on Mt Sion where Mary lived out her days under the protection of the Evangelist John can be traced back no further than the beginning of the seventh century. It followed the discovery of the Virgin's tomb in Gethsemane in the fifth century, which led to the need for the house in which she might have 'fallen asleep'. Mt Sion was located on a hill just outside the walls on the south-west side of the old city of Jerusalem. Christians mistakenly identified it with an important site in Jewish tradition, according to 2 Kgs 5: 7 (LXX); 2 Sam 5: 7, believing it to be the stronghold that had been known as the 'City of David'. During the early Christian period, the site was associated with important events both before and after the death of Jesus Christ, including the Last Supper (Mt 26: 17–29, etc.), his appearance to the apostles after the resurrection (Jn 20: 19–29), the period after the Ascension (Acts 1: 13), and Pentecost (2: 1–4). The Evangelists describe a house in which the disciples sheltered together, but do not associate it specifically with John or the Virgin Mary. At the end of the fourth century, a large basilica with five aisles was built to commemorate these events. After destruction during the Persian invasion of Jerusalem in 614, the church was rebuilt by the patriarch Modestos. The association of the house (which had been replaced by the basilica) on Mt Sion with the dormition of the Virgin Mary occurs in an anacreontic hymn by the early seventh-century patriarch of Jerusalem, Sophronios, the pilgrimage account of Arculf (dated to 670), the *Diegesis* or 'Guide' to the Holy Land by Epiphanios Hagiopolites (whose earliest recension dates to the mid-seventh century), the *Chronicle* of Hippolytos of Thebes (seventh–eighth century), various Late Antique accounts of Mary's dormition, and sermons by Andrew of Crete, John of Damascus, and Germanos of Constantinople (all dated to the early or mid-eighth century); for references, see Mimouni 1995, 533–48. For more information on the building, along with the churches that took its place, see Baldovin 1987, 49–50, 86–87.

138 Mingarelli provides a different version of this whole passage, beginning at 'But the high priests' and ending at '...and the rest'; see Appendix A (f).

139 Cf. Jn 18: 15.

LIFE OF MARY, THE THEOTOKOS 99

For half of his house was given to the high priest; meanwhile he occupied the other half, in which the Ruler Christ carried out the Passover and the mystical supper with his disciples. For they say that Christ sent his disciples there in order that they might prepare the Passover [meal]. For [Jesus's] statement, 'Go to a certain man',[140] referred, as some say, to John – in other words, to the master of the house who stayed in it. For John never separated himself from Christ but was with him until his world-saving crucifixion. So they remained there and there carried out the Passover and the mystical supper.[141] And the Theotokos also remained there, from the time when John took charge of her and stood with her at the cross of Christ, and heard from him the words, 'Behold your mother', while the Theotokos [heard] 'Behold your son.'[142] For the saying that 'that disciple took over the care of her and took her into his own home'[143] means, in veiled language, 'the holy Sion', [that is,] his house. It was there that Christ entered in through closed doors, [D 37] and stood in their midst and said, 'Peace be with you', and the rest.[144]

26. The myrrh-bearing women are seven in number:[145] (i) Mary Magdalen and (ii) Salome, also the mother of the sons of Zebedee,[146] and (iii) Mary,

---

140 Mt 26: 18.
141 Mt 26: 17–29; Mk 14: 12–25; Lk 22: 7–38; Jn 13: 1–30.
142 Jn 19: 26–27.
143 Cf. Jn 19: 27.
144 Jn 20: 19, ff.
145 Mingarelli provides a simpler reading here: Μυροφόροι δὲ ἦσαν ἑπτά ('There were seven myrrh-bearers'), along with some adjustments in the passage that follows; see Appendix A (g). In the list that follows, I have provided numbers that help to identify the individual women who attended Jesus Christ's tomb at the end of the sabbath, according to Epiphanios. The four Gospels meanwhile differ in their accounts. According to Matthew, they were only two in number: Mary Magdalen and 'the other Mary' (Mt 28: 1). Mark says that they were Mary Magdalen, Mary the mother of James, and Salome (Mk 16: 1). Luke describes them first as 'the women who had come with him from Galilee' (Lk 23: 55) but later, more precisely, as 'Mary Magdalen, Joanna, Mary the mother of James, and the other women' (Lk 24: 10). John, however, names only Mary Magdalen (Jn 20: 1). The tradition that there were seven (or sometimes eight) myrrh-bearers developed at a later date, with Mary, the mother of James, frequently being identified as the Virgin Mary (see below, n. 147). See, for example, the *SynaxCP*, 30 June, 789–90. The liturgical celebration of the myrrh-bearers took place on the second Sunday, along with the weekdays that followed it, after Easter; see *Pentekostarion* 1883, 82–136; Eng. trans. 1990, 105–53. I have not yet been able to determine exactly when the legend that there were seven myrrh-bearers developed in the Christian tradition.
146 According to Byzantine tradition, Salome was the wife of Zebedee and mother of the

the mother of James the Less,[147] and (iv) the wife of Judah, the brother of the Lord, and (v) the mother of Joses (she who reared the brother of the Lord, Joses, the son of Joseph),[148] and (vi) Joanna (who some say was the wife of Peter), and (vii) the sister [-in-law] of the Lord's mother, Mary, wife of Klopas who was Joseph's brother;[149] for Joachim and Anna produced no other child besides the supremely holy Theotokos. These all-famed myrrh-bearers came seven times that night to the tomb, and when [Christ] was resurrected, they did not recognise him.[150] But the Theotokos was not present at the tomb since she was laid up with unspeakable pain. While the angel was speaking with Mary Magdalen, Christ appeared first to his mother in the house of the Theologian, that is, on holy Sion.[151] And all

apostles James and John. On the two brothers, see Mt 4: 21; on Salome, cf. *SynaxCP*, 30 June, 790.

147 'James the Less' or 'James the Younger' (Ἰακώβου τοῦ μικροῦ) came to be identified as one of the sons (along with Joses, Simon, and Judas) of the Virgin Mary's betrothed husband Joseph, although this association is tenuous. Although the 'Mary' mentioned here should thus be the Theotokos (who was stepmother to the four men), Epiphanios does not appear to make this association – even though he named them earlier in the text; see above, n. 41. On Mary's maternal relationship to this James, cf. Mt 27: 56; Mk 15: 40; Mk 16: 1; Lk 24: 10.

148 Mingarelli's version of the text omits Ἰωσῆ υἱὸν Ἰωσήφ ('Joses, the son of Joseph') here; see M209C. It is not clear who this woman is, although the participle ἀναθρέψασα might provide a clue. I have translated this as 'reared', but it could also mean 'nursed' or 'educated' (from ἀνατρέφω).

149 Dressel's text, which must be defective, adds the phrase, …καὶ θυγάτηρ Ἰωσήφ, here. I have chosen to follow the reading in Mingarelli's version because Dressel's version simply makes no sense (the relationship would be incestuous); see PG 120, 209C. On Klopas or Kleopas, Joseph's brother, see the genealogy which Epiphanios provides at the beginning of the *LVM*, above, nn. 16 and 19.

150 The seven visits to the tomb are not mentioned in the Gospel accounts but provide a parallel with the number of the myrrh-bearing women, according to Epiphanios. This detail is repeated in the narrative of *SynaxCP*, 790 (30 June); see also above, n. 145.

151 On the Evangelist John's house at Sion, see above, n. 137. The statement here that Christ appeared first to his mother in this house (before appearing to Mary Magdalen or the apostles, as the canonical Gospels report) seems to be an invention of Epiphanios the Monk. It was not picked up by the tenth-century Marian hagiographers, nor was it adopted in most Byzantine iconography of the resurrection. It is noteworthy, however, that at least two ninth-century illustrated psalters depict the scene, providing inscriptions to show that Christ's post-resurrection appearance to his mother occurred at Sion; see, for example, Chludov Psalter, Cod. Mosqu. gr. D. 129, f. 100ᵛ; Barberini Psalter, Cod. Vat. Barb. gr. 372, f. 171ʳ. On the influence of Epiphanios's narrative in the West, following its translation into Latin, and the depiction of the scene in at least one English church, see Introduction, n. 158. On the appearance of the resurrected Christ to Mary after the resurrection in Eastern and Western texts and images, see also Breckenridge 1957.

LIFE OF MARY, THE THEOTOKOS 101

of the apostles were staying with her, together with the myrrh-bearing women and [Christ's] siblings, [engaging in] fasts, sleeping on the ground, prayers, [D 38] tears, and continuous hymnody.[152] It is there that Christ first appeared to them when the doors were closed. And it is there that Thomas came to believe.[153] There also the Holy Spirit visited the apostles.[154] And after being sent out from there into [many] places and having returned, they again gathered there.[155]

27. The Theotokos, on seeing the ascension of her Son into heaven, devoted herself even more [M 212] to asceticism and genuflexion. As Andrew, who was from Jerusalem and [became] archbishop of Crete, says, 'the indentations of her knees are visible even until now on the marble [floors] of holy Sion, along with the dent on the rock where she would take a natural sleep for a short time'.[156] She possessed honour and fear on the part of all human beings, as well as glory – not only from a faithful person, but also from a Jew and a Greek.[157] And not one of the Jews, the governors, the high priests, or any of the Greeks dared to say or do[158] anything with regard to her – or to approach at all the house where she was staying (since Sion and Gethsemane are the same place).[159] She was [meanwhile] accomplishing many cures, granting health to the sick, freeing those who were possessed by demons from these impure spirits, [D 39] performing acts of mercy and care for the poor, along with widows and orphans. Some say that not one of the twelve apostles went far away or even departed from Jerusalem during her life. But even in the course of the affliction that came to pass with the persecution of the Church at the time of the destruction of Stephen, the first

---

152 Mingarelli's version of the text differs slightly in this passage; see Appendix A (h).
153 Jn 20: 26–29.
154 Acts 2: 1–4. This is the scene that is celebrated in the Christian feast of Pentecost.
155 Epiphanios must be referring here to the scene of Mary's dormition, when the apostles miraculously returned from their various missions in order to attend her deathbed.
156 Andrew in fact writes: 'There marble slabs, laid out as a floor, shout aloud far and wide concerning the bending knees of her all-holy body'. See Andrew of Crete, *Homily I on the Dormition*, PG 97, 1073A; trans. Daley 1998, 104 (with adjustments). (Daley argues, p. 115, n. 1, that this is in fact the first, not the second, in a trilogy of homilies on the Dormition, as published by F. Combefis in 1648.)
157 Mingarelli's text renders these nouns in the plural, also leaving out 'a Greek': '...not only from faithful people, but also from Jews'; see PG 120, 212A.
158 This phrase, ἢ ποιῆσαι, does not appear in the Mingarelli version.
159 This statement is incorrect. It reveals the author's lack of familiarity with the topography of Jerusalem and its environs.

martyr, all [of the Christians] were dispersed into the cities of Judaea and Samaria – except for the twelve apostles, as the Evangelist Luke writes.[160] And the execution of the first martyr occurred six years after the ascension of Christ.[161] [The apostles] held James, the brother of the Lord, as the first in rank among them, on account of the piety that he possessed, and they did nothing without him. There were many women from different provinces who stayed with the Theotokos; some had been freed from illnesses, others from impure spirits, and yet others were moved by faith and love for her. Among them, so they say, was Paul's wife.

28. Hippolytos the Theban relates that she lived in the flesh for a full fifty-nine years.[162] [D 40] But the aforesaid Andrew, bishop of Crete, who came from Jerusalem, says that, according to tradition, she reached extreme old age;[163] as for the fifty-nine years, that is not 'extreme old age'. It is on account of the disturbances at that time, especially the subsequent destruction of Jerusalem by the Romans which happened thirty years after Christ's ascension, that no one wrote things down about her. But before the Roman armies came to Jerusalem, the apostles and all of those who believed in Christ went up out of Jerusalem by an angel's command and came to a city of Peraia that had been assigned the name of Pella.[164]

29. Dionysios the Areopagite says concerning the falling-asleep of the Theotokos that he was present at it, along with Timothy and Hierotheos and

---

160 Acts 7: 54–60.

161 According to Hippolytos of Thebes, the stoning of the first martyr, Stephen, took place *seven* years after the ascension of Christ; see idem, *Chronicle 3*, ed. Diekamp 1898, 4, 12, 16, 19, 27. Mingarelli's text also diverges in this respect from that of Dressel; see Appendix A (i).

162 Mingarelli's version adds 'but we find more' after this sentence, also substituting the present infinitive for the aorist ('lived'); PG 120, 212C. For the source of this statement, see Hippolytos of Thebes, *Chronicle* 3, ed. Diekamp 1898, 4, 12, 16, 19: ἔζησεν γὰρ τῇ ἀνθρωπότητι ἡ ἁγία Θεοτόκος ἔτη νθ´ ('for the holy Theotokos lived in her human state for fifty-nine years'). The passage is worded differently in the fifth version of the *Chronicle* (28. 9).

163 The Greek expression which Epiphanios uses here is βαθὺ γῆρας. For the statement that the Virgin Mary lived to 'extreme old age', see Andrew of Crete, *Homily II on the Dormition*, PG 97, 1060B, trans. Daley 1998, 126 (8). (Daley argues that this homily, which Migne published as the first in the trilogy, is in fact the second; see ibid., 135, n. 1.)

164 Epiphanios may have obtained this information from Eusebios's *Ecclesiastical History* III.5.3; ed. Schwartz, Mommsen, and Winkelmann 1999, 196; trans. Williamson 1965, 111. Pella lay to the east of Jerusalem in what is now north-western Jordan, seventeen miles south of the Sea of Galilee.

LIFE OF MARY, THE THEOTOKOS   103

the rest of the apostles.[165] This Dionysios and Timothy became disciples of Paul. Paul, however, was baptised six and a half years after Christ's ascension and began his preaching three years after that; after nine years, he taught Dionysios. The blessed Paul says that he went up into Jerusalem after fourteen years, in response to a revelation – so that all of these years numbered twenty-four.[166] [D 41] We find this revelation in certain memoirs, [which say] that the apostle was taken up from Ephesus [M 213] on account of the falling-asleep of the Theotokos.[167] And what he said to the Corinthians, namely, that Christ was seen at the same time by more than five hundred brothers after his resurrection,[168] means that this occurred at the falling-asleep of the holy Theotokos. A certain virtuous priest and monk, who was pious in deed and in word and who was pursuing divine things, recounted this, saying, 'Someone once appeared to me when I was engaged on these matters one night, saying that the apostle Paul had been taken up on a cloud from Ephesus [so as to attend] the falling-asleep of the Theotokos. And he went up into the third belt of the stars and he saw the things on the far side of the ocean,[169] along with paradise itself. And he heard ineffable words, the hymns of the angels and of the apostles.'[170] Some say that all of the apostles who were not in Jerusalem were present by means of clouds. But Dionysios the Areopagite, who was there at that time, does not say this. It is possible that they were gathered according to

---

165 See (ps-) Dionysios the Areopagite, *On the Divine Names* III. 2; ed. Suchla 1990, 141. 4–14; PG 3, 681D–684A; trans. Luibheid 1987, 70.
166 Cf. Gal 2: 1.
167 Epiphanios appears to be referring to the famous passage in (ps-) Dionysios's *Divine Names* again here. The latter claims that he, 'his saintly teacher' Hierotheos, and many of the apostles were brought together for 'a vision of that mortal body, that source of life, which bore God'. Whereas the apostles attempted 'to praise the omnipotent goodness of that divine frailty', Hierotheos 'was so caught up, so taken out of himself, experiencing communion with the things praised, that everyone who heard him, everyone who saw him, everyone who knew him (or, rather, did not know him) considered him to be inspired, to be speaking with divine praises'; see above, n. 165.
168 Cf. 1 Cor 15: 6.
169 That is, beyond the edge of the earth, according to a cosmology that envisages a flat earth.
170 Cf. 2 Cor 12: 4. It is possible that the 'certain virtuous priest and monk' to whom Epiphanios refers here is John of Damascus, who juxtaposes the scene of the Virgin's dormition with Paul's vision, or translation to heaven, in his first homily for the feast; see John of Damascus, *Homily I on the Dormition of the Virgin*, ed. Kotter 1988, 496.1–497. 24; trans. Daley 1998, 196 (11).

some dispensation before the time of her departure. Not one of the twelve apostles had died prior to her falling-asleep, except for James, the son of Zebedee, who was John's brother, [D 42] whom Herod (who has also become food for the worms) had killed.[171]

30. The all-praised and ever-virgin Theotokos predicted her departure fifteen days in advance, and the archangel Gabriel arrived and informed her of her departure from the world, as well as about the arrival of the Lord, three days before that. And she sent out [messengers] and summoned all of the apostles. But they arrived since they also had foreknowledge, through the Holy Spirit, of her departure. And many other people came to her. Women were also present, including Mary Magdalen, Joseph's daughters, and many others who were related to her by kinship. And she delivered a great speech to them, along with fearful mysteries, which she had placed and kept safe in her heart. She recounted the angel's greeting and his appearance – as well as the manifestation shortly before this, which she saw when she was praying in the Temple – as she travelled around with the apostles.[172] And she had made a testament, as the apostle Bartholomew says.[173] She was humbled by her asceticism from the very beginning. And when her hour came, Christ made himself visible to all. And they all fell to the ground [D 43] at the glory and splendour of the light that shone about him, becoming like corpses. And Christ said to them, 'Peace be with you.' They were overwhelmed with joy. An angelic and invisible hymn was heard. And the apostles were standing dumbfounded and were struck

---

171 This passage, beginning with 'Some say...' and ending '...had killed', is rendered differently (with some additions) in Mingarelli's version; see Appendix A (j).

172 Epiphanios refers both to the Lukan annunciation scene here (Lk 1: 26–38) here, as well as to the apocryphal story of an annunciation that took place in the Temple (see above, n. 38). The meaning of the phrase, 'as she travelled around with the apostles' (ὡς ἐν ταῖς τῶν ἀποστόλων περιόδοις ἐμφέρεται) is puzzling here – and is omitted in Mingarelli's version; M 213C. It is possible that the phrase originated in a marginal gloss since it does not fit easily into this sentence.

173 Epiphanios must be referring to the tradition that is recounted in the apocryphal *Gospel of Bartholomew* here; see also above, n. 38. According to this text, the apostles approached the Virgin Mary after Christ's ascension and asked her questions about her conception and how she could have contained the One 'whom the seven heavens scarcely contain'; see *Gospel of Bartholomew* II, esp. 12, translated in Schneemelcher 1991, 543–45. However, this text does not mention a 'testament'; it is possible that Epiphanios is referring here to another tradition, such as the dormition narrative that is attributed to John the Evangelist (*CANT* 102). The latter mentions a 'book' that Mary entrusted to John before her death. See *Transitus graecus* 'R', chap. 20, ed. Wenger 1955, 220–23.

with amazement at the miracle. Then the apostles burst into song. And as she opened her mouth in sweet sleep, she delivered her spirit to her Son and God; she was at this time seventy-two years old.[174] And the angels, after singing once more, went away with the Lord into heaven. Each one of the holy apostles, as Dionysios the Areopagite says, sang his own hymn and they were not all in unison.[175] For this reason, they all marvelled at the hymn of Hierotheos. [M 216] And after the singing, having tended to her [body], they placed her in a tomb at Gethsemane. After a short time when they were all present and watching, her holy and all-holy body was taken away from before their eyes.[176] And having celebrated her death, which was glorious in this way, they each departed to their own places.[177]

31. The years of the [Theotokos] were numbered as follows: her parents presented her to the Lord in Jerusalem when she was seven years old and she spent six and a half years in the Temple.[178] She was [then] in Joseph's

---

174 The calculation of Mary's age at the time of her death does not occur in most accounts of the dormition. Epiphanios disagrees with Hippolytos of Thebes here, since the latter states that she was fifty-nine years old; see above, n. 162; Hippolytos of Thebes, *Chronicle* 3, ed. Diekamp 1898, 4, 12, 16, 19, 27.

175 I have interpreted the sense of this passage somewhat loosely. It seems likely that Epiphanios is referring to (ps-) Dionysios the Areopagite's *Divine Names* III.2 here, in which the writer states that 'these hierarchs chose, each as he was able, to praise the omnipotent goodness of that divine frailty'; see (ps-) Dionysios the Areopagite, *The Divine Names* III. 2, ed. Suchla 1990, 141. 8–10; PG 3, 681D; trans. Luibheid 1987, 70.

176 It is interesting that Epiphanios describes the apostles' witness of the disappearance of Mary's body here. This is unusual in dormition narratives, which state either that Christ returned to take her body to heaven after three days or that the tomb was discovered to be empty after the same time lapse. Some traditions omit any mention of Mary's assumption into heaven; for summaries of all of these textual traditions, see Shoemaker 2002, 37–38 ('Palm of the Tree of Life' tradition), 51–52 ('Bethlehem' tradition), 58 (Coptic tradition), 67–68 ('Late Apostle' tradition). The Greek homiletic tradition usually adheres to the story of the tomb being opened and discovered to be empty after three days; see Cunningham 2021, 122. However, one notable exception, which may have influenced Epiphanios, is an early eighth-century homily in which the preacher writes, 'And it was from their hands, as all looked on, that the Virgin's body was taken away'; see Germanos of Constantinople, *Homily III on the Dormition*, PG 98, 369C; trans. Daley 1998, 177 (9). (It is worth noting that whereas the Migne edition numbers this as the third homily in a trilogy, Daley argues that it is the second and final one.)

177 Mingarelli's text is slightly shorter than that of Dressel here; see Appendix A (k).

178 Note again that Epiphanios changes the Virgin Mary's age at the time of her entrance into the Temple from three to seven years here, thus departing from the *Protevangelion of James* and most subsequent interpretations of that tradition; see also above, n. 25.

house for six months. And [D 44] she received [there] the announcement of cosmic joy. And she gave birth when she was fifteen years old. She passed thirty-three years with her Son, our Lord Jesus Christ, which means that she had by now become forty-eight years of age. And after the ascension of her Son she remained in the house of the Theologian, on holy Sion, with him for her remaining years, that is, for twenty-four more years. [She lived] a total of seventy-two years. After the falling-asleep of the holy Theotokos, all of the apostles were dispersed. And John went to Ephesus.[179] The Evangelist Matthew says that none of the apostles went far away until the destruction of Jerusalem.[180] But his Gospel was written after thirty years at the command of James, the brother of the Lord who lived on after the ascension of the Lord, so they say, for another twenty-eight years. This James divided up the lands for them.[181] And sending them out, he commanded each of them, even while he was teaching, to send word to him every year – which they all did – so that each might speak with one voice in the proclamation of Christ, to whom be glory with the Father and the Holy Spirit forever and ever. Amen.

---

179 The tradition that the Evangelist John went on to Ephesus (after his association with Mary in Jerusalem) appears frequently in early dormition traditions. Shoemaker notes that a tension between John's obligation to care for the Virgin after the crucifixion of Christ (Jn 19: 26–27) and his mission in Asia Minor is sometimes acknowledged in these texts; see Shoemaker 2002, 74–76, esp. n. 166. Another tradition which places both the tomb and the house of the Virgin Mary in Ephesus developed much later; according to Mimouni, these were only identified in the seventeenth and nineteenth centuries, respectively; see Mimouni 1995, 585–97.

180 It is possible that Epiphanios is referring to Mt 10: 23 here, in which Jesus tells his disciples to flee from one town to another when they are persecuted.

181 On the leadership of the followers of Jesus in Jerusalem by the apostle James ('brother of the Lord'), see Acts 12: 17, 15: 13–21, 21: 17–18. On his martyrdom, when he was thrown off the parapet of the Temple and then stoned, see Eusebios of Caesarea, *Ecclesiastical History* II. 23, ed. Schwartz, Mommsen, and Winkelmann 1999, 164–74, trans. Williamson 1965, 99–103.

2

[VIN 236; D 45; M 216] BY EPIPHANIOS, MONK
AND PRESBYTER, CONCERNING THE LIFE
AND ACTIONS AND DEATH OF THE HOLY AND
ALL-FAMED AND FIRST-CALLED OF THE
APOSTLES, ANDREW[1]

1. Although many [writers] have described the lives and actions of God-loving men and women [in order to promote] zeal and imitation among those who wish to travel the path to heaven and who hope to enjoy the kingdom of heaven through many afflictions and labours – such as the wrestling schools of the martyrs and struggles against the devil, along with brave deeds and miraculous acts, and not only this, but also the tranquillity of the holy ascetics, flights from worldly things, and bodily disciplines – no one has satisfactorily described the lives of the blessed apostles.[2] And it seemed good to me, as I longed and endeavoured to search out and select [information] about them here and there, [to employ] eyewitnesses and God-bearing [M 217] men including Clement of Rome,[3] Evagrios of

---

1 This translation is based on the critical edition of the text by Andrey Vinogradov 2005, 236–63. Page numbers are indicated in square brackets as [Vin 236], etc., throughout. However, in case readers do not have access to this Russian edition, I have indicated the page numbers of Dressel's 1843 edition as [D 45, etc.]. Dressel's text is reproduced in PG 120, 216–60, with some corrections. I have also included references to this publication, e.g. [M 216], etc., in the present translation. Readers should bear in mind, however, that Vinogradov's edition deviates from that of Dressel in many instances (as indicated below in footnotes).

2 This is scarcely an accurate statement on the part of Epiphanios. He must have been aware of the numerous *Acts* of the Christian apostles that circulated in Greek (with translations into many other languages) throughout the Christian world, dating from about the second century onward, and indeed he used versions of the second- or third-century *Acts* of St Andrew and of Andrew and Matthias (*AA* and *AAMt*) as inspiration for the *LAA*. He may have been aware however that many of these texts, including the *AA*, were condemned as heretical by the Christian fathers. For further discussion, see Introduction, 46–47; *Actes*, trans. Prieur 1995, 55–61.

3 According to A. Vinogradov, J.-M. Prieur, and D.R. MacDonald, Epiphanios is

Sicily,[4] and Epiphanios of Cyprus (for he says in the record of the seventy disciples,[5] '...as those who came before us handed this on to us' – that is to say, orally).[6] [And he used] not only apocryphal and historical writings, as well as the encomiasts, but also other sources.

2. It came to pass in the days of Hyrkanos, the priest and king of the Jews,[7] that there was a certain Jonas, from the tribe of Symeon and the village of Bethsaida (which the tetrarch Philip, the son of Herod Antipater, later founded), who had two sons, Simon and Andrew.[8] [This Jonas] was utterly poor [D 46] and in dire straits. Having survived for a fair number of years, he died, leaving his children in great poverty. So they let themselves out for hire. And Simon married the daughter of Aristoboulos, brother of the apostle Barnabas, and, as some say, produced a son and a daughter.[9] But

probably referring here to the *(ps-) Clementine Homilies*, ed. Rehm and Strecker 1992, and the *(ps-) Clementine Recognitions*, ed. Rehm and Strecker 1994; see Vinogradov 2005, 236; *AA*, ed. Prieur 1989, 18–19; ed. MacDonald 1990, 183. For orientation on the pseudo-Clementines, along with translations of the texts, see Schneemelcher (1992), vol. 2, 483–541.

4 Epiphanios alludes here to the author of the *Life* of St Pankratios of Taormina (*BHG* 1410–12) who calls himself 'Evagrios', although scholars treat this as a pseudonym. C.J. Stallman-Pacitti, who edited the *Life*, suggests that this author was active before 730, while some other scholars place him later in the eighth century. The text was known to ninth-century writers including Theodore of Studios, the patriarch Nikephoros, the author of the *Life* of Michael the Synkellos, and others. Epiphanios mentions the legend of Pankratios again later in the text; see below, n. 71; for the edition of the *Life* of St Pankratios, see Stallman-Pacitti and Burke 2018; for further analysis, see Kazhdan (with Sherry and Angelidi) 1999, 302–7.

5 Epiphanios refers here to (ps-) Epiphanios of Salamis, *Index apostolorum*, a pseudonymous work which was composed between the sixth and eighth centuries. The text, which provides a catalogue of the apostles and seventy disciples, also includes an account of Andrew's travels and visit to Byzantion; ed. Schermann 1907, 107–31; for discussion of its likely date and content, see Vinogradov 2005, 33.

6 Epiphanios uses the adverb ἀγράφως here. It is also possible that the adverb means 'unscripturally' or 'uncanonically', but I have opted for the idea of narratives that were handed down orally rather than in writing. I am grateful to Judith Ryder for suggesting this meaning.

7 John Hyrkanos II (76–30 BCE), high priest and ruler of Judaea from 67 to 66 BCE. For background, see Horbury, Davies, and Sturdy 1999, 216–23.

8 On the sibling relationship of Simon (Peter) and Andrew, see Mt 4: 18; Mk 1: 16; Jn 1: 40. The name of their father, Jonah or John, is also provided in Mt 16: 17, when Jesus calls Peter 'Simon Bar-Jonah' ('Simon, son of Jonah'), and Jn 21: 15, where the same appellation is used. On the village of Bethsaida, which was located on the northern shore of the Sea of Galilee, see Chap. 1, n. 123.

9 Peter's wife and children are not mentioned in the canonical Gospels. However, the

Andrew dedicated himself to chastity. Neither learned to read, but they became fishermen by trade.

3. [Vin 237] And when John was proclaiming baptism, Andrew saw his conduct, which was similar to that of the angels, and since he admired his nobility, became his disciple. When John had pointed his finger at Christ and said, 'Behold, the Lamb of God who takes away the sin of the world',[10] Andrew, on hearing and seeing [this], left John and followed Jesus. And, after bringing along his own brother, he showed him Christ, who renamed him Peter.[11] When Jesus went out into the desert to be tempted by the devil, Peter and Andrew returned to their own [homes] and worked as fishermen; but when Jesus returned from the desert, he immediately called them and they, after abandoning everything, followed him. Whereas Peter was utterly ardent in spirit and ready to attend to worldly needs, Andrew was gentle and spoke little. And when Peter's mother-in-law died, Peter entrusted his wife to the Theotokos.[12]

4. But when Christ suffered and was resurrected and raised into heaven, and Matthias was numbered among the eleven apostles instead of Judas,[13] and after the cure of the man who was crippled from birth,[14] the apostles,

---

late second-century *Acts of Peter* provide more details, including the story of the apostle's healing of his virginal and paralysed daughter; see *Acts of Peter*, trans. Schneemelcher 1989, vol. 2, 285–87. There are also mentions of Peter's wife in the *(ps-) Clementine Homilies* and *Recognitions*; see Chap. 1, n. 119. The martyrdom of his wife in Rome, during the reign of the emperor Nero, is briefly mentioned in Clement of Alexandria, *Stromata* VII.xi.63.3, ed. Stählin, Früchtel, and Treu 1970, 46, and quoted in Eusebios, *Ecclesiastical History* III. 30: 'We are told that when blessed Peter saw his wife led away to death, he was glad that her call had come and that she was returning home and spoke to her in the most encouraging and comforting tones, addressing her by name: "My dear, remember the Lord". Such was the marriage of the blessed, and their consummate feeling towards their dearest'; ed. Schwartz, Mommsen, and Winkelmann 1999, 262; trans. Williamson 1965, 140.

10 Jn 1: 29.

11 Cf. Mt 16: 17–19; Jn 1: 41–42.

12 For the story of Jesus's healing of Peter's mother-in-law from a fever, see Mt 8: 14–15; Mk 1: 29–31; Lk 4: 38–39. The Gospels do not recount, however, her later death or the dedication of Peter's wife to the care of the Virgin Mary. The latter story, with the addition that his mother-in-law joined Peter's wife in becoming a disciple of Mary, appears in the tenth-century *Lives*: see John Geometres, *Life of the Virgin* 69, ed. Constas and Simelidis 2023, 182–85; Euthymios the Athonite, *Georgian Life of the Virgin* 69, ed. Shoemaker 2012, 96–97.

13 Acts 1: 26.

14 Acts 3: 1–10.

having been mistreated and released,[15] went out into Antioch in Syria. They followed the command of the Teacher to go two by two, taking [D 47] Matthias, Gaios, and other disciples with them. And, having proclaimed the Word, performed many miracles, taught, and made disciples of many people, they came to Tyana, a city in Cappadocia. After staying there, they came to Ankyra of Galatia.[16]

5. After staying with a Jew named Onesiphoros, then raising a dead man and instructing many people, they travelled from there through cities, interpreting the scriptures, performing miracles, persuading many people, baptising, and transmitting the divine mysteries, [M 220] they reached Sinope, a city of the Pontos (the so-called Scythians),[17] as Peter himself says in his catholic epistle: 'Pontos and Galatia'.[18] There was a great crowd of Jews in that city, who held many heresies among themselves and who were men of barbaric and savage customs; on this account, they were called 'eaters of men'.[19] But, on arriving there, the apostles Peter and Andrew did not enter [Vin 238] the city; instead they took up their quarters at the furthest point of the island. It was a deserted place, about six miles from the city.[20]

---

15 Acts 4: 21.
16 On Tyana, see Hild and Restle 1981, *TIB*, 298–300. The preaching of the apostles in Tyana is not mentioned in any other sources. Ankyra (now Ankara) was an important episcopal see in Galatia. See Belke and Restle 1984, *TIB*, 126–30.
17 The legend that the apostle Andrew preached among the 'Scythians' is first attested by Eusebios of Caesarea, *Ecclesiastical History* III.1.1, ed. Schwartz, Mommsen, and Winkelmann 1999, 188; trans. Williamson 1965, 107. As MacDonald and Prieur have demonstrated, however, legends about the trajectory of Andrew's mission varied considerably, with the earliest apocryphal *Acts* differing in their account from that of Epiphanios. For a summary, see Introduction above, 49–62; *AA*, ed. Prieur 1989, 14–20; ed. MacDonald 1990, 15–47.
18 1 Pet 1: 1.
19 ἀνθρωποφάγοι. According to Dennis MacDonald, Sinope corresponds to 'Myrmidonia' ('city of the ants'), the name that Gregory of Tours and other Latin redactors of the *AAMt* assigned to the city of the cannibals where Matthias was imprisoned; see *AA*, ed. MacDonald 1990, 7–8. The early sixth-century Latin pilgrim Theodosius describes a stop in Sinope, on his way to Jerusalem, which he says was also called 'Myrmidona'. According to him, 'everyone who lived there devoured people for their food'; see Geyer 1898, 144, trans. MacDonald 2000, 8. However, none of the Greek apocryphal sources – or Epiphanios the Monk – give Sinope that name.
20 The city of Sinope was an important trading centre on the southern coast of the Black Sea. It stands on the north-east corner of a peninsula, which has sides of about nineteen miles. At the north-west corner, where Andrew and Matthias were probably believed to have

6. I, Epiphanios the monk and priest, along with James the monk, arrived there and discovered the holy apostle Andrew's house of prayer, [inhabited now by] two monastic presbyters, Theophanes and Symeon, as well as an icon of the holy Andrew, entirely marvellous, which was depicted[21] on marble. And Theophanes, who was more than seventy years of age, showed us the seats of the apostles and their imprints on the stones.[22] And he said that during the reign of [Constantine] the Horseman,[23] some icon-fighters had wanted to scrape off the icon. Although they contrived many [methods], they had no success; or rather, their hands were overpowered. [D 48] We have a tradition that the icon was drawn when the apostle was still alive. And it performs many healings.

7. When the apostles Peter and Andrew arrived and took up their quarters at the furthest point, the demons of that land[24] at once cried out, saying, 'The apostles of Jesus have come to chase us out of here!' On hearing this, they came out of the city towards them. But the people assembled, carrying those who were possessed by demons and those who were ill with incurable diseases. When the apostles came out to them, [the former] called on them, saying, 'Men, why do those of you who are Hebrews hold many

---

stayed, there was a 'fine cape (or promontory)' (Λεπτὴ ἄκρα). The peninsula is characterised by gently rolling, fertile hills. In addition to the apostle Andrew, who was believed to have evangelised the city, Christians in Sinope venerated St Phokas, a gardener who became first bishop of the city; see Bryer and Winfield 1985, vol. 1, 69–88, esp. 71.

21 The meaning of ὑλογραφουμένην is unclear in this context. The verb was sometimes used for encaustic painting, so Epiphanios may be suggesting that this technique was unusually applied to marble in this case. It is also possible, however, that he describes an image that was inscribed or carved onto a marble surface. Vinogradov comments that Byzantine icons painted on marble do survive; see Vinogradov 2005, 117, n. 236.

22 Dvornik, citing Lipsius, states that the legend whereby the city possessed an 'ambo' from which Andrew preached may predate the original *AA* and therefore be founded on fact; see Dvornik 1958, 200. In fact, Lipsius correctly refers to this object as a 'Lehrstuhl', that is, a throne or chair from which the apostle taught; see Lipsius, vol. 1, 1883, 604.

23 Constantine V (741–75). Various epithets were applied to this emperor by iconophile writers. These include Καβαλῖνος or Καβαλλῖνος ('Horseman' or possibly 'Groom'), as here, or the more pejorative Κοπρώνυμος ('Dung-named'). According to Stephen Gero, the latter nickname was not used by eighth- or early ninth-century writers; it appeared first in the late ninth-century *Chronicle* of George Hamartolos, which influenced a number of later chronicles; see Gero 1977, 169–75.

24 Χώρα may mean 'land', 'space', or 'place'; see Lampe, 1536. It is interesting to note here the localisation of demons: like human beings, they are considered to belong to a particular region and to display characteristics that are associated with it.

opinions and why do you not all adhere to the law of Moses, believing in those things which he wrote and handed on? For we proclaim these things: the One whom you say will arise as a prophet is that One whom we have seen. After eating together, he sent us to proclaim[25] repentance in his name and remission of sins for the whole world, refraining from all frivolity and baptising [people] in his name.' And, after confirming and illuminating the crowd, [who included] both Jews and Greeks, with many speeches, after laying their hands on those who were gathered together that they might hold fast to the faith, and after healing those who were ill, they dismissed them. And they baptised many of those who were assembled [there] in the name of the Father and of the Son and of the Holy Spirit, and they distributed the divine mysteries of Christ to them.[26]

8. When Matthias went down into the city because of some necessity, the Jews seized him and placed him in prison for three days, intending to do away with him on the next day.[27] But Andrew, having come down from the mountain during [Vin 239] the night, went to the prison. For the gate of the city, as well as of the prison, spontaneously opened for him. [M 221] Having led Matthias out, along with those believers who were locked up with him, [Andrew] hid them [D 49] for seven days outside of the city, at a distance of about one mile, by the sea. There was a thicket of both cultivated and wild fig trees that was difficult to penetrate, and it was the season of figs.[28] There was also a cave. Those who lived there showed us the cave and explained these things [to us]. After instructing [the people] for seven days, he baptised them

---

25 D provides the reading καρῦξαι instead of κηρῦξαι (aorist infinitive of κηρύσσω) in M 220C–D; this is probably a scribal error.

26 Epiphanios refers here to the Eucharist, which is often called 'the divine mysteries' in Byzantine texts.

27 The passage that follows, which describes the rescue of Matthias and his fellow prisoners from the prison in Sinope, may be a version of the much longer account that appears in the *AAMt*, as reconstructed by MacDonald 1990, 70–169. According to MacDonald, this narrative originally represented the beginning section of the *AA*; see ibid., 3–15, 22–47. J. Flamion and J.-M. Prieur dispute this hypothesis, believing that the *AAMt* and *AA* are separate texts; see Flamion 1911, 269–300; *AA*, ed. Prieur 1989, 32–35.

28 This section of the text, in particular the refuge of the escaped prisoners in a glade that includes fig trees, slightly resembles the *AAMt* 21, in which Andrew instructs the released prisoners (including Matthias) to wait for him under a fig tree in the lower section of the city of the cannibals; see *AA*, ed. MacDonald 2020, 118–19. According to Vinogradov, the sixth-century *Topography of the Holy Land* by Theodosius is the first text to identify Sinope with this city; see Vinogradov 2005, 117, n. 238; Wilkinson 1977, 67 (13).

by night on the seashore and, on the eighth day, having washed them clean, he dismissed them. And [Andrew] consoled and exhorted them, saying, 'My children, flee from the Scythian heresies, do not be associated with the Greeks at their idolatrous meals, and do not give heed to the Jews. Behold, the only holy, good, and benevolent God has chosen you out and marked you through the name and the baptism of his Son, Jesus Christ. For you have been reborn through water and Spirit; for this reason, I baptised you in the name of the Father and of the Son and of the Holy Spirit. He is the one God of all things, who exists in heaven and on earth and in all of the depths.[29] Venerate only this One and worship him alone.[30] Also be regulated and protected by the law of Moses, and the God of peace will be with you.' And he dismissed them. And taking Matthias, he departed for the east.

9. According to the holy Epiphanios, [arch]bishop of Cyprus, who says that he has it from tradition,[31] the blessed apostle Andrew taught the Scythians, the Sogdians, and the Gorsinoi in the great [city of] Sebastopolis, where the fortress of Apsaros, the harbour of Zekchos, and the Phasis river are [located].[32] Within this [area] live the Iberians and Sousa and Phoustians and Alans. Holding these [notes] in our hands and fleeing from communion

---

29 The Greek word ἄβυσσος was used in the LXX to refer to 'the deep' that was covered with darkness before God created light (Gen 1: 2–3). The Christian Fathers usually interpreted it positively since it was created by God along with everything else; however, the word could sometimes refer to the abode of demons or (with reference to Ex 14: 23–31) the Red Sea. Another, more allegorical interpretation was the 'depth' of God's wisdom; for references, see Lampe, 3. Epiphanios refers here to the creation story in Genesis, as Andrew stresses in his sermon God's creation of all things, including the 'depths'.

30 It is interesting to note that Epiphanios uses the words προσκυνέω ('to venerate') and λατρεύω ('to worship') as synonyms here. Iconophile theologians, beginning with John of Damascus, began to distinguish between the two verbs, suggesting that whereas God is worshipped, icons are venerated. In other words, there are relative degrees of paying honour to divine or holy subjects; see John of Damascus, *On the Divine Images* I. 6, 14, 16, II. 14, etc., ed. Kotter 1975, 79–80, 87, 89–92, 105–6; trans. Louth 2003, 23, 27–28, 29–31, 70–71; Parry 1996, 166–77.

31 (ps-) Epiphanios of Salamis, *Index apostolorum*, ed. Schermann 1907, 108.9: Ἀνδρέας δὲ ὁ ἀδελφὸς αὐτοῦ, ὡς οἱ πρὸ ἡμῶν παραδεδώκασιν, ἐκήρυξε Σκύθαις καὶ Σογδιανοῖς καὶ Γορσίνοις καὶ ἐν Σεβαστοπόλει τῇ μεγάλῃ, ὅπου ἐστὶν ἡ παρεμβολὴ Ἄψαρος καὶ Ὕσσου λιμὴν καὶ Φᾶσις ποταμός, ἔνθα οἰκοῦσιν Αἰθίοπες, θάπτεται δὲ ἐν Πάτραις τῆς Ἀχαΐας σταυρῷ προσδεθεὶς ὑπὸ Αἰγέα τοῦ βασιλέως Πατρῶν. This work is listed under 'Spuria' in *CPG*, vol. 2, 337. For background on this text, see Introduction, 55–56.

32 Sebastopolis was a large port city near ancient Dioscurias, on the eastern side of the Black Sea; see Mango 2002, 262, n. 34. It is worth noting that Epiphanios omits the reference to 'Ethiopians' which appears in (ps-) Epiphanios's account; see above, n. 31.

with the icon-fighters ([or rather the Christ-fighters], for the image and its archetype are the same thing in theory [even if not in substance] [Vin 240; D 50], since whereas we venerate Christ in an image, they insult him in his image – for, as the holy Basil says, 'the honour of the image passes on to its prototype'),[33] and then traversing lands and cities as far as Bosporos,[34] passing through with great longing, we searched for the holy inhabitants and wherever there might be a relic [of them], and we came upon many relics. And [concerning those places] which we did not reach, we questioned scrupulously whomever we happened to meet and learned [many things] with pleasure. And we will speak later about those in Nicaea. But when we came to Nikomedia,[35] we saw the relics of the holy martyr Panteleimon.[36]

33 Vinogradov suggests that the phrase 'communion with the icon-fighters' (τὴν κοινωνίαν τῶν εἰκονομάχων) may be inspired by Theodore of Studios's *Letter* 225 (to Naukratios), in which Theodore speaks of 'communion with the Christ-fighters'; see Theodore of Studios, *Letter* 225, ed. Fatouros 1992, vol. 2, 357. 85; Vinogradov 2005, 239. 25–26. On the destruction of images affecting their prototypes, see Basil of Caesarea, *On the Holy Spirit* 18.45, ed. Pruche 1986, 406–8; cf. Theodore of Studios, *Letter* 57 (to Plato), ed. Fatouros 1992, vol. 1, 164–65. 17–32. This passage from Basil's *On the Holy Spirit* was frequently used in iconophile polemical literature in order to counter iconoclast opposition to man-made icons; see Barber 2002, 74. The connection between the first and second halves of this paragraph (or between the sentence ending, 'Phoustoi and Alanoi', and that beginning, 'And we, holding these memorials in our hands...') is unclear. Such shifts in topic are not unusual in Epiphanios's text. Epiphanios probably refers here to (ps-) Epiphanios's *Index apostolorum*, which our hagiographer was using as a kind of guidebook on his travels. I am grateful to Marc Lauxtermann for pointing this out.

34 It is likely that Epiphanios refers here to the Crimean (Cimmerian) city of Pantikapaion (later called 'Bosporos'), located on the north coast of the Black Sea, rather than to the strait that links the Black Sea with the Propontis; see *ODB*, vol. 1, 313. He is implying that this city represented the furthest extremity of his travels to the east and north in search of holy relics.

35 Nikomedia, which was located at the eastern end of the Sea of Marmara, was an important Byzantine city – although it was eclipsed by the foundation of the New Rome (Constantinople) in the early fourth century and the choice of Nicaea and Chalcedon for the first and fourth Ecumenical Councils (325 and 451, respectively). As Epiphanios suggests on the basis of his visit to Nikomedia, the city possessed numerous shrines in honour of martyrs and other saints. Among those whom he does not mention were St Christopher and St Eleutherios; see Janin 1975, 77–104.

36 The feast day of St Panteleimon was celebrated on 27 July according to the Constantinopolitan liturgical calendar. Trained as a physician, he was believed to have served the poor, healed the sick, and visited captives in prison during his life. Having confessed his Christian faith and refused to sacrifice to the Roman gods, Panteleimon was martyred in Nikomedia during the reign of Diocletian's co-emperor, Maximian (286–305), probably in 304 or 305 CE; see *SynaxCP*, 847–48. The church of St Panteleimon τὰ Νάρσου (in the region of Constantinople) possessed his head and was regularly visited by Byzantine

LIFE AND ACTS OF ST ANDREW THE APOSTLE 115

And we touched with our hands as many things as his book contains.[37] And in a similar way, we touched [the relics of] Anthimos, who was bishop of those who were in that spot,[38] Indes, and [those of] the other martyrs who were with him.[39] [And so also] in Daphnousia, [the relics of] Zotikos, Aniketos, and Photios.[40] There were other wondrous things in Herakleia,[41] [as well as the relics] of Hyacinth in Amastris.[42] In Dorapin, we saw and venerated the relic of the martyr Christina.[43] And [we also venerated] that of Hypatios in Karousia.[44]

---

emperors; see Janin 1953, 401–2; Janin 1937; Majeska 1984, 383–84 (all cited in Gerstel 2012, 176, n. 17). On the church that honoured the saint in Nikomedia (but which contained an empty tomb), see Gerstel 2012, 178–79.

37 Epiphanios may be referring to one of several Greek passions of the saint that were in circulation during the middle Byzantine centuries (*BHG* 1412z–1413h). These were followed by versions attributed to Symeon the Metaphrast, John Geometres, Niketas the Paphlagonian, and other authors – all of which testify to the importance of this saint. For references, see *BHG*, vol. 2, 166–69; on the church in Nikomedia, see Janin 1975, 99.

38 St Anthimos was celebrated on 3 September, according to *SynaxCP*, 9. He served as bishop of Nikomedia under the emperors Diocletian and Maximian; cf. Eusebios of Caesarea, *Ecclesiastical History* VIII.6.6 and 13.1–2, ed. Schwartz, Mommsen, and Winkelmann 1999, 750, 772; trans. Williamson 1965, 334, 344; *Paschal Chronicle*, trans. Whitby and Whitby 1989, 5, 9, n. 24, which places his death in 303 at the start of Diocletian's persecution. Several *Passions* of St Anthimos (who is sometimes associated with companions including Indes and Domna), one of which is by Symeon the Metaphrast, recount his martyrdom (*BHG* 134y–135c). On the church of St Anthimos, which was located outside the eastern walls of Nikomedia, see Janin 1975, 83.

39 Indes, along with a group of other martyrs who died in Nikomedia during the persecution of the early fourth century, was celebrated on several dates in the Constantinopolitan liturgical calendar. See *SynaxCP*, 94, 275, 357–58. There is a Greek *Passion* of St Indes (or Indos) and St Domna (*BHG* 822z), as well as a metaphrastic version (*BHG* 823).

40 Daphnousia, on the Bithynian coast of the Black Sea, was a suffragan bishopric of Nikomedia; see Janin 1975, 78–79; Belke 1996, *TIB* 9, 149. Sts Photios and Aniketos were martyred at Nikomedia under the emperor Diocletian and their relics were housed at a shrine in Daphnousia; ibid., 104; see also *AASS*, Aug. II, 709.

41 Epiphanios is probably referring here to the city that was located on the southern coast of the Black Sea between Sinope and Trebizond (as opposed to one of the two cities by that name that were located along the northern coast of the Sea of Marmara, as described below, n. 159); see Bryer and Winfield 1985, vol. 1, 328.

42 This may refer to the St Hyacinth who was martyred in Rome during the reign of Trajan (98–117 CE), for whom a Greek *Passion* survives (*BHG* 758).

43 St Christina was believed to have been born in Tyre and to have been martyred ca. 300 CE. She was celebrated on 24 July; see *SynaxCP*, 839–40.

44 Hypatios, bishop of Gangra in central Anatolia, was martyred on his way home from the Council of Nicaea (325). A Greek *Passion* records his martyrdom (*BHG* 759d). It is worth

Having come to Sinope, as I said before, and spent a number of days there, the inhabitants showed us the habitual places [M 224] and seats of the blessed apostles Peter and Andrew, along with the icon of the [latter] apostle that was entirely marvellous, which had been drawn while he was still alive. [They also described] the wonders which he performed, and [showed us] the prison, which Andrew opened spontaneously by making a sign over it, and [from which] he led out Matthias along with those who were imprisoned with him and due to be executed on the following day. [And they showed us] also the fig trees in the place where he hid them, as well as the seashore where he baptised them. They said that in all they were seventeen in number, and [they spoke of] how seven of these, who were possessed by demons, were healed. And [they told us] about [D 51] the savage customs of the people of that time – or rather of the men who are there now. But the people of Amisos described other things to us. Then the two brothers divided the whole world between themselves. Whereas it fell to Peter's lot to enlighten the regions of the west, the east belonged to Andrew.[45]

10. After they were separated from one another, Andrew departed from Sinope with his disciples and Matthias, and came to Amisos, a city that is beside the sea.[46] And he entered it and approached one Dometianos, a Jew. And, on the Sabbath, he went into the synagogue. The local people there were both handsome and good, belonging to many faiths; [they were] Greeks and Jews, not unkind by nature, hospitable and lovers of goodness. And the place was truly agreeable;[47] it produced olives and all sorts of fruit.

11. [Vin 241] When Andrew entered the synagogue with his disciples, [the people] were asking where they had come from and what their message

---

noting, as discussed also in the Introduction, that the whole section in which Epiphanios describes his visits to the shrines and relics of martyrs in various cities is written in an almost telegraphic style. It may reflect his use of notes jotted down in the course of his travels.

45 On the apostolic claims of the Latin and Greek halves of Roman Christendom, see Introduction, 40–41.

46 Amisos (modern Samsun) was a coastal city on the Black Sea in Pontos. It belonged to the Anatolikon theme and played an important commercial role in supplying Cherson with grain; see *ODB*, vol. 1, 78; Bryer and Winfield 1985, vol. 1, 92–95.

47 Epiphanios uses wordplay here: the adjective ἄμισος ('agreeable' or 'not hateful') is similar to the name of the city (Ἀμισός).

LIFE AND ACTS OF ST ANDREW THE APOSTLE 117

was.[48] So he said, 'We are the disciples of Jesus of Galilee. You have surely heard the report that has come out of Jerusalem.' The Herodians were present and said, 'We have heard of Jesus, but we say that Herod was the Christ, since he brought down Hyrkanos and put on the high priesthood and the crown, and also raised up many trophies.'[49] Andrew replied, 'Herod [belonged to] another tribe since he was the son of Antipater, slave of the priest of Askalon. Herod was bloodstained, a killer of children, as well as being a wife-killer, bloodthirsty, and a womaniser.[50] And he was not a Jew since the prophets spoke about the tribe of Judah.' Others answered and said, 'John was from the tribe of Judah and he was the son of the high priest Zacharias.' And Andrew said, 'Brothers, listen to me. I was John's disciple at the start. I was taught first by John, along with others. And John, preaching a baptism of repentance, saw Jesus coming towards him, pointed his finger at him,[51] and said about Jesus, "Behold, the Lamb of God who takes away the sin of the world."[52] And Jesus said to him, "I need to be baptised by you and do you approach me?" And John bore witness concerning Jesus [D 52], [saying,] "I have seen the Spirit coming down and remaining on him. And I did not recognise him. But he who sent me to baptise is the One who said to me, 'He on whom you see the Spirit

---

48 Epiphanios uses λόγος in various contexts to mean 'teaching', 'message', or (more literally) 'word'. It refers here to Andrew's summary of the good news concerning Christ, which he uses to attract new converts to the faith.

49 The Herodians, who may have been members of Herod's household and/or supporters of his dynasty, are mentioned in Mk 3: 6 (in Galilee), Mk 12: 13, Mt 22: 16 (in Jerusalem); Rowley 1940; Bennett 1975. Epiphanios picks up here the probably erroneous view of some Christian writers that the Herodians believed Herod to be the true Messiah; see, for example, John of Damascus, *On Heresies* 20, ed. Kotter 1981, 25.20.1–2. It is also interesting that Epiphanios places members of the 'heretical' group in first-century Anatolia.

50 On Herod's humble origins, Vinogradov points out that the accusation originally referred to his father, Antipater, who, according to Eusebios, was a 'temple slave' of Apollo; see Eusebios of Caesarea, *Ecclesiastical History* I.6.2; Vinogradov 2005, 123, n. 285. The term γυναικομανής means literally 'mad for women'. On the massacre of the innocents, following the Magi's report to Herod about the birth of Jesus in Bethlehem, see Mt 2: 16. His bad reputation, as regards women, may reflect the fact that he had many wives and divorced or murdered a few of them; see *Life of the Virgin* above, n. 81; Josephus, *The Jewish War* I. 431–551, trans. Thackeray 1961, 204–13; Josephus, *Antiquities* XVII. 19–22; trans. Marcus and Wikgren 1963, 174–77.

51 Epiphanios also used this expression towards the beginning of the text; see above, section 2. The verb is δακτυλοδεικτέω ('to point with the finger'); see Lampe, 332.

52 Jn 1: 29.

descend like a dove and remain, this one is the Son of the living God.'"[53] On hearing these things from John, I, Andrew, left him and followed Jesus for three years. And Jesus worked miracles in front of us that surpassed those of Moses. After what had been foretold about him by the prophets, the high priests, who envied him, delivered him to Pilate, the governor of Judaea, [M 225] and crucified him while Pilate washed his hands like one who was free from blame.[54] And [Jesus] was placed in a new tomb and arose on the third day before dawn. And he appeared to us for forty days.[55] And he enjoined us to proclaim repentance and the remission of sins in his name to all the nations, baptising in pure water in the name of the Father and of the Son and of the Holy Spirit, setting [people] free from errors and making them heirs of the Kingdom of Heaven. And he went up into [Vin 242] heaven while we were watching. And he sat at the right hand of God. He will come to judge the living and the dead according to his commandments.'

12. Andrew, on departing from the synagogue, saw a great crowd standing there, carrying the sick and those who were troubled by impure spirits, which cried out, [saying,] 'The disciples of Jesus of Galilee have come to pursue us!' And they fell down before him, shouting, 'Servant of God, may God have mercy on us through you.' But Andrew, after climbing up on a rock, made a sign with his hand, and caused them to be silent.[56] And he began to speak:[57] 'Men who have ears to hear, listen to a message of life. Listen and understand and believe in order that you may experience eternal life. Distance yourselves from the multitude of doctrines and, on believing, approach the one [D 53] living and true God who is the God of the Hebrews. For he alone is the true and good Craftsman of all creation, who searches out the hearts and minds of each human being, having known everything since before their birth, as the Maker of all things. To him alone, gazing

---

53 Cf. Jn 1: 33–34.
54 Mt 27: 24.
55 The post-resurrection appearances of Christ are elaborated most fully in Jn 20: 1–21, 23; however, see also Mt 28: 9–10, 16–20; Mk 16: 9–20; Lk 24: 13–51.
56 Vinogradov's edition provides the third-person plural here: 'they became silent' (ἡσύχασαν). Since this form does not fit grammatically into the sentence, I have adopted the reading which appears in three manuscripts that transmit Version A of the text, thus: 'he caused them to be silent' (ἡσύχασεν). Cf. Vinogradov 2005, 242. 8.
57 The sermon that follows is influenced by that of the apostle Peter at Tyre from the *(ps-) Clementine Homilies* 7. 1–4, ed. Rehm and Strecker 1992, 117. 1–118. 24. Epiphanios the Monk noted his use of this source in section one of the *LAA*; see above, n. 3.

earnestly into heaven, fall down in the evening and the morning, and at noon. To him alone make a sacrifice of praise, avoiding the things that you yourselves hate; for example, if you do not wish to be wronged, do no wrong; and if [you do not wish] for your wife to commit adultery, do not yourself [commit it] with the wife of another man.[58] Do not do to others those very things that you hate. Display works of repentance, including mercy to slaves and to strangers, unqualified love towards everyone – honest and forgiving[59] – and obedience to that which is good. And if you follow my instructions you will be set free from illnesses and from the harm of demons, and you will spend the remaining time in your life in peace. So live thus in the future and gather together tomorrow in order that you may experience healing and that your souls may be illumined.' And he dismissed them.

13. And going in with his disciples, he ate and rested. There were eight disciples, so they say: Thaddaeus and Matthias,[60] Tychikos and Astachys, Evodios and Simon, Agapetos and Dometios. [The people] presented them with many goods and donations. But Andrew distributed everything to the poor. And he founded churches, dedicated sanctuaries, and appointed [Vin 243] priests. And they possessed only one garment and went barefoot in sandals, being fed on bread and water once a day, and they were equipped with pallets.

14. The next day, when the people had gathered together and [D 54] a certain person made this known [to him], Andrew went out and stood on a pedestal in order to be seen.[61] He was not young in age, [M 228] but rather of a great [age]; and he was slightly stooped, with a prominent nose,[62] and [he had] heavy eyebrows.[63] And he said, 'Separate those who are possessed with

---

58 This passage paraphrases (but does not quote directly) Jesus's teachings to the assembled crowd in Mt 5: 21–48.

59 Epiphanios uses alliteration in this phrase with words including ἁπλῆν... ἄδολον... ἀμνησίκακον... ἀγαθόν.

60 Thaddaeus and Matthias were among the twelve disciples of Jesus Christ (although Matthias was chosen later to replace Judas, according to Acts 1: 26); see above, Chap. 1, n. 136.

61 The meaning of θεωρεῖσθαι may mean 'contemplated' since Andrew is a holy man, the sight of whom would be considered spiritually uplifting.

62 The word ἐπίρρινος ('a prominent nose') is used with reference to Christ in (ps-) John of Damascus, *Epistola ad Theophilum imperatorem* 3, PG 95, 349C.

63 On the significance of physical descriptions of characters in Byzantine chronicles and other narrative sources, see Introduction, 17–18.

demons into one group.' And when this came to pass, the demons began clamouring. But Andrew turned to them and said, 'Be silent!' And at once they were quiet. And he said to the people, 'Peace be with you, brothers.' And they said, 'And with you.'[64] And he began to speak in a gentle way, [saying,] 'There is one God who is without beginning, eternal, and good. [He is] the Craftsman of all creation, of heavenly and earthly things, and of things in the underworld. He alone fashioned the heavens and the earth. He alone also made ranks of angels. Being Light, he brought them into light; being Fire, [he made them] fiery; being good, [he made them] good; without malice; rational; with free will; hymn-singing; and not lacking anything that is good. For the olive tree does not bear figs; nor does fire [cause] water; nor does light [bring about] darkness. But one of the ten ranks [of angels] (the leader of his rank), who was unable to bear the abundance of such benefits, turned voluntarily to evil since he possessed free will; and from being light, he became dark; and instead of [being] good, [he became] evil; instead of fragrance, stench; instead of [being] pure and holy, he was impure and profane. And let no one say that there was darkness from the beginning. For God is eternal light without a beginning, while darkness is a shadow of light. If there was nothing producing a shadow before heaven, how was it possible for there to be darkness? Having exalted himself against the Creator and been unwilling to sing his praises with the rest, the Devil wilfully shut his eyes and was deprived of the divine light; and in place of many blessings, he became the perpetrator of many evils; [he was] a cheat and a liar. Then the good God and Craftsman, after [the Devil] had fallen with those who were under him, decided to create a human being with free will, according to his own image and likeness, to oppose him. [He made him] radiant, wise, with foreknowledge, a prophet, guileless, good, hymn-singing, master of everything on earth, an initiate of heavenly things, incorruptible, and eternal. Then the wicked Satan, on seeing the human thus honoured instead of himself by the Craftsman, envied him and hastened to bring him down. But the good God, knowing the villainy of the Evil One, as well as human free will and simplicity, gave him a helpful rod as a support, a tree of nourishment, saying, "You are master of all things; only do not touch this. And may you not die, on becoming arrogant or distancing yourself from me. For that is what death is." Then the Devil

---

64 These utterances are reminiscent of liturgical greetings between clergy and laity in Byzantine worship; see Brightman and Hammond 1965, 320 ('The Byzantine Liturgy of the Ninth Century').

knew that the human being would give birth to an incorruptible offspring and that even if he should first [V in 244] go astray, the second incorruptible one would be saved. He hastened that [the human] should, before the birth, arrogantly disobey the God who had created him and he [first] beguiled the woman and then the wife [beguiled] her husband. Having eaten [the fruit], they were deprived of many blessings including God and angelic discourse. And having denuded themselves of these things, they recognised their own shame and also death. And they bore a son from their disobedience, who was Cain; he manifested the wicked disposition of the Devil. For Cain was born ungrateful, wicked, envious, false, unjust, insatiable, misanthropic, a fratricide, wrathful, a perpetrator of many evils which I exhort you to renounce. And when the people had multiplied in number, he taught them to do likewise. And, since he was not satisfied by these things, the Devil taught them idolatry. After distancing them even to this day from worship of God, their Maker, he has taught them to believe in their own demons; [and] he dwells among them as if with his own servants and introduces every infirmity. Therefore, if you renounce your idols, your abominable meals, and your lawless activities, and if you believe in the God who created you, you will be delivered from illnesses and the demons will flee from you. And when you are cleansed of your ancient pollutions by the water of the divine baptism, you will become partners with the heavenly angels.'[65] After saying these things, Andrew ordered the crowds to be brought towards him and, having placed his hand on each person, he healed them all. He expelled the demons having only rebuked them with a fierce glance and, having washed with water those who were maimed, he made them as healthy as young children. After laying his hands on those who were lame, hump-backed, withered, blind, crippled, maimed, and paralytic, he delivered them all from their sufferings.

15. The people, on seeing the apostles who were humble, underfed, pale, barefoot except for sandals, and wearing only one garment, but flowing with divinely inspired speech, granting cures, and carrying out hymnody for God in the evening, morning, and at midday, were amazed and did not want to be parted from them. Each day, a crowd of men and women joined in believing in the Lord. And Andrew ordered his disciples to instruct them. But he, along with two disciples, made the circuit of the

---

65 A large section of this sermon (from 'There is one God...' to 'introduces every infirmity') is omitted in V3 (and Dressel's edition of the *LAA*).

nearby villages in order to meet those who were unable [D 55] to come to him. And having instructed [Vin 245] them for many days, they baptised great crowds. In fact many of the people in charge [of each village] also came to believe and were baptised. The emperors at that time, Tiberius, Gaius, and Claudius, did not prevent [faith in Christ];[66] instead, many of the well-born women and Jews believed and were baptised. Therefore, having baptised them in the name of the Father and of the Son and of the Holy Spirit, [Andrew] dedicated a sanctuary and temple of the holy Theotokos, which to this day can be seen by everyone.[67] He ordained presbyters and deacons from among them. And it came to pass that there was great joy in that city, for he imparted to them the divine mysteries of Christ and handed on the service and the rule of psalmody, [namely] to come together in the evening and morning, to bend the knee to the east and then to pray in a standing position, and to sing the psalter of David and the rest of the prophets, [to fast,] and to pay no attention to the myths of the Greeks, but rather to remain steadfast to the law of Moses and to safeguard the things that had been established by the apostles. Both by acting and teaching thus, Andrew brought many cities and villages [of the Pontos] to Christ.

16. After departing from Amisos, he came to Trebizond and to Phasis, a city of Lazica.[68] The people there were ignorant [M 229] and irrational like beasts. Having departed from there, he spent time in Iberia. And after bestowing light on many people, he went up to Jerusalem through Parthia, on account of Easter.[69]

---

66 Epiphanios is correct in stating that the emperors Tiberius Caesar Augustus (14–37), Gaius (Caligula) (37–41), and Claudius Tiberius (41–54) did not initiate any persecution of Christians.

67 It is unlikely that a church would have been dedicated to the Virgin Mary during the lifetime of the apostle Andrew. There is no record of official veneration of the Theotokos before the fourth century; churches or shrines in her honour began to appear during the fifth century. See Shoemaker 2002, 78–141 (on Palestine); Mango 2000 (on Constantinople).

68 Trebizond was located on the south-eastern coast of the Black Sea. It was the most important Pontic city throughout Late Antiquity and the Byzantine period since it possessed a harbour and offered one of the best routes to the east. Justinian I based his Armenian campaigns in Trebizond, also restoring its walls and building an aqueduct. Trebizond had its own bishops from the third century onward, became an archbishopric in the ninth century and a metropolis in the diocese of Lazike in the early tenth. See *ODB*, vol. 3, 2112–13; Bryer 1980, I, 23–30; Bryer and Winfield 1985, vol. 1, 178–250.

69 Epiphanios uses the Greek word Πάσχα to refer to this important feast. The Byzantines

LIFE AND ACTS OF ST ANDREW THE APOSTLE

17. And after Pentecost, Peter, Andrew, John [son of] Zebedee, and Philip (of the twelve), along with Bartholomew, went down into Antioch, in Syria.[70] And whereas Peter [D 56] remained [there] and tonsured, with Paul's help, Markianos and Pankratios as bishops of Sicily,[71] the rest departed and continued to travel through the cities of the interior. Philip (of the twelve) and [Vin 246] Bartholomew remained in upper Phrygia and Pisidia [and Lycia]. Andrew and John went down to Asia, and Philip, one of the seven deacons, went down to Caria, to Samaria. Then the apostle Andrew and John passed some time in Ephesus and were teaching there. But the Lord said to Andrew, 'Go up into Bithynia. And I am with you wherever you go since Scythia is waiting for you.' When Andrew told John about the vision, they embraced each other. And taking his own disciples, [Andrew] went up to Laodikeia of Phrygia Kapatiane[72] and from there [went on] into Mysia, as far as Odyssoupolis.[73] And having passed a few days there, he appointed Apion as bishop for them. After passing over [Mount] Olympos he arrived in Nicaea, a town in Bithynia.[74] At that time [the town] was not fortified

---

usually employed the term (νομικὸν) Φάσκα for the Jewish Passover – unless they meant the celebration of Passover in the Old and New Testaments, which they viewed as the precursor of their Easter. By 'Parthia', Epiphanios means the region south of the Caucasus which constituted the Persian empire in antiquity and became modern Iran, Iraq, and Syria.

70 Patristic, as opposed to apocryphal, sources provide further evidence concerning the trajectories of the apostles' missions in Europe, Asia Minor, N. Africa, the Near East, and India. For orientation concerning these sources, see *AA*, ed. Prieur 1989, 67–72; Junod 1981. On the Christianisation of Georgia, along with doubts about Andrew's mission to that region, see Peeters 1932, esp. 12. On the legendary aspects of Andrew's mission, see Dvornik 1958, 181–222. Vinogradov's edition omits a few words (which appear in Dressel's edition) at the beginning of this section ('…along with Bartholomew, returned to Upper Phrygia. And Philip went down into Antioch…'). This appears to be a 'saut du même au même' omission and should perhaps be restored to the text.

71 This mention of St Pankratios reveals Epiphanios's awareness of the early eighth-century *Life of St Pankratios*, ed. Stallman with Burke 2018, 33. See also above, n. 4.

72 For a map of this region, see Moulet 2016, 88.

73 Mango suggests that 'Odyssoupolis in Mysia' may refer to Odessopolis in Moesia (located between Laodikeia and Nicaea); see Mango 2002, 256.

74 The city of Nicaea (modern Iznik) remained an important commercial and ecclesiastical centre throughout the Byzantine period. It was the seat of two important Ecumenical Councils (325 and 787 CE), also serving as a refuge for various emperors (Anastasios II in 715; Theodore Lascaris between 1206 and 1261). For further background, see *ODB*, vol. 2, 1463–65; Janin 1925; Janin 1975, 105–25; Peschlow 2017; Lichtenberger, Agtürk, Winter, and Zimmerman 2020.

or adorned, but later it was fortified under [the emperor] Trajan.[75] And the lake was then small and at a great distance from the town.[76]

18. Andrew, on entering [Nicaea], proclaimed Christ to them and called on them to accept the Lord's word. But the people of that place are liars, mockers,[77] arrogant, and false[78] to the present day; this includes both Jews and Greeks. And there was a great synagogue for the Jews, since it was a large town; but for the Greeks there was an idol of Apollo, which produced oracles and visions. Those who received an oracular response from it delivered the oracle but were not able to say anything else because the demon was speaking into their ears and through their mouths, and they remained mute and speechless. There were many weaknesses among them and many people were possessed by demons. But Andrew said to them, 'You will not be able to be released from your demons and illnesses [D 57] unless you approach the teaching that heals.' But while some took heed, others were false.

19. There was a very high rock, about nine miles away. On it, so they say, there lived an immense dragon,[79] and it injured many people. But Andrew went out to it, holding an iron staff with a cross on top on which he always leaned, in the company of two disciples. And as they approached, the dragon came out towards him. But Andrew thrust his iron staff into the [Vin 247] dragon's eye, and it came out of the other [eye], and [the dragon] at once expired.[80] When this happened, many people believed in the Lord. But Andrew returned to Nicaea and began his teaching.

---

75 The walls of Nicaea were completed in 270 CE, not during the reign of Trajan (98–117). They were rebuilt many times during the middle and late Byzantine centuries.

76 The Ascanian lake was in fact quite close to the city of Nicaea during the early Christian and Byzantine periods; see Foss with Tulchin 1996, 225, Fig. 1.

77 Μοῦκοι derives from the verb μουκίζω (to 'mock' or 'jeer'); cf. Leontios of Neapolis, *Life of Symeon the Fool* 41, PG 93, 1721A.

78 Lampe provides the meaning 'characteristic of a beggar or imposter' for ἀγυρτώδης; cf. Epiphanios of Salamis, *Panarion* 26.3, 30. 21, ed. Bergermann, Collatz, and Holl 2013, 279. 17, 361. 18; Lampe, 24.

79 Δράκων may mean 'serpent', 'snake', or 'dragon. The animal is often identified with the devil in Jewish and Christian literature. This story parallels an episode in Gregory of Tours' *Epitome* 19, which is probably based on the earlier *AA* (see Introduction, 54); *AA*, ed. MacDonald 2020, 262–63.

80 There are three changes of subject in this sentence (Andrew, the iron staff, and the dragon). This is characteristic of Epiphanios's relaxed approach to syntax.

20. After the dragon on the rock of Lokous was killed [M 232],[81] eight robbers came to live on [the rock], for it was wooded. And they committed many murders since two of them were possessed by demons. Andrew, having been summoned by the inhabitants of that place, approached them. But those who were possessed by demons came forward to meet him with cries. And Andrew rebuked them and the demons came out before he got near to them. Those who had been purified of the demons then folded their hands and presented themselves in sound mind to Andrew. And the rest, on witnessing these things, were contrite and, after throwing down their weapons, came and threw themselves at Andrew's feet. And he, with a gentle tone[82] of voice, said, 'Why do you act in such a way, my children? What is it that you hate? Why are you a nuisance to others? Do you not know that there is one God in heaven who watches over all things and that he is the Creator of small and great things who will render to each according to his actions? You do not want to be beaten, so why do you beat and even kill [others]? You do not want to be wronged, so why do you offend [others]? You do not want to be ruined, so why do you steal? God has given you health and bodily strength in order that you may work and gain [D 58] from your labour and have need of nothing – or rather, that you may supply those who do not have [these things]. Stand back in future from these wicked things that you are doing, go back to your homes, and God will have mercy on you, the [town] leaders will have occasion to praise you, and you will meet with rewards.' And he spoke the word of God to them. But they, having been stung [by these words], remained with him for days and so he baptised them.

21. Katzapos was a very high rock on the same road, on which there was an idol of Artemis. Many spirits lived in it, and they both caused visions and [Vin 248] sought sacrifices. From the ninth hour of the day until the third hour of the following day, they prevented anyone from passing along that road.[83] Therefore Andrew came and remained in that place with his disciples. The demons fled, just like ravens, crying, 'O, force from Jesus of Galilee! For his disciples are pursuing us everywhere!' Andrew, having

---

81 Clive Foss identifies the rock called Lokous with modern Karacakaya on the southern shore of the lake near Nicaea; see Foss 1996, 22, ff; cf. Mango 2002, 257. See also Kahl 1989, 101.
82 Κατάστασις means literally a 'condition' or 'state'.
83 The hours, according to Byzantine calculations, were numbered from daybreak, thus representing different times of day in the course of the solar year; see *ODB*, vol. 2, 952.

thrown down the idol, set up a cross, and the rock, as well as the place, was cleansed of demons.

22. And there was a region to the left of Nicaea called Daukomis.[84] Near it there was a wooded place[85] in which a dragon and a multitude of demons lived, and the Greeks sacrificed to them. For there was a statue of Aphrodite. Andrew went out with his disciples to the place and, having kneeled down, prayed and got up, stretched out his hand and sealed the place.[86] And the dragon and the demons fled. And from that time forward, that place has been inhabited.

23. And so Andrew taught those who came to him by day and healed those who were ill while at night he went out to the mountain, called Klithos, that was in the east.[87] There, together with his disciples, he prayed to God that he might assist him since many people were opposing him. A feast of the Greeks took place [D 59] and they offered sacrifices to their gods. And on the next day, the demons entered the men and, after going mad, the whole crowd [of people] were eating their own flesh.[88] And they at once went out to the mountain towards Andrew, wailing, screaming, and crying, 'Have mercy on us, apostle of the good God.' The local people [M 233] say these things, along with some other [stories], from what has been passed down.[89] Then Andrew came down from the mountain and, going out, stood

---

84 Dressel omits the name 'Daukome' (Δαύκωμης χωρίον), although it does appear in the Vatican manuscript that he was using (V3).

85 The adjective δασύς may mean 'hairy' or 'shaggy'; however, according to LS, 370, it may also mean a rough, wooded area.

86 One meaning of the verb σφραγίζω is 'to make the sign of the cross'. See, for example, the second-century *Apocryphal Acts of John* 115, ed. Junod and Kaestli 1983, 343; trans. Schneemelcher 1992, vol. 2, 204 ('and having sealed himself in every part'); John Moschos, *Pratum spirituale* 56, PG 87, 2912A, trans. Wortley 1992, 45 ('...so [the brother] laid his hand [on the diseased part] and sealed [it with the sign of the cross] and she was immediately healed').

87 Although he is unable to identify 'the mountain called Klithos', Gerhard Kahl sees no reason to doubt the existence of such locations in connection with the apostle Andrew's legend; see Kahl 1989, 101.

88 This episode, which involves the eating of human flesh (although in this case it is that of the instigators themselves), may be inspired by the earlier text known as the *AAMt* in which cannibalism plays an important part; see Introduction, 47–48 and above, n. 19.

89 Epiphanios provides the source for the story that he is telling about demons in Nicaea here, which is ἐκ παραδόσεως, an expression that he normally uses to refer to oral tradition. The use of the present tense suggests that the story was still being told in Epiphanios's own

in their midst, stretched out his hand, and sealed them.[90] And they stopped eating their own flesh. After climbing up onto a pedestal, he began to say, 'How can God have mercy on you and stop this anger of yours, when you do not wish to receive him? Or indeed, how will he hearken to me when I summon him on your behalf when you are not accepting the faith or renouncing your wicked deeds? I am teaching you the way of salvation and you mock me. I have told you many things: distance yourselves from the [Vin 249] idols, and you do not agree. You continue to worship gods, or rather demons, who, on taking up residence in you like domestic slaves, have displayed their innate wickedness. For they are incapable of doing anything good. Wash [yourselves] and approach the living and true God, and seal [yourselves] with the sign of the cross,[91] and the demons will flee from you. Renounce their works and acts of worship, since these are dark, with words and take up weapons of light in order that you may now live in peace and health, and that you may enjoy future benefits.'[92] Admonishing them with these and many other words, he said to them, 'Take these things to heart and contemplating them, always venerate and thank the God and Father of our Lord Jesus Christ, along with his holy [D 60] Spirit, and the demons and every illness will flee from you.' Then, as they took heed and were asking him to approach them, he placed his hand on each and healed them all. And blowing through the ears of the mutes, he made them speak and [then] dismissed them.

24. And on the next day at dawn, the whole people, both insignificant and great, men and women, Jews and Greeks, assembled – for they all came together. Andrew went out to them and stood in the place [where he had stood] the previous day and said, 'Peace to all.' Those who had been given strength cried out with one voice, 'And with your spirit.' And Andrew began to speak [as follows], 'When the good and only benevolent God and Creator of all things honoured the [first] man with his own image, he planted paradise to the east and placed the man there after giving him a commandment of immortality. But the wicked devil, who was envious, caused the man, through arrogance and pride (for he said, "You will be

---

day – and perhaps that he had heard it from the local people whom he interviewed on his travels. The statement is rather awkwardly inserted into the middle of the narrative.

90 Or 'made the sign of the cross on them'; see above, n. 86.

91 Epiphanios is more explicit here, using the words, σφραγίσθητε τῷ σημείῳ τοῦ σταυροῦ, instead of simply using the verb 'to seal' (σφραγίζω) as he did above; see nn. 86 and 90.

92 Version A of the *LAA* adds a longer section to this sermon; see Appendix B (a).

like gods"), to disobey[93] the God who had created him; and for this reason, [Adam] was turned from incorruption to corruption. And he bore a son of disobedience, Cain, who [Vin 250] bore the stamp of the devil.[94] For Cain became an inventor of all evil things. After murdering his own brother, who was righteous and blameless, [Cain] took seven punishments since he had committed seven wicked acts.[95] For when he offered up the first of his fruits to God, he first ate the best things himself and made an offering to God in this way; behold, this is the first wicked act. The second was envy, for he envied Abel, his own brother. The third was deceit since he deceived both God and his parents. The fourth was hatred, for it was while hating that he deliberated about how he would kill him. The fifth was his disobedience to God and to his parents. For they were telling him constantly not to deceive God. The sixth was trickery, [M 236] for he tricked his own brother, saying, "Let us go out into the field," evidently to distract him.[96] The seventh was falsehood, [D 61] for God said to him after the murder, "Where is your brother Abel?"[97] [God] was not ignorant but was giving him space for remorse; however, [Cain] was not only not swayed, having been moved by the isolation and separation from his brother, but he even lied shamelessly, saying, "I do not know. Am I my brother's keeper?",[98] thus mocking God. The righteous God dispensed seven punishments for seven wicked acts. And the first was estrangement from God, for Cain departed from the face of God. And secondly, the fact that he settled[99] on cursed land since he had stained it with fraternal blood. Third, there was unceasing labour, for he had no rest either by night or by day. Fourth was the barrenness of the land, for, [God] says, "You will till the earth and it will not continue to give its strength to you." Fifth is the groaning of groans

---

93 This is the meaning of παρακούω, according to Lampe, 1020. The word is frequently used to refer to Adam's disobedience; see, for example, Clement of Alexandria, *Stromata* 2.11.

94 Epiphanios is referring obliquely here to the mark of Cain; see Gen 4: 15.

95 Cf. Gen 4: 15. Epiphanios may have borrowed the theme of Cain's seven sins and seven punishments either from Basil of Caesarea's Letter 260. 3 to the bishop Optimos (ed. and trans. Courtonne 1966, 106–9) or from John Chrysostom's *Homily 19 on Genesis* (PG 53, 159–66, trans. Hill 1990, 31–33). However, Epiphanios lists slightly different sins under the seven headings from those mentioned in the earlier sources.

96 Cf. Gen 4: 8. For the metaphorical meaning of μετεωρίζω, see Lampe 864, d.

97 Gen 4: 9.

98 Gen 4: 9.

99 In accordance with his rather loose use of syntax, Epiphanios has neglected to provide a main verb in this phrase.

and ceaseless agony. Sixth is the trembling, "for you will be groaning and trembling upon the earth,"[100] since when trembling he was unable with his own hand to bring either food or drink to his own mouth or do anything else for his body. Seventh is his continuation of life, for he wished to be slain and separated from many evil things – for death becomes a gain for those who are being punished since it leads to swift release. But God said, "Not so. Anyone [Vin 251] who kills Cain will avenge those things that have [already] been avenged; that is, he will cancel the seven vengeances and thereby abandon the murdered Abel."[101] Seth was born like Adam: he was righteous, wise, innocent, gentle, and knowledgeable. For he invented the sciences.[102] He begot Enos, who was like himself,[103] and they called him God on account of his virtues. His sons, on seeing Cain's daughters, took them as wives since the daughters of a leper's family are beautiful in appearance.[104] But these women taught [D 62] them their paternal wicked ways, [including how] to steal, murder, quarrel, divide, draw up boundaries, build cities (for Cain was the first man to build a city), to wage wars on account of one woman,[105] and to do battle with women on account of one man.[106] And then the giants were born and the earth could no longer bear the evil deeds of humanity. When he saw this, God brought about the flood and washed sin out with water and purified the earth. But he saved one righteous man who was from righteous seed, Noah, along with his wife and three sons with their wives, after ordering him to construct a great boat and to bring on board, along with himself, one of every creature and of every seed. But he destroyed the rest of the world in its entirety.[107] And when

---

100 Gen 4: 12.
101 Cf. Gen 4: 15. In other words, God did not want Cain to die so that he would fully experience his seven punishments.
102 According to Josephus, Seth's descendants developed the science of astronomy and built the 'pillars of the sons of Seth', two pillars that were inscribed with scientific discoveries and inventions. See Josephus, *Antiquities* I. 69–71, trans. Thackeray 1930, 32–33.
103 Cf. Gen 4: 25–26.
104 Κελεφός ('leper') is used as an insult here, with reference to Cain.
105 Epiphanios must refer here to the Trojan War, which, according to legend, was started on account of the Menelaus's wife, Helen.
106 It is possible that Epiphanios is thinking of several women who were believed to have fought in the Trojan War. These included Epipole of Carystus, Penthesilia, and others; see Mayor 2014, esp. 291–92 (Epipole), 287–304 (Penthesilea). Alternatively, he may be referring to the legendary Amazons, a tribe of warrior women who were believed to live in Asia Minor. For background, see Blok 1995.
107 For the story of Noah and the flood, see Gen 6: 9–8: 22.

humanity had once again multiplied, the author of evil,[108] the devil, did not cease waging war on the race of human beings. For he taught them idolatry and instead of venerating[109] the good God who created all things, [M 237] men who were both good and wise venerated created things, or rather demons, that were senseless and evil. Abraam alone fled from idolatry and worshipped the true God, Maker of heaven and earth and of all the stars. For on seeing and understanding these things, he recognised their Creator. For this reason, he was loved by God and [God] blessed his seed.[110] And God raised up pious teachers and prophets out of him, including Joseph, who was prudent.[111] And when a famine occurred, he fed Egypt for seven years.[112] After this, the Egyptians made the righteous offspring their slaves. [Vin 252] For this reason, the good God established an avenger for his own people, Moses, who performed miracles and great signs in Egypt.[113] For after dividing the sea [D 63], he led his own people across on dry land.[114] And the Egyptians who pursued them also entered the sea on dry land. But Moses turned and brought back the water so that the Egyptians remained in the depths.[115] And the people of Moses, having been released from slavery, remained in the desert for forty-two years being fed from heaven; they received sayings and commandments from the living God.[116] But Moses, on reaching the end of his life, said to the people, "The Lord God will raise up a prophet like me from among your relatives. But whoever disbelieves this prophet will be blotted out from a book of the living."[117] And he gave them his successor, Joshua, the son of Naue.[118] And the judges came in succession, as far as Samuel and King David, to whom God swore that the everlasting kingdom would be given, from the fruit of his loins. And after David, [God raised up] all the prophets, who prophesied about the coming

---

108 Epiphanios uses the adjective ἀρχέκακος here, which literally means 'originating evil'; see Lampe, 233.
109 In this context, Epiphanios uses the word προσκυνέω ('to venerate') rather than λατρεύω ('to worship'). On this author's flexibility with regard to the two terms, see above, n. 30.
110 Gen 12–13. The subject changes from Abraam to God in this sentence, reflecting Epiphanios's habitual disregard for correct syntax.
111 Gen 37–50.
112 Gen 41: 47–57.
113 Ex 7–12.
114 Ex 14: 21–22.
115 Ex 14: 26–28.
116 Ex 15: 22–24: 18.
117 Cf. Deut 18: 15–22; cf. Ex 32–33; Ps 68: 29 (LXX).
118 Num 14: 6. English Bibles render the name 'Naue' as 'Nun'.

LIFE AND ACTS OF ST ANDREW THE APOSTLE 131

of Christ. And when the weeks of Daniel had been fulfilled,[119] God sent his Son into the world and he dwelt in a spotless maiden from the seed of David who [lived with] an elderly guardian in Galilee. And when the Son of God was born in Bethlehem of Judaea, heaven announced his birth by means of a star and summoned the Magi from Persia. And the angels sang, and the shepherds saw, heard, and were given the good news of joy for the world and the overthrow of the Devil. When Jesus, the Son of God, reached the age of thirty, he sent John the son of Zacharias the priest, who came before him, to preach to the world the baptism of repentance for the remission of sins. By water the sin of the old world was destroyed; by water the people of Israel were freed from Egyptian slavery; by water and fire the Jewish people was purified of the delusion of Baal by Elijah.[120] By the water of baptism you will be purified from your ancient defilements and your names will be inscribed in heaven, and the demon will no longer touch you since he drowns in water that has been sanctified by the invocation of the Father and the Son and the Holy Spirit.' And praying again and laying his hands on them, [Andrew] dismissed them, saying, 'Go in peace and come back soon tomorrow.' And they, encouraged by his teaching and healing, departed joyfully.

25. [Vin 253] And when they had come together again on the next day, Andrew, supported by his iron staff, resumed his teaching, saying, 'There is only one God, Almighty, Creator, wise, holy, who sanctifies and makes wise by his Spirit. He made the prophets wise, he gave wisdom to the Greeks, he gave Moses a law for [divine] grace, along with the commandments of salvation. And Moses commanded about the prophet: Jesus Christ is the prophet whom Moses spoke about according to the prophets; for no other enacted so many powers or fulfilled the law. Moses parted the sea with a staff, but Christ walked about on the sea for thirty stades while we watched and were afraid, for it was at night. But he cried, "I am [the One]. Do not be afraid." And my brother Peter, impelled towards him, stepped down from the boat and walked about on the sea. Moses fed the people in the desert with manna from heaven by means of his prayer, but Jesus satisfied five thousand people with five loaves and we collected twelve hampers of what was left over. And again [there were] seven loaves for four thousand,

---

119 Dan 9: 24; cf. Origen, *On First Principles* IV.1.5; Eusebios, *Demonstratio evangelica* 8.2, ed. Heikel 1913, 374.
120 Cf. 3 Kgs 18: 20–40 (LXX); 1 Kgs 18: 20–40.

and seven baskets of leftovers. Elijah raised one dead man through prayer; Jesus raised the son of the widow in Nain by his command. Elisha, having warmed him seven times, raised up the child;[121] Jesus took the hand of the daughter of the ruler of the synagogue and raised her.[122] And lest I should enumerate [such miracles] individually, Jesus Christ alone performed the works of all the prophets after his baptism. When Jesus approached John to be baptised by him, John said to him, "I need to be baptised and you are coming to me?" And seeing Jesus coming towards him, he said, "Behold the Lamb of God who takes away the sin of the world; for I have seen the Spirit descending from heaven upon him."[123] And John bore witness, saying, "This is the Son of the living God."[124]

26. I, Andrew, heard these things from John. But on seeing the miracles which he was working, the chief priests envied him and sought to kill him. We said that he could bring fire down from heaven against the impious but that the benevolent One did not consent to this. And he knew everything and told us in advance about what would happen to him, including his resurrection after three days, and how we would see him, and about his coming again with much glory when he will come to judge the living and the dead and reward each according to his works. But while he was teaching the people in the Temple, he was censuring the high priests, along with their reckless deeds and unlawful acts.[125] Since they could not bear [Vin 254] this, they gave thirty pieces of silver to my fellow disciple Judas and he delivered him to them in the night. And having seized him, they delivered him to Pilate, the governor of Judaea. When he had examined him and understood that they had delivered him up to him out of envy, [D 64] he wished to release him. But the high priests cried out, "You are not a friend of Caesar if you release him; his blood [will be] on us and on our children."[126] So Pilate delivered him up in accordance with their will and

---

121 Cf. 4 Kgs 4: 32–37 (LXX); 2 Kgs 4: 32–37.
122 The ruler of the synagogue is named as Jairus in two of the synoptic Gospels; see Mt 9: 18–19, 23–26; Mk 5: 22–24, 35–43; Lk 8: 40–42, 49–56.
123 Cf. Jn 1: 29–34.
124 Cf. Jn 1: 34. This version (B) of the *LAA* omits the section 26 that appears in version A. I have therefore introduced a new section in order to bridge the numerical gap. On the missing paragraph, see below, n. 133.
125 Mt 21: 23–22: 22; Mk 11: 27–12: 34; Lk 20: 1–26.
126 Cf. Jn 19: 12. Epiphanios substitutes the phrase 'his blood [will be] on us and on our children' for John's words, 'Everyone who claims to be a king sets himself against the emperor' (πᾶς ὁ βασιλέα ἑαυτὸν ποιῶν ἀντιλέγει τῷ Καίσαρι).

LIFE AND ACTS OF ST ANDREW THE APOSTLE   133

crucified him, according to [Christ's] own will. [M 240] And having placed him in a new tomb, they sealed it and placed guards beside it. For he said, "I shall rise on the third day."[127] In the night, at the dawn of the third day, he arose, having left his graveclothes as witnesses. An angel rolled away the rock of the tomb and, having benumbed the guards with sleep, sat on top of it. But women from our group went out very quickly to the tomb with myrrh.[128] And the angel said to them, "The Lord has risen. Go and tell the disciples." And while they were on their way to us, Jesus himself met them and said, "Rejoice! Tell the disciples that they should go out into Galilee and they will see me there, as I told them before."[129] And we often beheld him when he had arisen from the dead, and we ate and drank with him for forty days.[130] And he urged us in his name to proclaim repentance and remission of sins to all the nations, baptising in the name of the Father and of the Son and of the Holy Spirit.[131] And he was raised up at the third hour of the day while we were watching; and he ascended into heaven and sat at the right hand of his Father.[132] We expect him at the end of the [present] age and now we are raising the dead in his name, banishing demons, and healing every illness.' When Andrew had said these things, the whole people cried out, 'A holy spirit is in your mouth! Truly you are an apostle of the holy and true God! Make haste that we may be saved.' And he, having prayed in his usual way and placed his hands on them, dismissed them.[133]

27. [Vin 255] Andrew was [D 65] acting and teaching in this way for two whole years, also admonishing and healing both places and people. He destroyed idols and converted the synagogue into a church, dedicating it as a sanctuary of the Theotokos.[134] He set up an altar, baptised people,

---

127 Cf. Mt 17: 23; Mk 9: 31.
128 The three synoptic Gospels describe the arrival of the myrrh-bearing women at the tomb; however, Epiphanios follows the account in Matthew 28: 1–10 most closely here.
129 This version of the resurrection story is closest to that which appears in Mt 28: 1–7.
130 On the post-resurrection appearances of Christ, see Mk 16: 9–20; Lk 24: 13–49; Jn 20: 19–21: 23.
131 Mt 28: 19.
132 Lk 24: 51; Acts 1: 9–11. Biblical references to Christ's position at the right hand of the Father in heaven occur in numerous passages of the Old and New Testaments, including Ps 109 (110): 1; Mt 22: 44; Mk 16: 19; Lk 22: 69; Acts 2: 33; Romans 8: 34.
133 Version A of Epiphanios's *Life* adds a paragraph (26) here; see Appendix B (b). Vinogradov includes this passage in his translation of the text; see Vinogradov 2005, 140.
134 Epiphanios is probably referring here to the church of the Dormition in Nicaea, which was founded as part of the monastery of Hyakinthos. This was a rectangular structure with

and ordained presbyters, deacons, and a bishop, Drakontios (although others say that this was another [man]). Drakontios was then martyred on the twelfth day of the month of May.[135] On this account, the clerics of the Great Church told me not only of these events, but also of Andrew's many miracles.[136]

28. After departing from Nicaea, Andrew went to Nikomedia,[137] and the brothers came out to meet him.[138] And when a certain Kallistos was struck by a demon and had died, Andrew raised him up by means of a prayer and denounced the wiles of the demons' ruler. After supporting them for a few days, he sailed along the coast to Chalcedon.[139] Having crossed into the same city of Bithynia, he established Tychikos as bishop.[140] And after departing again and sailing in the Pontic Sea, he came to Herakleia.[141] And

---

a cruciform nave, surmounted by a dome, set on massive pillars. It was founded between the late sixth and early eighth century (not, as Epiphanios suggests, during the lifetime of the apostle Andrew); the church was rebuilt and redecorated after an earthquake in 1065 but was finally destroyed by fire in 1922; see Janin 1925; Schmit 1927; Janin 1975, 121–24; Foss with Tulchin 1996, 97–101; Peschlow 2017; Lichtenberger, Agtürk, Winter, and Zimmerman 2020. On the important mosaic images in the apse of the church of the Dormition, see Barber 2002, 63–69, Figs. 20–23; James 2017, 317, Fig. 103.

135 St Drakontios is not listed in *BHG* or in *SynaxCP* (for 12 May). He was believed to be the first bishop of Nicaea and was later martyred. See Foss with Tulchin 1996, 23. It is possible that the name Drakontios reflects Andrew's killing of the dragon near Nicaea; see Vinogradov 2005, 141, n. 387.

136 Epiphanios indicates here that he received information about the apostle Andrew from oral sources, including the clerics of the main church (St Sophia) in Nicaea; see Vinogradov 2005, 43.

137 On Nikomedia, see above, n. 35.

138 It is not clear to which 'brothers' Epiphanios refers here; it is possible that he means that Nikomedia was largely inhabited by Christians in this period. Thus the inhabitants were 'brothers' of each other and of Christ.

139 Chalcedon was located across the Bosphoros from Constantinople and hosted the fourth Ecumenical Council in 451. After this, Chalcedon became a metropolitan see, having been detached from the ecclesiastical province of Bithynia (under Nikomedia). The city was a popular residence for imperial dignitaries from the fourth century onward; *ODB*, vol. 1, 403–4; Janin 1975, 31–60.

140 Tychikos is mentioned in the Acts of the apostles and the Epistles of Paul; see Acts 20: 4; Eph 6: 21; Col 4: 7; 2 Tim 4: 12; Titus 3: 12. Epiphanios the Monk takes his information about Tychikos becoming bishop of Chalcedon from (ps-) Epiphanios of Salamis, *Index apostolorum* 57, ed. Schermann 1907, 125.

141 Epiphanios refers again to the city of Herakleia that was located on the southern coast of the Black Sea; see above, n. 41.

having taught some people there, he went up to Kromna, which is now called Amastris,[142] and after a few days to Sinope.

29. On entering the city, he found a few disciples and stayed with them. But the city was otherwise full only of Jews. On hearing that Andrew was present, the man who had opened the prison and led out the prisoners, they assembled together, rose up, and were intending to set his house on fire. And seizing Andrew, they beat him with stones, dragged him along, and were biting his flesh like dogs. One of them bit and cut off the finger of one of his hands. And to this day, they are called 'finger-eaters' on account of this.[143] When they had dragged Andrew through the whole city, beating, stoning, and biting him, they then threw him down, half dead, outside [M 241] the city. And at once the Lord appeared to him, saying, 'Arise, my disciple, advance towards [D 66] them, and do not be afraid of them. For I am with you.' And he restored his finger to health. Andrew then got up and entered the city. [Vin 256] And, on seeing his patient endurance and gentleness and how he called on them, they were stung[144] and began to listen to him. And they were amazed when they heard his teachings.[145] He interpreted the scriptures and they received the word of Christ until, having gathered together multitudes in the early morning, they brought the sick whom Andrew healed by calling on Christ. A man was found murdered in the middle of the city, and, while the murderer was being hunted, his wife was wailing, and the people were surging about. Andrew, on being called, approached, prayed, and by calling on Christ, raised the dead man. And many believed in the Lord. And so the word of the Lord was exalted and

---

142 Amastris (modern Amasra) was a city on the coast of the Black Sea in Anatolia. It became an important centre of trade and communications in the course of the ninth century, also functioning as a military base. Amastris was a suffragan bishopric of Gangra and was made a metropolis before 940; see *ODB*, vol. 1, 74–75; Ruggieri and Zäh 2016, 57. On 'Kromna' as the ancient name for Amastris, see Mango 2002, 261.

143 Cf. Acts 14: 19–20. This episode may also reflect the preoccupation with cannibalism (associated with the cities of Myrmidonia or Sinope) in early texts on the apostle Andrew; see Introduction, 47–48; above, n. 88. It is worth noting that Dressel's text substitutes ἀνθρωποφάγοι ('man-eaters') for δακτυλοφάγοι ('finger-eaters') here. In private correspondence, Vinogradov suggested 'date-eaters' as a possible meaning for the word.

144 The verb κατανύσσω literally means 'to goad' or 'to spur on'; in the Christian context, it came to mean experiencing a change of heart or compunction. See Lampe, 713.

145 Version A of Epiphanios's *Life* adds a short passage here in which Andrew delivers another sermon to the people; see Appendix B (d); Vinogradov 2005, 222. 9. Vinogradov includes this passage in his translation of the text; see ibid., 143.

spread further. [Andrew] ordained presbyters and deacons from among them, after handing down to them the whole tradition and ecclesiastical order.

30. And so he departed for Zalichos.[146] And, on hearing this, the people of Amisos advanced joyfully to meet him and, praising him, led him into the hostel.[147] Having sent on ahead from Amisos, he departed for Trebizond.[148] The people there were without understanding, except that some had accepted the word. And he went to Neokaisareia.[149] And as he was proclaiming the word to them, a few accepted it.

31. From there he went up to the great Parthian city of Samosata.[150] There were many Greeks and philosophers in it who opposed Andrew. But he said to them, 'Observe for yourselves the disorder of your gods, since they fight with each other. Things that fight with each other are corruptible. But the one God who is good confers good things. Observe then who made and unified the elements [D 67] and established the earthly creation out of them. Observe the course of the luminaries and stars and consider who has set up the unending and equal course for them since they are lifeless and do not move of their own accord – and also because this is a rule of many that is [intrinsically] disordered and irregular. Take up the good way through the law of Moses since it offers peace to those who conform to it. Take up the prophets since [Vin 257] they teach truth and peaceful and eternal life. Consider that the dead are raised in the name of Christ and that demons and suffering are put to flight.' After spending many days in their midst and teaching many people, he took leave of them and departed for Jerusalem.

32. And after Pentecost, Andrew, Simon the Canaanite, Matthias, and

---

146 Zalichos, Zalekon, or Leontopolis was a suffragan bishopric of Amaseia and was thus also located in the Pontos. Epiphanios implies that it was very close to the coastal city of Amisos here. See Bryer and Winfield 1985, vol. 1, 89–90.

147 On the city of Amisos, see above, n. 46. According to Epiphanios, Andrew had visited Amisos earlier on his travels and had converted both Jews and 'Greeks' to Christianity.

148 On Trebizond, see above, n. 68.

149 Neokaisareia was situated in the Lykos Valley on one of the main northern routes across Anatolia. It became the civil and ecclesiastical metropolis of Pontos Polemoniakos. See *ODB*, vol. 2, 1453–54; Bryer and Winfield 1985, vol. 1, 107–10; Hild and Restle 1981, *TIB* 2, 100, 110, 120.

150 Dressel's edition substitutes παραθαλασσίας for Παρθίας. This led Mango to note that Samosata is not near the sea; see Mango 2002, 256. On Samosata, see also Bryer 1980, II, 83–84.

LIFE AND ACTS OF ST ANDREW THE APOSTLE 137

Thaddaeus, with the rest of the disciples, went down into Edessa. And Thaddaeus remained there near Abgar.[151] But the rest, having passed through the cities teaching and working miracles, went down into Iberia as far as [the river] Phasis;[152] after some days [they entered] Sousania.[153] The men of that race were then ruled by their wives. Their feminine nature was acquiescent and they swiftly obeyed [them].[154] Matthias remained in those villages with his disciples, teaching [M 244] and performing many miracles. But Simon and Andrew departed for Alania and to the city of Phousta. And having worked many miracles and taught many people, they departed for Abasgia.[155] And after entering the great Sebastopolis,[156] they taught the word of God and many accepted it. Andrew then left Simon there and went with his disciples to Zekchia.[157] The Zekchians were harsh people and barbarians; half of them remain unbelievers even until now. They were about to murder Andrew except that they observed his poverty, gentleness, and asceticism. And then, after leaving them, he went to the Sougdaians [D 68] who lived further up.[158] The people were obedient and civilised and they accepted the word with joy.

---

151 Epiphanios refers here to the Syrian king Abgar who lived in the city of Edessa at the time of Christ. On the legend of Abgar, see Eusebios of Caesarea, *Ecclesiastical History* I. 13, ed. Schwartz, Mommsen, and Winkelmann 1999, 82–86, in which the author transcribes a letter describing how Thaddaeus, one of the 'seventy' followers of Christ, healed the king of his ailment (gout).

152 Vinogradov suggests that the masculine article τὸν here indicates the river Phasis. However, there was also a city by the same name on the eastern coast of the Black Sea (modern Poti, Georgia, on the river Rioni). It was founded in the seventh or sixth century BCE as a colony of the Milesian Greeks at the mouth of the eponymous river in Colchis. See *ODB*, vol. 3, 1647; Bryer and Winfield 1985, vol. 1, 326.

153 It is possible that Epiphanios (or a scribe) substituted 'Sousania' for 'Sousarmia' here. On the latter, which was probably a port at the mouth of the Hyssos river, see Bryer and Winfield 1985, vol. 1, 324–25. However, a more likely explanation is that Epiphanios meant a mountainous region in what is now north-western Georgia called Σουάνια (today Svaneti). I am grateful to Dr Vinogradov for this suggestion.

154 This sentence is interesting from the point of view of gender. Epiphanios understands 'male' or 'female' gender as a set of attitudes or behaviours rather than as a biological state; cf. Neville 2019, 23–31. Epiphanios is also referring here to the ancient concept of γυναικοκρατέομαι ('to be ruled by women'); see LS 363 for references.

155 Abasgia was a region in the Caucasus (modern Georgia); see Bryer and Winfield 1985, vol. 1, 346–47.

156 On the port city of Sebastopolis, see above, n. 32.

157 Also known as Zichia; see Bryer and Winfield 1985, vol. 1, 325.

158 The meaning of τοὺς ἄνω is enigmatic. Epiphanios may mean either that this tribe lived

33. And [from there] he went to Bosporos, a city on the other side of the Pontos, which we also reached.[159] And those who were there immediately obeyed [him], having seen the miracles which he was performing and [heard] the God-inspired word, as they have told us. They showed us a coffer that was buried in the foundations of the very large temple of the holy apostles, which has an inscription of the apostle Simon, and it contains [Vin 258] relics. And they gave some of them to us. There is another tomb for Nikopsis of Zekchia, which has an inscription of Simon the Canaanite, and it also contains relics.

34. However, Andrew departed from Bosporos into the city of Theudesia,[160] which is both populous[161] and philosophical, and which was home of the king Sauromates.[162] But few of these people were believers. On departing from them, he went on to the city of Cherson, as [the people of Cherson] have told us.[163] Theudesia today contains no trace of a human being in it. Meanwhile, the people of Cherson, who belonged to a nation that is

---

on higher ground or that it was located further inland from Zekchia. On the mention of these peoples in (ps-) Epiphanios's *Index apostolorum*, see above, n. 31. Sougdaia (Sudak), in the Crimea, is also mentioned in relation to a commercial voyage in 1274; see Bryer and Winfield 1985, vol. 1, 112. It appears in many texts from the eighth century onwards.

159 The city of Bosporos was located on the peninsula of Crimea on the northern side of the Black Sea; see also n. 34 above. It submitted to Byzantine rule ca. 530 when Justinian I used it as a base for resisting the Huns. The region became a province of the Khazar empire between the seventh and tenth centuries, after which it was ruled by the Rus', followed by the Mongols, the Genoese, and finally the Ottoman empire; see *ODB*, vol. 1, 313; Bryer and Winfield 1985, vol. 1, 347–49. On Andrew's mission here, which was carried out with the help of Simon the Canaanite, see also Dvornik 1958, 209–10.

160 The city of Theodosia (which Epiphanios calls 'Theodesia') is located until the present day on the south-eastern side of the Crimean peninsula; see Millar, Cotton, and Rogers 2004, 239.

161 Literally 'full of men' (πολύανδρον).

162 Tiberius Julius Sauromates II was a prince and Roman client king of the Bosporan kingdom (174–210 CE). He was named in honour of Sauromates I, a paternal ancestor and previous Bosporan king. For background on the Bosporan kingdom, see Millar, Cotton, and Rogers 2004, 239–45.

163 Cherson was a Greek colony that was located within the precincts of modern Sebastopol on the Crimean peninsula. Christianity was established there by the beginning of the fourth century, not in the first, as Epiphanios suggests here. The Byzantines used Cherson as a place of exile for important figures, including Pope Martin I and Justinian II in the late seventh century; see *ODB*, vol. 1, 418–19. It is interesting to note that Epiphanios, presumably with his companion, reached this distant region on his travels around the Black Sea during a period when it was subject to the Khazars.

LIFE AND ACTS OF ST ANDREW THE APOSTLE   139

unstable and without strength in their faith to the present day, false and carried about by every [heretical] wind.[164] However, Andrew spent a fair number of days with them before returning to Bosporos; there he found a Chersonese ship and crossed to Sinope. And the Chersonese compiled an alphabetic [text] for Andrew in which they called the people of Sinope 'cannibals'.[165]

35. Andrew crossed to Sinope where he strengthened them for a few days,[166] appointed the bishop Philologos on their behalf, and thus strengthened the churches; after this he went down to Byzantion.[167] At that time Argyropolis was flourishing and confident.[168] He appointed Stachys of Argyropolis as their bishop, and consecrated a sanctuary of the holy Theotokos on the acropolis of Byzantion, which remains there to the present day.[169] After departing from there, he went down into Herakleia, in Thrace.[170] And

164 This negative assessment of the Chersonese is not uncommon among Byzantine writers; see Vinogradov 2005, 146, n. 426.
165 Vinogradov believes that this text (τὸ ἀλφαβητάριν) was a hymn with an alphabetical acrostic (perhaps a kontakion or a kanon); see Vinogradov 2005, 147, n. 427.
166 The verb στηρίζω (to 'confirm' or 'strengthen') recalls Acts 15: 32.
167 Epiphanios reveals here his knowledge of the history of Constantinople, which was called 'Byzantion' before it became the capital city of the eastern Roman empire and was renamed by Constantine I in 324 CE. As the hagiographer suggests, the city would still have been known by its original name when Andrew was carrying out his mission during the second half of the first century.
168 Argyropolis ('Silver City') was a suburb of Constantinople, situated opposite Chrysopolis ('Golden City'). According to the early fifth-century historian Socrates, it was named by the patriarch Attikos (406–25) because he liked its beautiful situation; Socrates, *Historia Ecclesiastica* VII. 25. 11–12, ed. Hansen 1995, 373; PG 67, 796B–C; cf. Dvornik 1958, 219. On Argyropolis, see also Külzer 2008, *TIB* 12, 263–64.
169 Epiphanios shows the influence of (ps-) Epiphanios of Salamis' *Index apostolorum*, which also mentions Andrew's ordination of Stachys to the bishopric of Byzantion in Argyropolis; see *Prophetarum vitae fabulosae*, ed. Schermann 1907. For discussion of this text, along with analysis of its testimony concerning the legend that St Andrew founded the bishopric of Constantinople, see Dvornik 1958, 175–78, 225–26. The story may be based on a figure named Stachys who is greeted by the apostle Paul in Rom 16: 9 along with numerous other followers of Christ. As for the church of the Virgin Mary which Epiphanios mentions here, this may have been located in the quarter of Armasios near the acropolis (named after the Praetorian Prefect of the East in 469–70); see Mango 2002, 263. Although legend associated the construction of this church with the apostle Andrew, it was actually built in the late tenth or early eleventh century; see Vinogradov 2005, 147, n. 431.
170 This Herakleia was located on the north shore of the Sea of Marmara at the junction of the Via Egnatia and the main route to Naissus (modern Niš in Serbia). The sixth-century historian Procopius states that Constantinople replaced Herakleia as the most important city

having passed some days there, he departed. As he was travelling around the cities of Macedonia, teaching, summoning, healing, founding churches, [D 69] purifying pagan places of sacrifice, and anointing priests, he went as far as Patras in the Peloponnese, at the time when [it was ruled] by the proconsul[171] Aigeates of Achaia.[172]

36. Andrew, along with his disciples, entered [the city], and a man named Sosios, whom Andrew had cured of a mortal illness, received them. As he was passing through the city, he saw a man who had been abandoned and thrown onto a dungheap. And Andrew approached him, gave him his hand, and raised him up by calling on Christ. When this had been made widely known, Maximilla, [Vin 259] the wife of the proconsul Aigeates, sent her faithful [servant] [M 215] Ephidama since she was ready to see, speak with, and listen to Andrew. Ephidama arrived and met with Sosios, who had become a disciple of Andrew and with whom she was acquainted.[173] He instructed her in the word of God and about his own healing, and then led her to Andrew. And falling at his feet, she listened to his words. And departing, she reported back to her mistress.

---

in the province of Europa, following Constantine's choice of the former as his capital city; see Prokopios, *Buildings* IV.9.14, trans. Dewing 1940, 294–97; *ODB*, vol. 2, 915; Külzer 2008, *TIB* 12, 398–408. Another city by the same name was located further to the west on the northern coast of the Sea of Marmara; see Külzer 2008, *TIB* 12, 408. It is difficult to determine which of the two cities Epiphanios indicates here since he provides no description or geographical details in this passage.

171 The title ἀνθύπατος is attested in various early Christian texts, including the *Martyrdom of St Polycarp* 4; Palladios, *Lausiac History* 62, and others; see Lampe, 144.

172 Patrai or Patras is situated on the north-western coast of the Peloponnesian peninsula, at the mouth of the Gulf of Corinth. This is the city where the apostle Andrew was believed to have been martyred, according to the earliest *Acts* of the saint. Patras was important not only as a result of St Andrew's cult, but also because of its position as a commercial port on trade routes between the Latin West and Byzantium. The bishop of Patras, originally suffragan of Corinth, was elevated to the rank of metropolitan from ca. 805. It was also at about this time (when Epiphanios was active as a hagiographer) that the city was saved from an attack by Arab and Slavic forces, purportedly with the help of St Andrew. Epiphanios's narrative closely follows that of the third-century *AA* from this point onward; see Introduction, 62–68; *AA*, ed. Prieur, 18–20; *Actes*, trans. Prieur 1995, 24–25.

173 The verb ξενίζω is associated with ξένος ('guest'); according to LS, 1188, it may mean 'to entertain' or sometimes (in the passive) 'to be astonished'. I have interpreted the meaning somewhat loosely here in order to make sense of its place within the narrative. It is possible that (according to Epiphanios) Ephidama is only allowed to meet Sosios, as opposed to St Andrew himself, because she is merely a servant.

37. After some days, Maximilla, the wife of the proconsul, fell ill. And since the doctors despaired and gave up hope, she sent Ephidama out and summoned Andrew. He came back with her along with his disciples. And when he entered the house, he found the proconsul holding a knife and waiting for the death of his wife because he wished to kill himself [and thus] to die along with her. But Andrew said to him with a gentle voice, 'Return the knife to its place, my child, and call on the Lord God of heaven and earth, having come to believe in him, and be saved.' But [Aigeates] did not answer him. Then Andrew rebuked the fever, saying, 'Fever, depart from her.' And he set his hands on her and [D 70] she at once began to sweat and sought to eat and forthwith got up [out of bed]. And many who saw this became believers [in God]. But the proconsul treated Andrew as if he were a doctor. For he was a Greek and he did not wish to hear the word of God. He gave him a thousand pieces of gold, saying, 'Take your pay.' But Andrew rejected it, saying, 'We have received freely and we give freely.[174] Offer yourself instead to God, if you are capable of this.'

38. On departing from there, they were supporting Andrew, for he was an old man. And he saw someone lying down on the colonnade and begging; he had lived for many years as a paralytic. And Andrew said to him, 'Jesus Christ heals you.'[175] And he gave him his hand. The man was at once healed and ran through the middle of the city, gesturing to himself and glorifying God. And having advanced from there, [Andrew] saw a man who, along with his wife and [Vin 260] child, was blind. And he touched their eyes and at once they saw again and followed him, glorifying and thanking God.[176] The crowd, on seeing this, were astounded and, marvelling, many came to believe. And they called on him to go to the harbour, since a well-born man from one of the ancient families had caught leprosy and, not being able to support his stench, they had placed him on the dunghill. And no one was able to approach him except when they brought food to him, holding their noses and quickly withdrawing. When Andrew heard about these matters,

---

174 Andrew uses the 'royal we' here; however, he is referring to himself when he makes this remark.
175 This miracle is reminiscent of Christ's healing of the paralytic man in the synoptic Gospels, Mt 9: 1–8, Mk 2: 1–12, and Lk 5: 17–26.
176 The healing of the blind man recalls miracles worked by Christ according to Mk 8: 22–26 and Jn 9: 1–7. However, whereas Christ used saliva (either applied directly to the man's eyes or mixed first with earth), Andrew simply touches the family's eyes and their sight is restored.

he was deeply moved and went out to [the man]. And many others from among the people went with him. Andrew approached him and said, 'Jesus Christ heals you. Arise.' And at once he arose in a healthy state.[177] Having taken hold of him, [Andrew] washed him in the sea and his flesh became like that of a small child, and he was cleansed. And when he was healed, he did not take clothes to put on, but ran naked through the middle of the city gesturing to himself. Andrew then said [D 71] to him, 'Put on your garment and wash away your sins, having come to believe in Christ and been baptised.' And he, giving thanks, followed him.

39. [M 248] Then, when his miracles were proclaimed and those who had been healed were shouting [about it] throughout Patras of Achaia and in the whole of that land, they brought him people who had been possessed by demons and who were ill. And, bearing witness to the word of grace and teaching them, he laid hands on them and healed them all by calling on Christ. And there was great joy in that city. They trampled on the temples of idols, broke up the gold and silver statues, and burned the books. And they offered much property to Andrew, but he gave this, through his disciples, to the orphans and widows, as well as for the foundation of churches. And nothing was used from these sources unless it was necessary. He bestowed the Old Testament and the Gospel on them.[178] And he ordained presbyters and deacons for them, and ordered that there should be a great church. And he commanded that the Old and New Testaments should be written on the walls,[179] as local people, who have [this] tradition, are witnessing until today.

40. [Vin 261] The proconsul Aigeates travelled to Rome to see the Caesar Nero at the time when his wife had been healed. [Aigeates] had a brother

---

177 Christ also healed lepers according to Mt 8: 2–4, Mk 1: 40–45, and Lk 5: 12–16.

178 Παρεδίδου δὲ αὐτοῖς τὴν παλαιὰν διαθήκην καὶ τὸ εὐαγγέλιον: it is interesting that Epiphanios describes the 'Old Testament' or 'Ancient Covenant' as if it were one unit. The various books of the Old Testament, according to the Septuagint version, were usually divided into separate volumes, such as the Pentateuch, the Octateuch, the Prophets, the Psalter, and others during the Byzantine period; see Magdalino and Nelson 2010, 1. 'The Gospel' refers here to the four Gospels attributed to Matthew, Mark, Luke, and John. For recent study of their role in the Byzantine Church and culture, see Krueger and Nelson 2016.

179 Using the verb γράψαι ('to write'), Epiphanios means that narrative scenes from the Old and New Testaments were painted on the walls of the church. Two later (nineteenth- and twentieth-century) churches remain shrines to St Andrew in Patras. The larger and more modern cathedral possesses relics of the saint, including a finger, part of the apostle's skull, and small portions of the cross on which he was martyred. For recent discussion of the saint and his cult, see Saranti and Triantaphylopoulos 2013.

LIFE AND ACTS OF ST ANDREW THE APOSTLE 143

by the name of Stratokles who was in Athens for the sake of his education. While the proconsul was in Rome, Stratokles returned from Athens to Patras. He had a very beloved slave by the name of Alkmanas. But after being stricken by a demon, Alkmanas rolled about, foaming at the mouth. When Stratokles saw this, he was sorrowful unto death[180] and was at a loss for what to do. But Maximilla, his sister-in-law,[181] reported to him the news about Andrew and how she had been cured of her life-threatening fever. After hearing this [D 72], he summoned Andrew. Andrew arrived and rebuked the impure spirit, saying, 'In the name of Jesus Christ, come out of the man and do not enter him again.' And at once the spirit came out and the boy was healed from that hour. Then Stratokles believed [in God], along with his whole household, and he was baptised along with Maximilla, his sister-in-law, Ephidama, and a whole crowd [of others]. And they were rejoicing on account of everything with Andrew and his brothers. But Andrew summoned and admonished many people, by night and by day, to remain in the faith, to keep the law and the Gospel, to attend to the soul, to give no thought to the body, to be pure, to have self-control, to remain virginal, to be prudent, to be wronged but not to do wrong, and to avoid talking nonsense and lying but to pray without ceasing. And Maximilla did not deviate from these [practices].

41. While these events were taking place, Aigeates returned from the Caesar in Rome and immediately approached his wife, Maximilla. But she did not receive him since she had adopted the way of Christ;[182] she pretended instead to be ill. As the days passed and she was unwilling to sleep with him, he did not know what to do. And one of the household slaves[183] told him about Andrew, [saying,] 'Your brother and your wife, along with your whole [M 249] household, have approached Andrew's God and promised

---

180 Cf. Mt 26: 38.
181 The noun ἡ νύμφη means, according to Gen 11: 31 and Mt 10: 35, a 'daughter-in-law'. However, it may refer to any female relation by marriage in post-Classical Greek.
182 It is noteworthy that Maximilla (and also, by implication, St Andrew) interprets the Christian way of life as celibate. This is probably an aspect of the original *AA* that appealed to Epiphanios because of his monastic background. Earlier Christian writers, however, including Eusebios of Caesarea and Epiphanios of Salamis, condemned the text for its Encratite and other heretical tendencies; see *Actes*, trans. Prieur 1995, 18–23. For further discussion, see Introduction, 46–47, 67–68.
183 Vinogradov's edition has τις τῶν οἰκοπαίδων whereas Dressel substitutes τις τῶν οἰκογενῶν ('one of those born in the household') here.

to live in chastity.'[184] Then the proconsul said to Maximilla, his wife, 'Obey me and sleep with me, and you will be mistress of everything in my house; however, if you do not, [Vin 262] I shall deliver the man who deceived you to the cross.' When she did not give her consent to him, he placed Andrew in prison. But Maximilla went out to him and was taught by him to endure the afflictions, for in them the demonstration of firm faith is made manifest. The proconsul, on learning that the brothers were coming to [help Andrew], was upset and said to Maximilla, 'If that old man changes your mind about sleeping with me, I shall release him. But if not, I shall quickly destroy both of you.' Maximilla, on entering the prison, reported every one of her husband's words to Andrew. But Andrew fortified her even more in the fear of God and in the care of the flesh, that is, not to be drawn into desire, saying to her, 'Endure for a short time in order that you may be eternally joyful. As for me, [that] joy is to gain for myself the death of my Lord and to be with him.' And she returned and reported these things to her husband, saying, 'I am more inclined to die than to surrender my chastity to you.'

42. When the proconsul heard these words, he was enraged, and after going out to the prison, he closed it securely, sealing the locks and bolts with his own ring and placing guards there as well. But the brothers, along with Stratokles and Maximilla, came to [the apostle] at the dead of night.[185] When they knocked, Andrew understood and made a sign of the cross[186] from within and at once all of the doors opened of their own accord and the guards cowered with fear. Andrew said, 'Do not be afraid, for the proconsul will not know.' The brothers accompanied him and kindled many lamps. And he preached about many things to them and, since they had brought bread, gave them a share in the undefiled mysteries of Christ. And he ordained Stratokles a bishop and gave him the rule of the liturgy and of the psalmody for Orthros and Vespers,[187] [Vin 263] of holy baptisms,

---

184 Literally, 'to be pure' (ἁγνεύειν); for this meaning, see Lampe, 21.
185 Vinogradov's edition omits this sentence, which appears in Dressel's version of the text. I have included it since it is necessary for the sense of the passage – as does Vinogradov in his translation; see Vinogradov 2005, 151.
186 Epiphanios uses the verb σφραγίζω here, which means, as elsewhere in the text, 'to make the sign of the cross'; see above, nn. 86 and 90.
187 On the liturgical rites of Orthros (morning service or 'Matins') and Vespers; see Taft 1986, 27–83; Getcha 2012, 70–82, 86–92, 100–16.

LIFE AND ACTS OF ST ANDREW THE APOSTLE   145

and the whole order of services.[188] And, having embraced them all, he sent them away. And [D 74] after he had sealed everything again [with the sign of the cross], all the doors were closed along with the seals.

43. The proconsul spared his wife on account of her family since he feared them; however, he handed Andrew over to the soldiers to be crucified. And he commanded that he should be bound with ropes, not with nails, so as to stretch out the punishment to a greater extent in order that, after growing quite weary, [Andrew] would change Maximilla's mind about sleeping with [her husband].[189] But as he was hanging on the cross, he summoned everyone and taught them not to fear death, but to rejoice since those who have finished the contest well shall enter their repose. And the entire people stood watching. And, when a night and a day had passed, Stratokles, the brother of the proconsul, wished to release [Andrew] from the cross. But the blessed man did not consent to this. And when the third day arrived, while Andrew was still speaking and teaching the people, all the people ran together to the proconsul, crying, 'What sin did this man commit that he must die so unjustly by a cruel death? He has not sinned against Caesar or his laws.'[190] The proconsul, who was frightened by the tumultuous gathering of the people, then came to release him. But the blessed man, on seeing [him], said, 'Turn back and be saved. I do not take your wickedness into account and nor does my God. For you are sending me forward into good things. But if you will not repent and will not believe in him, you will die by a wicked death.' And after embracing all the brethren and praying, he expired[191] as he hung on the cross. And Maximilla, as soon as he stopped breathing and while everyone was weeping, approached with Stratokles, untied him, and, along with the rest of the brethren, buried him with honour.

44. But Aigeates, when he missed [the presence of] Maximilla in the night,

---

188 Ἀκολουθία refers to the whole set of services, including the Divine Liturgy, that would later be contained in Byzantine service books, including the *Euchologion*. On the service books, see Velkovska 1997; Getcha 2012, 15–66.

189 It is at this point that Dressel's edition of Epiphanios's *LAA* (following the text in V3) borrows the conclusion of the anonymous *Narratio* (probably 8th century); see Introduction, 72–73. All other manuscripts that contain versions A or B of the *LAA* provide the shorter ending that follows (with some variations).

190 I have paraphrased this sentence slightly since it is difficult to render the Greek syntax literally into English.

191 The Evangelist Luke uses the same word, ἐξέπνευσεν, to describe Jesus's death on the cross; cf. Lk 23: 46.

threw himself off a high place and thus died a cruel death without having his inheritance.[192] And [Vin 264] his brother Stratokles distributed his wealth[193] to the needy. He took nothing from these [goods], since [they belonged to] a most impious and idolatrous man, and he said, 'It is better for me to cleave to God.'[194] Many healings took place when the blessed apostle Andrew expired and they continue to happen at his tomb to the present day. The blessed apostle of Christ, Andrew, died on the thirtieth day of the month of November. Meanwhile, Maximilla and Ephidama did not leave his tomb throughout their lives. And, together with the male brethren and the bishop, they distributed their substance, which was great, to the poor and for the maintenance of the see. After founding monasteries both for men and for women, they endured for a sufficient [number of] years, giving thanks and glorifying the Father and the Son and the Holy Spirit, now and forever and to the ages of ages. Amen.

---

192 The noun κληρονόμος means a Christian reward in this context – not a material or monetary inheritance.
193 Literally 'substance'.
194 Cf. Ps 72 (73): 28 (LXX).

APPENDIX A:
VARIANT READINGS IN THE *LVM*

Appendix A

a) D 25. 2–12:
13) After a short time the Magi from the temperate east came out of Persia, having seen the star from the left-hand side of Jerusalem – for Persia lies beside Judaea in this way. But the star was not from among the rest of the stars or even from the height to which the other stars are fixed; rather, it appeared to be close to the earth and unusual compared with those that manifest themselves normally or under some particular circumstance – nor had it ever appeared before, as both the great Basil and John Chrysostom say.

M 201B:
...and on the second day, the Magi from the temperate east came from the Persian city of Babylon, having seen the star from the left-hand side of Jerusalem – for Persia lies beside Judaea in this way. And the star was not from among the rest of the stars but was near the ground. And it had never appeared before, as John Chrysostom says.

b) D 26. 6–29:
14) But Herod, having been tricked by the Magi, sent out a decree and then killed all the children in Bethlehem who were two years of age or less on the basis of what he learned from the Magi. And his whole household and the nearest and dearest of his family were immediately overthrown since he slaughtered his wife, from whom he had begotten two sons, Alexander and Aristoboulos, along with the two sons themselves, and another, Antipater, whom he had begotten from another woman. And Herod himself succumbed to a divinely sent illness, enduring a putrefaction around both his genitals and his intestines; teeming with worms, he expired, as Josephus testifies in his history about him.
15) The soldiers killed Zacharias when he was performing his duties between the nave and the altar. The reason for his murder was double: for some say that he was destroyed because of the disappearance of his son, who was being sought by Herod; but others say that it was on account of the holy Virgin and Theotokos, since Zacharias led her into [the part of the Temple] which virgins were allowed to enter – and it was in the same place that he was killed by the scribes, as one who had clearly transgressed the law since he was telling everyone of the matters relating to her, that is, how she had remained a virgin and was just as she had been before giving birth.

M 201C–D:
But Herod had his own battle in those days with Salome, the daughter of the high priest Hyrkanos, who was also his wife, as well as with her sons, Alexander and Aristoboulos. After murdering his wife, he went to the Caesar in Rome. On taking authority from him, [Herod] returned and also strangled his sons in the river since he had meanwhile forgetfully neglected what the Magi had said. When he took time to remember, wrath washed over him and, two years after the Magi [had come], Herod carried out the slaughter of the infants.

And the soldiers killed Zacharias while he was performing his duties within the sanctuary.

APPENDIX A

c) D 29. 1–24:
18) His age, or rather, the growth of his body had reached six full feet; he had tawny hair which was not completely bushy, but rather had a close-curling tendency; his eyebrows were dark and not entirely curved; his eyes were tawny and sparkling with joy – just as the story of his forefather David relates, when it says, 'And he was ruddy with beauty of eyes.' And so [Christ] also had well-shaped eyes, a prominent nose, a tawny beard, and long hair. For never did a razor encounter his head, nor did a human hand – apart from that of his mother when he was nursing [as a baby]. He inclined his neck slightly so that he might not entirely achieve the straight and erect stature of his body. His complexion was fair; he did not have a round face but one that, like his mother's, was somewhat long and was ruddy, enough to give an indication of his piety, his intelligence of character, his gentleness, and his unequivocal lack of anger; and [his face was] of the same sort as the sketch that this text, a little earlier, drew of his mother.

M 204C:
...at his age, he had reached a height of six feet; [he was] fair-haired, [and had] a prominent nose, light-coloured eyes that were well shaped, dark hair,[1] a tawny beard, and long hair; for never did a razor encounter his head, nor a human hand [touch him] – apart from that of his mother when he was nursing [as a baby].

---

1 The author or scribe contradicts himself in mentioning dark hair (μαυρόθριξ), having just stated that Christ had fair hair (ξανθόθριξ). This may be a scribal error.

d) D 32. 16–28:
21) ...they went up into a certain city of Galilee in which there is the lake that is called Gennesa, which is also Gennesaret. Many kinds of trees grow in this area, but it contains especially both balsam and flax, which have been cultivated in this land. And Gennesa is also called 'Bowl' (Phiale), because it is equal on all sides and spherical. And its waters are finer than the muddy thickness [of other lakes]. Nevertheless, it nurtures every kind of fish. And those of the trees that bear fruit differ even more from the rest; for they have very many trunks and are extremely productive. And there is a surfeit of wine and oil.

M 205D–208A:
...they came to the village of Bethsaida, a city of Galilee in which there is the lake that is called Gennesaret and 'Bowl' (Phiale), on account of its roundness on all sides. And the water is entirely transparent and pure. And its circumference is seven miles long. The olive oil is utterly marvellous, as is the fruit around the lake and the good-smelling fish.

e) D 35. 7–16:
23) The disciples who followed Jesus were as follows: Peter and Andrew, who were brothers from the city of Bethsaida; James and John, the sons of Zebedee; Philip and Bartholomew; James, the son of Alphaeus, and Judas, who were brothers of the Lord (for Joseph, their father, had the surname Alphaeus); Simon from Cana in Galilee and Thomas, who was called Didymos; along with Matthew the Evangelist and Judas the Iscariot.

M 208D–209A:
The disciples were Andrew and Peter, the brothers from the city of Bethsaida; Philip and Bartholomew; James and Judas, brothers of the Lord (for Joseph was called by the name Alphaeus); Simon from Cana; and Matthew the Evangelist; Judas from Jerusalem; Thaddaeus from Edessa in Syria; Judas the traitor from the city of Skara;[2] [and] James and John from Zebedee.

---

2 Judas is called 'the Iskariot' in the Gospels, although some versions use the form 'Skariotes'; see *New Testament*, ed. Aland, Black, Martini, Metzger, and Wikgren 1983, 34 (with reference to Mt 10: 4).

APPENDIX A   151

f) D 35. 22–37. 2:
25) But the high priests of the Jews at that time used to change each year and they procured the priesthood by means of money. For this reason, even Caiaphas did not originate from Jerusalem, but rather from a certain one of the external eparchies; he was a high priest for that year, but they say that he did not have a residence in his own house – but [stayed] instead in John's inherited property (κληρονομίᾳ). It is on this account that the Evangelist John himself says in his Gospel that 'that disciple was known to the high priest'. For half of his house was given to the high priest; meanwhile he occupied the other half, in which the Ruler Christ carried out the Passover and the mystical supper with his disciples. For they say that Christ sent his disciples there in order that they might prepare the Passover [meal]. For [Jesus's] statement, 'Go to a certain man', referred, as some say, to John – in other words, to the master of the house who stayed in it. For John never separated himself from Christ but was with him until his world-saving crucifixion. So they remained there and there carried out the Passover and the mystical supper. And the Theotokos also remained there, from the time when John took charge of her and stood with her at the cross of Christ, and heard from him the words, 'Behold your mother', while the Theotokos [heard] 'Behold your son.' For the saying that 'that disciple took over the care of her and took her into his own home' means, in veiled language, 'the holy Sion', [that is,] his house. It was there that Christ entered in through closed doors, and stood in their midst and said, 'Peace be with you', and the rest.

M 209B–C:
But the high priests then used to change each year, and they were not local but came from different eparchies. For this reason, even Caiaphas, who came from Kios in the eparchy of Bithynia, became high priest for that year [and] stayed in the purchased [house] (ἀγορασίᾳ) of John the Theologian. On this account [the latter] said, 'he was known to the high priest'. And in one half [of the house] he prepared the Passover, that is, the mystical supper, for Christ, along with his disciples and female students (ταῖς μαθητρίαις). But whenever [Jesus] said, 'Go to a certain man', he meant John the Theologian. They completed the mystical supper there and remained there after the resurrection of the Lord. For John took over charge of the mother from Jesus after standing at the cross [with her] and 'took her to his own home', which was the holy Sion. And it was there that Christ entered in through closed doors and stood in their midst and said, 'Peace be with you', and the rest.

g) D 37. 3–13:
26) The myrrh-bearing women are seven in number: (i) Mary Magdalen and (ii) Salome, also the mother of the sons of Zebedee, and (iii) Mary, the mother of James the Less, and (iv) the wife of Judah, the brother of the Lord, and (v) the mother of Joses (she who reared the brother of the Lord, Joses, the son of Joseph), and (vi) Joanna (who some say was the wife of Peter), and (vii) the sister [-in-law] of the Lord's mother, Mary, wife of Klopas who was Joseph's brother; for Joachim and Anna produced no other child besides the supremely holy Theotokos.

M 209C:
There were seven myrrh-bearing women: (i) Mary Magdalen, and (ii) Salome, also the mother of the sons of Zebedee, and (iii) Mary, the mother of James the Less, (iv) the wife of Judah, the brother of the Lord, and (v) Joses (she who reared the brother of the Lord), (vi) Joanna (some say that she was the wife of Peter, but others [say that] she was the mother of Clement), and (vii) the sister [-in-law] of the Lord's mother, Mary, wife of Klopas who was Joseph's brother, since Joachim and Anna bore no other child.[3]

h) D 37. 21–38. 6:
26) And all the apostles were staying (ἔμενον) with her, together with the myrrh-bearing women and [Christ's] siblings, [engaging in] fasts, sleeping on the ground, prayers, tears, and continuous hymnody. It is there that Christ first appeared to them when the doors were closed. And it is there that Thomas came to believe. There also the Holy Spirit visited the apostles. And after being sent out from there into [many] places and having returned (ὑποστρέφοντες), they again gathered there.

M 209D:
All of the apostles stayed (ἔμειναν) there with her, with the women and with [Christ's] siblings, in order to pray with fasts, sleeping on the ground, and tears, along with continuous hymnody with great joy. And Christ often (πυκνότερον) appeared to them there. And they were sent out to [many] places and, on coming [back] (πορευόμενοι), they again gathered there.

---

3 The divergences of Mingarelli's text from that of Dressel are fairly slight in this passage. However, the former provides only six names after stating that there were seven myrrh-bearers, which may reflect a lacuna in the text.

APPENDIX A

i) D 39. 5–20:
27) But even in the course of the affliction that came to pass with the persecution of the Church at the time of the destruction (τῇ ἀναιρέσει) of Stephen, the first martyr, all [of the Christians] were dispersed into the cities of Judaea and Samaria – except for the twelve apostles, as the Evangelist Luke writes. And the execution of the first martyr occurred six years after the ascension of Christ. [The apostles] held James, the brother of the Lord, as the first in rank among them, on account of the piety that he possessed, and they did nothing without him. There were many women from different provinces who stayed with the Theotokos; some had been freed from illnesses, others from impure spirits, and yet others were moved by faith and love for her. Among them, so they say, was Paul's wife.

M 212B:
But even at the stoning (τῇ λιθοβολίᾳ) of Stephen, the first martyr, which happened seven years after the ascension of Christ, all [of the Christians] were dispersed except for the twelve. And [the apostles] held James, the brother of the Lord, as their leader (πρῶτον) and did nothing without him. Pious women from different provinces were with the Theotokos; some [were converted] by [the expulsion of] impure spirits, others by faith. Among them, so they say, was Paul's wife.

j) D 41. 17–42. 2:
29) Some say that all of the apostles who were not in Jerusalem were present by means of clouds. But Dionysios the Areopagite, who was there at that time, does not say this. It is possible that they were gathered according to some dispensation before the time of her departure. Not one of the twelve apostles had died prior to her falling-asleep, except for James, the son of Zebedee, who was John's brother, whom Herod (who has also become food for the worms) had killed.

M 213B:
...he[4] says that the twelve were present by means of clouds. But he lies. For how did those who were there, [namely,] James and John and Matthew, come by means of clouds? Perhaps they [did come] from far away? Dionysios was present at that time, although he does not say this. Nor had any of the twelve died beforehand, except for James, the brother of John the Theologian, whom Herod had killed. And Agrippa, the son of the first Herod from Mariamme, had also become food for worms. Meanwhile, from among the remaining saints who had died before this, their souls were all present.

k) D 43. 16–20:
30) After a short time when they were all present and watching, her holy and all-holy body was taken away from before their eyes. And having celebrated her death, which was glorious in this way, they each departed to their own places.

M 216A:
After a short time, when all who were present were watching, the body became invisible to their eyes. After singing a hymn once again, they each departed to their own places.

---

4 The verb λέγει is in the third person singular in Mingarelli's text, whereas Dressel's text gives the plural, 'Some say...'. The subject of the former version seems to refer back to 'A certain virtuous priest and monk...' at the beginning of this passage.

APPENDIX B:
VARIANT READINGS IN THE *LAA*

As stated in my Introduction, Andrey Vinogradov argues that Epiphanios himself produced the two surviving versions (A and B) of the *LAA*.[1] I have chosen not to translate both versions in full, owing to the amount of overlapping material that they contain. However, it is worth including translations of a few passages (mostly containing sermons or parts of sermons that the apostle Andrew is said to have delivered in the course of his travels) that appear only in version A of the text. I do not include the original Greek since this is accessible in Vinogradov's edition of both versions.

a. The following passage (in version A, section 23) forms part of a sermon which Andrew delivers during his stay in the city of Nicaea. He has visited a mountain near the city where people were sacrificing to demons. After expelling these, Andrew mounts a pedestal and preaches against idolatry. The passage appears after the word 'you may enjoy' (ἀπολαύσητε) (Vinogradov 2005, 209. 18 [version A], 249. 7 [version B]):

'Destroy your revered objects, which are dead statues, and worship, [turning to] the east, the one God in heaven and on earth, who created you in accordance with everything that is in heaven and on earth and who made the water and strengthened the earth in the middle of it. And by the word of his command [he made] the firmament and suspended the water above it and, collecting everything beneath into a single group (while the dry earth appeared), he did not base it on anything. He made the stars and the light, the sun and the moon (and they do not sink by their weight, nor do they ascend in flight [Vin 210] although they are larger than the earth in size and inanimate, yet they move endlessly on an equal course and seasons, months, and years are measured by them). [God] brings forth his spirit

---

1 See above, 70–73.

and clouds, waters, winds, snows, ice, lightning, thunder, and storms come from it. [And he] leads rivers out of the earth, which gush and endlessly flow (and neither do they overflow wherever they enter the boundless [expanses] of the seas, nor do they empty it when they flow out). And [he made] the earth, like pumice, with corresponding great caves, countries, and great lakes within it, along with gloomy places in which spirits and the souls of idolators dwell. [There is] a sea of fire under the earth (and this is attested by the Lipari and the fires of Etna in Sicily, as well as by Photaria in Lycia). [And he made] the cave of Tartarus, high mountains, and uninhabited places within which swarms of demons have been banished to live. [He made] four-footed beasts, elephants, snakes, and reptiles; he created boundless species of four-footed beasts and birds and takes care of them all. [This includes] the flowers of the earth, fruits, all tastes, plants, and every kind of energy, kinds of precious stones, transparent and coloured marble, gold, silver, and every fine thing, the varieties of water and every kind of fish, colours and every visible hue, and every fragrance and every perfume. And all these things are for the sake of humanity whom he has honoured with his own image and [for whom] he has regulated all things, to whom he gave wisdom and intelligence to [whoever] seeks [this]. He enacted and is enacting countless miraculous things. This is the one and only God, [Vin 211] who brought all things from non-being into being by his wisdom and by his Spirit.'

b. This passage (in version A, section 26) also belongs to the narrative that deals with Andrew's stay in Nicaea. The apostle delivers a final sermon to the assembled people. The passage begins after the word αὐτούς (Vinogradov 2005, 218. 15 [version A]; 254. 27 [version B]):

And on the next day the whole people again gathered at his door and were causing a disturbance. Andrew went out and said to them, 'Do not make noise, but demonstrate works of repentance. Purify your hearts from dependence on wine and from malicious treachery, purify your mouths from deceit and from demonic songs and from all uneducated nonsense, and open [yourselves up to] the word of God [Vin 219] in order that you may attract the Holy Spirit. Cleanse your hands from unjust robbery and stolen goods, as well as from the yoke of deceit, and stretch them out to provide mercy for the poor, as well as for strangers and slaves. Take up the law of God, which [was given] through Moses, in order that you may live in peace. Receive the yoke of Christ since it is holy and contains abundant recompense. If you desire holy baptism, turn your souls and bodies away from Satan with his idols, works, and all his pomp. Approach Christ willingly and demonstrate the things that he loves: this means loving God and one another without guile, not being wronged or doing wrong, being merciful, practising self-restraint and not being arrogant; but instead to be humble, to be pure, to live in peace with everyone [and] to abstain from the things of others. Do not murder, do not steal, do not swear falsely, do not commit adultery, flee from lust and every impurity in order that you may become the new people of God, chosen, holy, [and] zealous for good deeds. Think and do heavenly things where Christ is and where you will come to dwell with him. Worship him with the Father and the Spirit each day and stand in prayer, facing the east.'

c. This passage occurs a few lines later (in version A, section 27), providing more discourse towards the end of Andrew's sojourn in Nicaea. It is inserted after μηνὸς (Vinogradov 2005, 219. 21 [version A]; 255. 6 [version B]):

He became the first bishop. But when Andrew was about to depart from Nicaea, he gathered them together and said, [Vin 220] 'You yourselves understand how much I have called on you and how much you have scorned me, how much I have kept vigils on your behalf and how many signs God performed through me. And you were not taught unless he dispersed the demons in order to teach you. God, since he loves humankind, does not act by compulsion but calls on everyone as if they were sovereign and wants each person to be saved. Behold, I have stayed with you for two whole years. Preserve as immoveable tradition whatever you have seen in me and heard from me. The Lord God, through his Son Jesus Christ, has marked you out and sealed you with his holy Spirit. See that you do not turn back to your former customs or fight over your faith and priests. For Satan will tempt you to see whether you are steadfast; for this is why he is allowed to test the gold of your faith – to see whether it is genuine. Demonstrate the firmness of your faith; for each of you, according to what he has, must offer your first fruits to God with joy and comfort by means of the priests. Obey them and ask that they joyfully perform prayers to God on your behalf. Do not judge the priests, ignorant people, for it is written, "Do not touch my anointed ones and among my prophets do no harm." Priests, educate the people [Vin 221] by means of your way of life, word, and command. Do not speak against each other. Let everyone bear each other's burdens. Let all be patient with each other. Love one another in order that you may be loved by God.'

d. This passage occurs later in the *LAA* (version A, section 29) after Andrew has travelled to Nikomedia, Chalcedon, Herakleia, Amastris, and back to Sinope. It is in the last of these cities that the apostle is attacked and even has his finger bitten off by one of the inhabitants. After his wound is healed by Christ, Andrew converts the local people. The following short passage, which is inserted after the word ἐξεπλάγησαν (Vinogradov 2005, 222. 9 [version A]; 256. 3 [version B]), provides another short homily, which he delivers to them from a pedestal:

For mounting a pedestal that was in their midst, he said to them, 'Men, I see that you are experienced and wise in all ways – so why are you mastered by anger? I came not to rebuke you, but to summon you, to heal the sick [and] to proclaim a message of life. And if you wish to come together into one faith, which Abraham, Isaac and Jacob, Moses, and all the prophets handed down (for I see that you are acquainted with them), I will add nothing to what they have said: I proclaim the law of Moses and [I proclaim] the prophets. The prophecies have been fulfilled: Christ has come, truth has been revealed, the signs testify.'

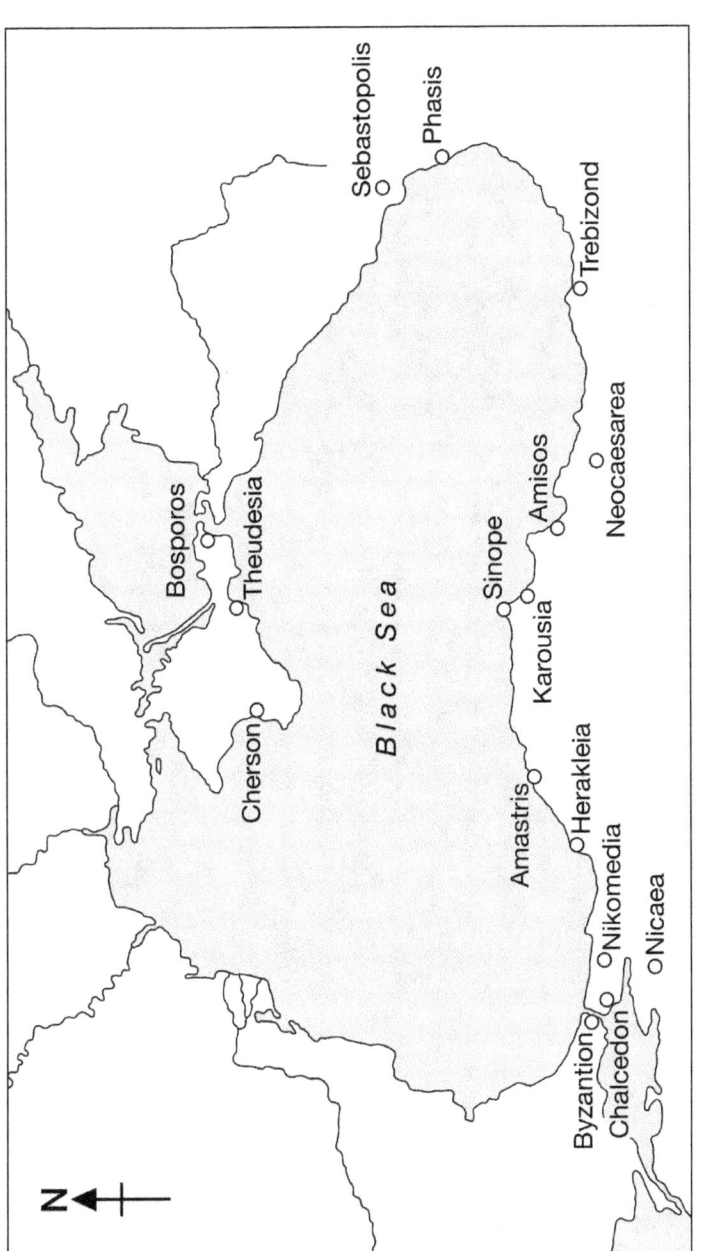

1. Map of Black Sea

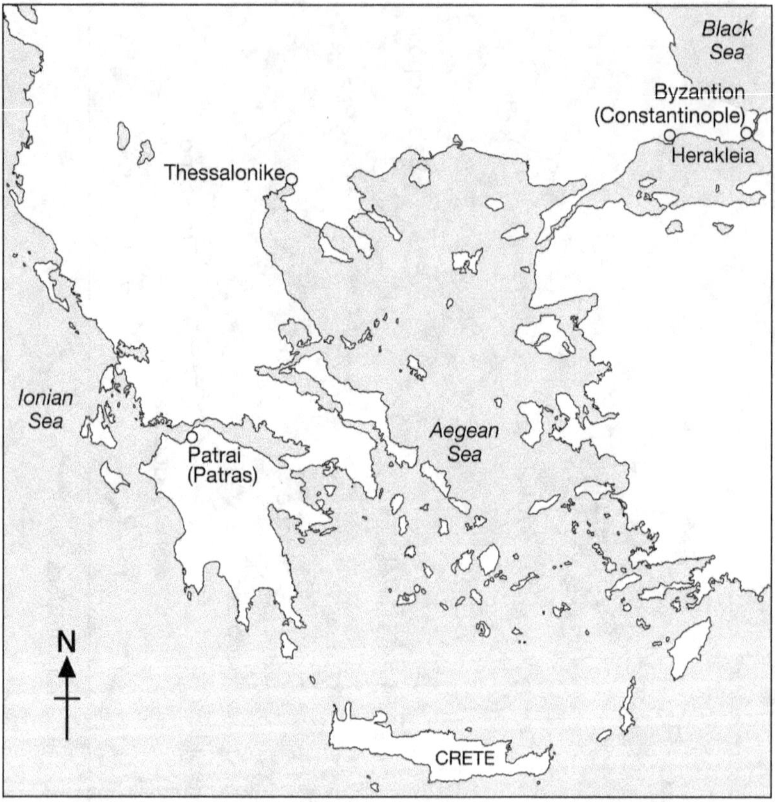

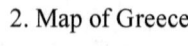

2. Map of Greece

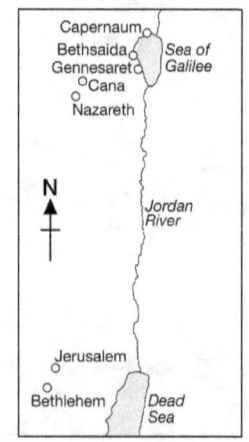

3. Map of Holy Land

LIST OF MANUSCRIPTS CITED IN BOOK

C = Paris, Bibliothèque nationale, Cod. Coisl. gr. 296, ff. 1^r–1^v, 13^v–22^v, 23–25^v (12th c.): *LVM*

E = Escorial Library, Cod. Esc. y–II–6, ff. 226^v–246^r (12th c.): *LAA*

J = Jerusalem: Patriarchal Library, Cod. Hag. Sab. 60, ff. 18–31^v (12th c.): *LVM*

N = Cod. Marc. gr. II. 42 (coll. 1123), ff. 237–250 (13th–14th c.): *LVM*

O = Oxford, Bodleian Library, Auct. E.5.12 (Misc. 77), ff. 235–250 (12th c.): *LVM*

P1 = Paris, Bibliothèque nationale, Cod. Paris. gr. 1510, ff. 1–19^v (10th c.): *LAA*

P2 = Paris, Bibliothèque nationale, Cod. Paris. gr. 1521, ff. 79^v–91^v (12th c.): *LVM*

P3 = Paris, Bibliothèque nationale, Cod. Paris. gr. 1538, ff. 2–7 (fragment) (10th c.): *LVM*

V1 = Rome, Vatican Library, Cod. Vat. gr. 442, ff. 330–349 (11th c.): *LVM*

V2 = Rome, Vatican Library, Cod. Vat. gr. 634, ff. 162^v–173^v (13th–14th c.): *LVM*

V3 = Rome, Vatican Library, Cod. Vat. gr. 824, ff. 105^v–128 (11th c.): *LAA*

BIBLIOGRAPHY

Primary Sources

Acta Andreae (= *AA*) (*CANT* 225. I), ed. and trans. Prieur (1989), vol. 2, CCSA 6, 443–549; ed. and trans. Macdonald (1990), 321–441
Acta Andreae et Matthias (= *AAMt)* (*CANT* 236; *BHG* 109), ed. Bonnet (1898), 65–116; ed. and trans. Macdonald (1990), 63–177; see also Elliott (1993), 283–99
Actes de l'apôtre André. Présentation et traduction du latin, du copte et du grec (= *Actes*), see Prieur (1995)
Acts of the Council of Chalcedon, ed. E. Schwartz (1938), *Concilium universal chalcedonense*, *ACO* I.6 (Berlin: De Gruyter); trans. R. Price and M. Gaddis (2005), TTH 45, 3 vols (Liverpool: Liverpool University Press)
Acts of John (*CANT* 215. I; *BHG* 900–9), ed. Bonnet (1898), 160–203; ed. E. Junod and J.-D. Kaestli (1983), *Acta Iohannis*, CCSA 1–2 (Turnhout: Brepols), 161–293
Acts of Peter (*CANT* 190. IV; *BHG* 1483–85); ed. R.A. Lipsius (1891), *Acta apostolorum apocrypha* I (Leipzig: H. Mendelssohn), 78–103; trans. W. Schneemelcher (1992), 271–321
Andrew of Crete, *Homilies I–IV on the Nativity of the Virgin* (*CPG* 8170–73), PG 97, 805–81; trans. Cunningham (2008), 71–138
—, *Homilies I–III on the Dormition of the Virgin* (*CPG* 8181–83), PG 97, 1045–1110; trans. Daley (1998), 103–52
—, *Kanon on the Nativity of the Virgin*, PG 97, 1316–29
Anonymous, *Martyrium Andreae alterum* A (*CANT* 225. I (d); *BHG* 97), ed. Bonnet (1898), 58–64; ed. Prieur (1989), 507–49
—, *Martyrium prius* (= *Mart. pr.*) (*CANT* 227; *BHG* 96), ed. Bonnet (1898), 46–57; ed. and trans. Prieur (1989), 675–703
—, *Narratio (Martyrium S. Apostoli Andreae)* (= *Narratio*) (*CANT* 229; *BHG* 99), ed. M. Bonnet (1894), *AB* 13, 354–72; repr. Bonnet (1895), 46–64; ed. Vinogradov (2005), 178–96 (references are made to this edition in the present book)
Arabic Infancy Gospel (*CANT* 58; *BHO* 619), ed. J.C. Thilo (1832), *Codex apocryphus Novi Testamenti*, vol. 1 (Leipzig: F.C.G. Vogel), 66–131

Armenian Passion of St Andrew, ed. C. Tchérakian (1904), *Écrits apostoliques non canoniques* (Venice), 146–67; French trans. L. Leloir (1986), *Écrits apocryphes sur les apôtres*, CCSA 3 (Turnhout: Brepols), 228–57

Athanasios of Alexandria, *First Letter to Virgins* (*CPG* 2147), ed. L.T. Lefort (1955), *S. Athanase: Lettres festales et pastorales en copte* (Louvain: L. Durbecq), 73–99; trans. D. Brakke (1995), *Athanasius and Asceticism* (Baltimore and London: Johns Hopkins University Press), 277–79

—, *On the Incarnation* (*CPG* 2091), ed. C. Kannengiesser (1973), *Sur l'incarnation du Verbe*, SC 199 (Paris: Éditions du Cerf)

Basil of Caesarea, *On the Holy Spirit* (*CPG* 2839), ed. B. Pruche (1986), *Basile de Césarée. Traité du Saint-Esprit*, SC 17bis (Paris: Éditions du Cerf); trans. D. Anderson (1980) (Crestwood, NY: St Vladimir's Seminary Press)

—, *Homily on the Nativity of Christ* (*CPG* 2913; *BHG^a* 1922), PG 31, 1457–76

—, *Letters* 219–366, ed. and trans. Y. Courtonne (1966), *Saint Basile. Lettres*, vol. 3 (Paris: Les belles lettres)

Bonnet, M., ed. (1895), *Acta Andreae cum laudatione contexta et Martyrium Andreae graece: Passio Andreae Latine, Supplementum codicis apocryphi*, vol. 2 (Paris: Klincksieck)

—, ed. (1898), *Acta apocryphorum apocrypha* II, I (Leipzig: H. Mendelssohn)

Brightman, F.E. and Hammond, C.E. (1965), *Liturgies Eastern and Western*, vol. 1: *Eastern Liturgies. Syrian, Egyptian, Persian, Byzantine Rites* (Oxford: Clarendon Press)

Clement of Alexandria, *Stromata* (*CPG* 1377), ed. O. Stählin and L. Früchtel (1960), Bks 1–6, GCS 52 [15] (Berlin: Akademie); O. Stählin, L. Früchtel, and U. Treu (1970), Bks 7–8, GCS 17² (Berlin: Akademie)

Clement of Rome and (ps-) Clement, *1–2 Clement, Letters to the Corinthians* (*CPG* 1001 and 1003), ed. and trans. M.W. Holmes (2007), *The Apostolic Texts and English Translations*, 3rd edn (Grand Rapids, MI: Baker Academic), 44–165

(ps-) Clementine Homilies, ed. B. Rehm and G. Strecker (1992), *Die Pseudoklementinen*, vol. 1: *Homilien* (Berlin: Akademie; Berlin and Boston: De Gruyter); extracts trans. J. Irmscher and G. Strecker in W. Schneemelcher (1992), 504–30

(ps-) Clementine Recognitions, ed. B. Rehm and G. Strecker (1994), *Die Pseudoklementinen*, vol. 2: *Rekognitionen in Rufins Übersetzung* (Berlin: Akademie; Berlin and Boston: De Gruyter), extracts trans. Irmscher and Strecker in Schneemelcher (1992), 531–41

Cunningham, Mary B. (2008), *Wider Than Heaven: Eighth-Century Homilies on the Mother of God* (Crestwood, NY: St Vladimir's Seminary Press)

Cyril of Alexandria, *Commentary on Twelve Minor Prophets* (*CPG* 5204), ed. P.E. Pusey (1868), *Cyrilli archiepiscopi Alexandrini in XII prophetas* (Oxford: Clarendon Press), 2 vols; PG 71, 9–1061, PG 72, 9–364

Daley, Brian E. (1998), *On the Dormition of Mary: Early Patristic Homilies* (Crestwood, NY: St Vladimir's Seminary Press)

Detorakis, T., ed. (1981–82), 'Τὸ ἀνέκδοτο μαρτύριο τοῦ ἀποστόλου Ἀνδρέου', *Acts of the Second International Congress of Peloponnesian Studies*, vol. 1 (Athens), 325–52

(ps-) Dionysios the Areopagite, *The Celestial Hierarchy* (*CPG* 6600), ed. Heil and Ritter (1991), vol. 2, 5–59; PG 3, 120–369; trans. Luibheid (1987), 143–91

—, *The Divine Names* (*CPG* 6602); ed. Suchla (1990); PG 3, 585–984; trans. Luibheid (1987), 47–131

—, *The Ecclesiastical Hierarchy* (*CPG* 6601), ed. Heil and Ritter (1991), 61–132; PG 3, 369–569; trans. Luibheid (1987) 193–259

—, *Epistles* (*CPG* 6604–13), ed. Heil and Ritter (1991), 151–210; trans. Luibheid (1987), 263–89

Doctrina Jacobi nuper baptizati, ed. V. Déroche (1991), TM 11, Centre national de la recherche scientifique (Paris: Boccard), 47–229

(ps-) Dorotheos of Tyre, *Index apostolorum discipulorumque Domini* (*BHG* 151–52h), ed. Schermann (1907), 131–63

Dressel, A., ed. (1843), *Epiphanii Monachi et Presbyteri: edita et inedita* (Paris and Leipzig: Brockhaus and Avenarius)

Elliott, J.K., ed. (1993), *The Apocryphal New Testament: A Collection of Apocryphal Christian Literature in an English Translation* (Oxford: Clarendon Press)

Epiphanios Hagiopolites, *Diegesis of a Journey to Syria and Jerusalem*, ed. Dressel (1843), 1–12; PG 120, 259–72; trans. Wilkinson (1977), 117–21

Epiphanios the Monk, *Life of the Virgin Mary* (= *LVM*) (*CANT* 91; *BHG* 1049), ed. Dressel (1843), 13–44; G.L. Mingarelli with G.C. Amaduzzi and G.L. Bianconi, eds (1783), *Anecdota litteraria ex mss codicibus eruta* (Rome: Antonio Fulgoni), 39–83; repr. PG 120, 185–216

—, *Life and Acts of Andrew* (= *LAA*, Version B) (*CANT* 233; *BHG* 102), ed. Dressel (1843), 45–82; PG 120, 216–60; ed. and trans. (Russian) in Vinogradov (2005), 236–64; trans. (Modern Greek) Archimandrite Nikodemos and the Monastery of the All-Holy Virgin Chryssopodaritisses (2023), *Περί του βίου και των πράξεων και τέλους του αγίου και πανευφήμου και πρωτοκλήτου των αποστόλων Ανδρέου* (Chalandritsa: 'Tinos')

Epiphanios of Salamis, *Panarion* (*CPG* 3745), ed. M. Bergermann, C.-F. Collatz, after K. Holl (2013), *Epiphanius. Band 1, Ancoratus und Panarion haer. 1–33*, GCS n.f. 10/1 (Berlin and Boston: De Gruyter); trans. F. Williams (2009), *The Panarion of Epiphanius of Salamis, Book I (Sects. 1–46)*, Nag Hammadi and Manichaean Studies 63 (Leiden and Boston: Brill, 2nd edn)

(ps-) Epiphanios of Salamis, *Index apostolorum discipulorumque Domini Epiphanio attributus* (*CPG* 3780; *BHG* 150), ed. Schermann (1907), 107–31

Euchologion sive rituale graecorum, ed. J. Goar (2nd edn, 1730) (Venice: Bartholomew Javarina)

Eusebios of Caesarea, *Demonstratio evangelica* (*CPG* 3487) ed. I.A. Heikel (1913), *Eusebius Werke*, vol. 6: *Die Demonstratio evangelica*, GCS 23 (Leipzig: J.C. Hinrich)

—, *Ecclesiastical History* (*CPG* 3495), ed. E. Schwartz, T. Mommsen, and F. Winkelmann (1999), *Eusebius Werke*, vol. 2. 1–3: *Die Kirchengeschichte*, GCS 9. 1–3 (Berlin: Akademie); trans. G.A. Williamson (1965), *Eusebius: The History of the Church from Christ to Constantine* (Harmondsworth: Penguin Books)

—, *Life of Constantine* (*CPG* 3496), ed. F. Winkelmann (1991), *Über das Leben des Kaisers Konstantin, Eusebius Werke*, vol 1. 1, GCS, 2nd edn (Berlin: Akademie), 3–148; trans. Av. Cameron and S. Hall (1999), *Eusebius: Life of Constantine* (Oxford: Oxford University Press)

—, *Onomastikon*, ed. E. Klostermann (1904), *Das Onomastikon der biblischen Ortsnamen* (Leipzig: J.C. Hinrichs)

Euthymios the Athonite, *Georgian Life of the Virgin* (*CANT* 90), ed. M. van Esbroeck (1986), *Maxime le Confesseur: Vie de la Vierge*, 2 vols, CSCO 478–79, Scriptores Iberici 21–22 (Louvain: Peeters); ed. and trans. S.J. Shoemaker (2012), *Maximus the Confessor: The Life of the Virgin* (New Haven and London: Yale University Press)

(ps-) Evagrios of Sicily, *Life of St Pankratios of Taormina* (*BHG* 1410–12), ed. Cynthia J. Stallman-Pacitti and John B. Burke (2018), Byzantina Australiensia 22 (Leiden and Boston: Brill)

Flamion, J., ed. (1911), *Les Actes apocryphes de l'apôtre André. Les Actes d'André et de Mathias, de Pierre et d'André et les textes apparentés*, Recueil de travaux d'histoire et de philologie 33 (Louvain: University of Louvain)

Gelasian Decree, ed. E. von Dobschütz (1912), *Texte und Untersuchungen* 38. 4 (Leipzig), 49–52

Germanos of Constantinople, *Homilies I–III on the Dormition* (*CPG* 8010–12; *BHG* 1119); PG 98, 340–72; trans. Daley (1998), 153–81

The Greek New Testament, 3rd edn, ed. B. Aland, M. Black, C.M. Martini, B.M. Metzger, and A. Wikgren (1966) (Stuttgart: Biblia-Druck)

Gregory the Great, *Forty Homilies on the Gospels* (*CPL* 1711), PL 76, 1075–1312; trans. D. Hurst (1990), *Gregory the Great: Forty Gospel Sermons*, Cistercian Studies 123 (Kalamazoo, MI: Cistercian Publications)

Gregory of Tours, *Epitome = Liber de miraculis beati Andreae apostoli* (*BHL* 430) ed. M. Bonnet (1885), *Monumenta Germaniae historica. Scriptores rerum Merovingicarum*, vol. 1 (Hannover: A. Hahn), 826–46; repr. and trans. Prieur (1989), 564–651; repr. and trans. MacDonald (1990), 188–317

Heil, G. and Ritter, A.M. (1991), *Corpus Dionysiacum*, vol. 2: *Pseudo-Dionysius Areopagita. De coelesti hierarchia, De ecclesiastica hierarchia, De mystica theologia, epistolae*, PTS 36 (Berlin and New York: Walter de Gruyter)

BIBLIOGRAPHY 167

Hippolytos of Thebes, *Chronicle*, ed. F. Diekamp (1898), *Hippolytos von Theben, Texte und Untersuchungen* (Münster: Aschendorff), 1–55; PG 117, 1027–56

Ignatius of Antioch, *Epistle to the Ephesians* (*CPG* 1025), ed. K. Lake (1912; repr. 1959), 2 vols (Cambridge, MA: Harvard University Press)

Itinera Hierosolymitana, ed. P. Geyer (1898; repr. 1964), *Corpus scriptorum ecclesiasticorum latinorum* 39 (Prague: F. Tempsky; New York: Johnson Reprints)

Jacob of Voragine, *The Golden Legend*, ed. G.P. Maggioni (1998), *Legenda Aurea* (Florence: SISMEL–Galluzzo), 2 vols; trans. W.G. Ryan, intro. E. Duffy (2012), *Jacobus de Voragine: The Golden Legend. Readings on the Saints* (Princeton, NJ: University of Princeton Press)

John Chrysostom, *Homilies on Genesis* (*CPG* 4409–10), PG 53, 23–386, PG 54, 385–630; trans. R.C. Hill (1986), *St John Chrysostom: Homilies on Genesis 1–17*, FOTC 74 (Washington, DC: Catholic University of America Press); trans. idem (1990), *Homilies on Genesis 18–45*, FOTC 82 (Washington, DC: Catholic University of America Press); trans. idem (1992), *Homilies on Genesis 46–67*, FOTC 87 (Washington, DC: Catholic University of America Press)

—, *Homilies on the Epistle to the Hebrews* (*CPG* 4440), ed. F. Field, ed. (1862), *Ioannis Chrysostomi interpretatio omnium epistularum Paulinarum*, vol. 7 (Oxford: J. Wright)

—, *Homilies on Matthew 1–45* (*CPG* 4424), PG 57, 13–472; F. Field, ed. (1839), *Joannis Chrysostomi, Homiliae in Matthaeum* (Cambridge: Cambridge University Press)

—, *Homily on the Nativity of Christ* (*CPG* 4334; *BHG*^{a} 1892), PG 49, 351–62

—, *On the Priesthood* (*CPG* 4316), ed. J.A. Nairn (1906), *De sacerdotio of John Chrysostom* (Cambridge: Cambridge University Press); trans. G. Neville (1964), *Saint John Chrysostom: Six Books on the Priesthood* (London: SPCK)

John of Damascus, *On the Divine Images* (*CPG* 8045; *BHG* 1391e–g); ed. Kotter (1975), vol. 3, PTS 17; trans. A. Louth (2003), *St John of Damascus: Three Treatises on the Divine Images* (Crestwood, NY: St Vladimir's Seminary Press)

—, *On the Two Wills of Christ* (*CPG* 8052), PG 95, 128–85

—, *Exposition of Faith* (*CPG* 8043) ed. Kotter (1973), vol. 2, PTS 12, 3–239; trans. F.H. Chase, Jr (1958), *Saint John of Damascus: Writings* (Washington, DC: Catholic University of America Press); trans. N. Russell (2022), *Saint John of Damascus: On the Orthodox Faith* (Yonkers, NY: St Vladimir's Seminary Press)

—, *On Heresies* (*CPG* 8044), ed. Kotter (1981), *Die Schriften*, vol. 4, PTS 22

—, *Homily I on the Dormition of the Virgin* (*CPG* 8061; *BHG*^{a} 1114), ed. B. Kotter (1988), vol. 5, PTS 29, 483–500

—, *Homily on the Nativity of Christ* (*CPG* 8067; *BHG*^{a} 1912), ed. B. Kotter, vol. 5, PTS 29, 324–47

(ps-) John of Damascus, *Epistola ad Theophilum imperatorem de sacris imaginibus* (*CPG* 8115), PG 95, 345–85; on the inauthenticity of this text, see Hoeck (1951), 26, n. 42 (secondary sources)
(ps-) John the Evangelist, *Transitus* (*CANT* 101; *BHG* 1055–56), ed. K. Tischendorf (1866), *Apocalypses apocryphae* (Leipzig: H. Mendelssohn), 95–112; trans. Elliott (1993), 701–8
John Geometres, *Life of the Virgin* (*CANT* 92; *BHG* 1102g–h, 1123m, 1143c; *BHG*^{a} 1102g); ed. and trans. Fr Maximos Constas and Christos Simelidis (2023), *Life of the Virgin Mary by John Geometres*, DOML 77 (Cambridge, MA: Harvard University Press). For the last section of the text, including the Dormition and Assumption of the Virgin Mary (based on Vat. gr. 504, ff. 190–194^v), see also ed. and trans. Wenger (1955), 363–415 (secondary sources); also ed. A. Benia (2019), *Ιωάννη Γεομέτρη, Εξόδιος ή προπεμπτήριος εις την Κοίμησιν της υπερενδόξου Δεσποίνης ημών Θεοτόκου: Πρώτη έκδοση και μελέτη του κειμένου* (unpubl. PhD thesis, University of Athens)
John Malalas, *Chronicle*, ed. L. Dindorf (1831), *Malalas, Chronographia* (Bonn: Weber); trans. E. Jeffreys, M. Jeffreys, and R. Scott, with B. Croke, J. Ferber, S. Franklin, A. James, D. Kelly, A. Moffatt, and A. Nixon (1986), *The Chronicle of John Malalas*, Byzantina Australiensia 4 (Melbourne: Australian Association for Byzantine Studies)
John Moschos, *Pratum spirituale* (*CPG* 7376; *BHG* 1441–42); PG 87, 2851–3116; trans. John Wortley (1992), *The Spiritual Meadow of John Moschos*, Cistercian Studies 139 (Kalamazoo, MI: Cistercian Publications)
John of Thessalonike, *Homily on the Dormition* (*CANT* 103; *CPG* 7924; *BHG* 1144a–c); ed. M. Jugie (1925; repr. 1990), *Homélies Mariales byzantines*, vol. 2, PO 19, fasc. 3, no. 93 (Paris: Graffin; repr. Turnhout: Brepols), 344–437; trans. Daley (1998), 47–70
Josephus, Flavius. *Jewish Antiquities. Books I–IV*, trans. H.S.J. Thackeray (1930); *Books XV–XVII*, trans. R. Marcus, ed. A. Wikgren (1963; repr. 1998), Loeb Classical Library (Cambridge, MA: Harvard University Press)
—. *The Jewish War*, ed. and trans. H.S.J. Thackeray (1961), *Books 1–3*, Loeb Classical Library (Cambridge, MA: Harvard University Press)
(ps-) Julius Africanus, *De rebus persicis post Christum natum* (*CPG* 6968; *BHG*^{a} 806); PG 10, 97–108 (see *Legend of Aphroditianus*)
Justin Martyr, *Dialogue with Trypho* (*CPG* 1076), ed. G. Archambault (1909), *Justin. Dialogue avec Tryphon. Texte grec, traduction française, introduction, notes et index*, Textes et documents pour l'étude historique du christanisme 8, 2 vols (Paris: Alphonse Picard et Fils); J. Goodspeed (1915), *Die ältesten Apologeten* (Göttingen: Vandenhoeck und Ruprecht), 90–265; trans. T.B. Falls (2003), *St Justin Martyr: Dialogue with Trypho* (Washington, DC: Catholic University of America Press)

BIBLIOGRAPHY 169

King James Version of the Bible, ed. D. Norton (2005), *The New Cambridge Paragraph Bible with the Apocrypha: King James Version* (Cambridge: Cambridge University Press)

Kotter, B., ed. (1969–88), *Die Schriften des Johannes von Damaskos*, 5 vols, PTS 7, 12, 17, 22, 29 (Berlin and New York: De Gruyter)

Legend of Aphroditianus (*CPG* 6968; *BHG* 802–6; *CANT* 55); various versions exist, including: *Narratio de rebus in Persia gestis*, ed. A.A. Vasiliev (1893), *Anecdota graeco-byzantina*, vol. 1 (Moscow: University of Moscow), 73–125; *De gestis in Perside*, ed. E. Bratke (1899), *Das sogenannte Religionsgespräch am Hof der Sasanid*, TU IV.3 (Leipzig: J.C. Hinrichs); P. Bringel, ed. and trans. (2007), *Une polémique religieuse à la cour perse: le De gestis in Perside. Histoire du texte, edition critique et traduction*, 2 vols. (PhD thesis, Université de Paris I, Panthéon Sorbonne); K. Heyden, trans. (2016), 'The Legend of Aphroditianus: A New Translation and Introduction', in T. Burke and B. Landau, eds, *New Testament Apocrypha: More Non-Canonical Scriptures* (Grand Rapids, MI: Eerdmans), 3–18; a version of the text is falsely ascribed to Julius Africanus in PG 10, 97–108

Leo I ('the Great'), *Tomus ad Flavianum*, ed. C. Silva-Tarouca (1932), *S. Leonis Magni Tomus ad Flavianum Episc. Constantinopolitanum (Epistula XXVIII)*, Textus et documenta, Series Theologica 9 (Rome: Pontifical Gregorian University); also see *Acts of the Council of Chalcedon*)

Letter of the Three Patriarchs to Emperor Theophilos and Related Texts, ed. and trans. J.A. Munitiz, J. Chrysostomides, E. Harvalia-Crook, and C. Dendrinos (1997) (Camberley: Porphyrogennetos Press)

Life of St Pankratios of Taormina (see [ps.-] Evagrios of Sicily)

Luibheid, C., trans. (1987), *Pseudo-Dionysius: The Complete Works* (London: SPCK)

MacDonald, D.R., ed. and trans. (1990), *The Acts of Andrew and the Acts of Andrew and Matthias in the City of the Cannibals* (= *AA* and *AAMt*) (Atlanta, GA: Scholars Press)

Menologion of Basil II, PG 117, 19–614; Vat. gr. 1613

Monastic *Typika*, ed. J. Thomas and A.C. Hero (2000), *Byzantine Monastic Foundation Documents*, 5 vols (Washington, DC: Dumbarton Oaks Research Library and Collection)

Niketas David the Paphlagonian, *Enkomion of St Andrew* (*BHG* 106), PG 105, 53–80

—, *Laudatio* (*CANT* 228; *BHG* 100), ed. Vinogradov (2005), 265–307; M. Bonnet (1894), 'Acta Andreae apostoli cum laudatione contexta', *AB* 13, 309–52; ed. idem (1895), 2–44; cf. *AA*, ed. Prieur (1989), 708–33, 738–45

Origen, *Commentary on Matthew*, trans. R.E. Heine (2018), *The Commentary of Origen on the Gospel of Matthew*, vols 1–2 (Oxford: Oxford University Press)

—, *On First Principles* (*CPG* 1482), ed. P. Koetschau (1913), *Origenes Werke*, vol. 5: *De principiis*, GCS 22 (Leipzig: J.C. Hinrichs); trans. G.W. Butterworth (1973), *Origen: On First Principles* (Gloucester, MA: Peter Smith)

Paschal Chronicle, ed. L.A. Dindorf (1932), *Chronicon paschale* (Bonn: E. Weber); trans. Michael Whitby and Mary Whitby (1989), *Chronicon Paschale, 284–628 AD*, TTB 7 (Liverpool: Liverpool University Press)

Paschal Romanus, *Historia beate virginis Mariae* (*CANT* 91; *BHL* 5345ᵛ), ed. E. Franceschini (1938), *Studi e note di filologia Latina medievale* (Milan: Società editrice 'Vita e pensiero'), 111–24

Pentekostarion (1883) (Rome); Eng. trans., *The Pentecostarion* (1990) (Brookline, MA: Holy Transfiguration Monastery)

Photios of Constantinople, *Bibliotheca*, ed. and trans. R. Henry (1959–91), *Photius, Bibliothèque*, 9 vols (Paris: Les Belles Lettres)

Prieur, J.-M., ed. and trans. (1989), *Acta Andreae. Praefatio–Commentarius* (= *AA*), CCSA 5 and 6 (Turnhout: Brepols)

—, trans. (1995), *Actes de l'apôtre André. Présentation et traduction du latin, du copte et du grec* (= *Actes*) (Turnhout: Brepols)

Prokopios, *Buildings*; trans. H.B. Dewing (1940), *Procopius: On Buildings*, Loeb Classical Library 343 (Cambridge, MA: Harvard University Press)

Protevangelion of James (*CANT* 50; *BHG* 1046); ed. E. de Strycker (1961), *La forme la plus ancienne du Protévangile de Jacques*, Studia Hagiographica 33 (Brussels: Société des Bollandistes); ed. C. Tischendorf (1876; repr. 1987), *Evangelia apocrypha* (Leipzig: H. Mendelssohn; repr. Hildesheim), 1–50; ed. and trans. J.K. Elliott and P.M. Rumsey (2022), *The Protevangelium of James* (Turnhout: Brepols)

Questions of Bartholomew (*CANT* 63; *BHG* 228) various editions; trans. F. Scheidweiler in W. Schneemelcher (1991), 537–57; J.-D. Kaestli and P. Cherix (1993), *L'Évangile de Barthélemy d'après deux écrits apocryphes* (Turnhout: Brepols). A critical edition is being prepared for the Corpus Christianorum Series Apocryphorum (Turnhout: Brepols) by Kaestli and Cherix

Schermann, T., ed. (1907), *Prophetarum vitae fabulosae indices apostolorum discipulorumque Domini Dorotheo, Epiphanio, Hippolyto aliisque vindicate* (Leipzig: Teubner)

Schneemelcher, W., ed. (1991), *New Testament Apocrypha*, vol. 1: *Gospels and Related Writings*: idem, ed. (1992), *New Testament Apocrypha*, vol. 2: *Writings Relating to the Apostles; Apocalypses and Related Subjects*, rev. edn (Cambridge: James Clarke & Co.; Louisville, KY: Westminster/John Knox Press)

Septuagint, ed. A. Rahlfs et al. (1926–), *Septuaginta*, 16 vols (Stuttgart: Vandenhoeck and Ruprecht); trans. L.C.L. Brenton (1851), *The Septuagint with Apocrypha: Greek and English* (London: S. Bagster and Sons; repr. Hendrickson); trans. A. Pietersma and B.G. Wright (2007), *A New English Translation of the Septuagint* (Oxford: Oxford University Press)

Socrates Scholasticus, *Historia ecclesiastica* (*CPG* 6028); ed. G.C. Hansen (1995), *Sokrates Kirchengeschichte*, GCS, n.f., 1 (Berlin: Akademie Verlag); PG 67, 33–841

Stephen the Deacon, *Life of St Stephen the Younger* (*BHG* 1666), ed. and trans. M.-F. Auzépy (1997), *La Vie d'Étienne le Jeune par Étienne le Diacre*, BBOM 3 (Aldershot and Brookfield, VT: Ashgate)

Symeon the Metaphrast, *Commemoration of St Andrew*, ed. *Menaia Novembris* (Venice, 1843), 235–45; repr. Μηναῖον τοῦ Νοεμβρίου (Athens, 1926), 318–25; Vinogradov (2005), 308–22

—, *Life of the Virgin* (*CANT* 93; *BHG* 1047–48); ed. B. Latyshev (1912), *Menologii anonymi byzantini saeculi X quae supersunt*, vol. 2 (St Petersburg: Imperial Academy), 346–83

Synaxarion of Constantinople (= *SynaxCP*), ed. H. Delehaye (1902), *Propylaeum ad Acta Sanctorum Novembris. Synaxarium Ecclesiae Constantinopolitanae* (Brussels: Société des Bollandistes)

Testament of the Twelve Patriarchs, ed. M. de Jonge (1978), *The Testaments of the Twelve Patriarchs: A Critical Edition of the Greek Text*, Pseudepigrapha Veteris Testamenti graece 1.2 (Leiden: Brill)

Theodore of Studios, *Letters*, ed. G. Fatouros (1992), *Theodori Studitae Epistulae*, 2 vols (Berlin: Walter de Gruyter)

Theophanes Confessor, *Chronographia*, ed. Carl de Boor (1883–85), *Theophanis Chronographia*, 2 vols (Leipzig: Teubner); trans. C. Mango and R. Scott (1997), *The Chronicle of Theophanes Confessor: Byzantine and Near Eastern History, AD 284–813* (Oxford: Oxford University Press)

Tomadakis, N.B. (1965), Ἡ Βυζαντινὴ Ὑμνογραφία καὶ Ποίησις ἤτοι Εἰσαγωγὴ εἰς τὴν Βυζαντινὴν Φιλολογίαν, 3 vols (Athens: Myrtides)

Typikon of the Great Church, ed. J. Mateos (1962–63), *Le Typikon de la Grande Église: Ms. Sainte-Croix no. 40, Xe siècle*, 2 vols (Rome: Pontifical Institute of Oriental Studies)

Vinogradov, Andrey, ed. (2005), *Grecheskie predaniia o sv. Apostole Andree*, Biblioteka 'Khristianskogo Vostoka' 3 (St Petersburg: University of St Petersburg Press)

Wilkinson, John (1977), *Jerusalem Pilgrims before the Crusades* (Warminster: Aris and Phillips)

Wright, W. (1871; repr. 1990), *Apocryphal Acts of the Apostles: Edited from Syrian Manuscripts in the British Museum and Other Libraries* (London and Edinburgh: Williams and Norgate; repr. Hildesheim: Orm)

Secondary Sources

Adler, William (2016), 'On the Priesthood of Jesus: A New Translation and Introduction', in T. Burke and B. Laudau, eds, *New Testament Apocrypha: More Non-Canonical Scriptures* (Grand Rapids, MI: Wm B. Eerdmans), 69–108

Allen, P., Külzer, A., and Peltomaa, L.M., eds (2015), *Presbeia Theotokou: The Intercessory Role of Mary across Times and Places in Byzantium (4th–9th Century)* (Vienna: Österreichischen Akademie der Wissenschaften)

Alwis, Anne (2020), *Narrating Martyrdom: Rewriting Late-Antique Virgin Martyrs in Byzantium*, TTB 9 (Liverpool: Liverpool University Press)

Antonopoulou, Theodora (1998), 'Homiletic Activity in Constantinople around 900', in P. Allen and M.B. Cunningham, eds, *Preacher and Audience: Studies in Early Christian and Byzantine Homiletics* (Leiden, Boston, and Cologne: Brill), 317–48

Arentzen, Thomas (2017), *The Virgin in Song: Mary and the Poetry of Romanos the Melodist* (Philadelphia, PA: University of Pennsylvania Press)

Arentzen, Thomas and Cunningham, Mary B., eds (2019), *The Reception of the Virgin in Byzantium: Marian Narratives in Texts and Images* (Cambridge: Cambridge University Press)

Auzépy, M.-F. (1992), 'L'analyse littéraire et l'historien: l'exemple des vies de saints iconoclastes', *Byzantinoslavica* 53, 57–67

Baldovin, John F., S.J. (1987), *The Urban Character of Christian Worship: The Origins, Development, and Meaning of Stational Liturgy*, OCA 228 (Rome: Pontifical Institute of Oriental Studies)

Barber, Charles (2002), *Figure and Likeness: On the Limits of Representation in Byzantine Iconoclasm* (Princeton and Oxford: Princeton University Press)

Bauckham, R.J. (1990), *Jude and the Relatives of Jesus in the Early Church* (Edinburgh: T. & T. Clark)

— (2002), *Gospel Women: Studies of the Named Women in the Gospels* (Grand Rapids, MI and Cambridge: Wm B. Eerdmans)

Belke, K. and Restle, M., eds (1984), *Galatien und Lykaonien*, TIB 4 (Vienna: Österreichischen Akademie der Wissenschaften)

Bennett, W.J. (1975), 'The Herodians of Mark's Gospel', *Novum Testamentum* 17, 9–14

Blok, J.H. (1995), *The Early Amazons: Modern and Ancient Perspectives on a Persistent Myth* (Leiden: Brill)

Bonnet, M. (1894), 'La Passion de l'apôtre André en quelle langue a-t-elle été écrite?', *BZ* 3, 458–69

Booth, Phil (2015), 'On the *Life of the Virgin* attributed to Maximus the Confessor', *JTS*, n.s. 66, pt. 1, 149–203

Boss, Sarah Jane, ed. (2007), *Mary: The Complete Resource* (London and New York: Continuum)
Bovon, F., ed. (1981), *Les Actes apocryphes des apôtres: Christianisme et monde païen* (Geneva: Labor et Fides)
— (1994), 'The Words of Life in the "Acts of the Apostle Andrew"', *HTR* 87.2, 139–54
— (1999), 'Byzantine Witnesses for the Apocryphal Acts of the Apostles', in F. Bovon, A.G. Brock, and C.R. Matthews, eds, *The Apocryphal Acts of the Apostles*, Harvard Divinity School Studies (Cambridge, MA: Harvard University Press), 87–100
— (2003), 'Canonical and Apocryphal Acts of the Apostles', *JECS* 11.2, 165–94
— (2012), 'The Corpus Christianorum Series Apocryphorum and the Association pour l'étude de la littérature apocryphe chrétienne', *Early Christianity* 3, 137–43
Bovon, F. and Snyder, G., eds (2009), *New Testament and Christian Apocrypha: Collected Studies II* (Tübingen: Mohr Siebeck)
Bratke, E. (1899), *Das sogenannte Religionsgespräch am Hof der Sasaniden*, TU NF IV, 3a (Leipzig), 61–127
Breckenridge, James D. (1957), '"Et Prima Vidit": The Iconography of the Appearance of Christ to His Mother', *The Art Bulletin* 39.1, 9–32
Bremmer, J.N., ed. (2000), *The Apocryphal Acts of Andrew* (Leuven: Peeters)
Brightman, F.E. and Hammond, C.E., eds (1965), *Liturgies Eastern and Western*, vol. 1: *Eastern Liturgies: Syrian, Egyptian, Persian, Byzantine Rites* (Oxford: Clarendon Press)
Brock, Sebastian P. (2006), 'The Genealogy of the Virgin Mary in Sinai Syr. 16', *Scrinium* 2, 58–71 (open access at http://www.scrinium.ru/lib/tome_2)
Brooks, Kenneth R. (1961), *Andreas and the Fates of the Apostles* (Oxford: Clarendon Press)
Brown, Raymond (1993), *The Birth of the Messiah: A Commentary on the Infancy Narratives in Matthew and Luke*, rev. edn (London: Chapman)
Brown, Raymond E., Donfried, Karl P., Fitzmyer, Joseph A., and Reumann, John, eds (1978), *Mary in the New Testament* (New York and Mahwah, NJ: Paulist Press)
Browning, Robert (1981), 'The "Low Level" Saint's Life in the Early Byzantine World', in S. Hackel, ed., *The Byzantine Saint: University of Birmingham Fourteenth Spring Symposium of Byzantine Studies* (London: Fellowship of St Alban and St Sergius), 117–27
Brubaker, Leslie and Cunningham, Mary B., eds (2011), *The Cult of the Mother of God in Byzantium: Texts and Images* (Farnham and Burlington, VT: Ashgate)
Brubaker, Leslie and Haldon, John (2011), *Byzantium in the Iconoclast Era, c. 680–850: A History* (Cambridge: Cambridge University Press)

Bryer, A.A.M. (1980), *The Empire of Trebizond and the Pontos* (London: Variorum Reprints, Ashgate)

Bryer, A.A.M. and Herrin, Judith, eds (1977), *Iconoclasm: Papers Given at the Ninth Spring Symposium of Byzantine Studies, University of Birmingham, March 1975* (Birmingham: University of Birmingham)

Bryer, A.A.M. and Winfield, David (1985), *The Byzantine Monuments and Topography of the Pontos* (Washington, DC: Dumbarton Oaks Research Library and Collection)

Burnet, R. (2014), *Les douze apôtres: Histoire de la réception des figures apostoliques dans le christianisme ancient*, Judaïsme ancien et origines du christianisme 1 (Turnhout: Brepols)

Callon, Callie, ed. (2019), *Reading Bodies: Physiognomy as a Strategy of Persuasion in Early Christian Discourse* (London: Bloomsbury T. & T. Clark)

Cameron, Averil (1979), 'The Virgin's Robe: An Episode in the History of Early Seventh-Century Constantinople', *Byzantion* 49, 42–56

— (1991), *Christianity and the Rhetoric of Empire: The Development of Christian Discourse* (Berkeley, Los Angeles, and Oxford: University of California Press)

Constas, Fr Maximos (2019), 'The Story of an Edition: Antoine Wenger and John Geometres' *Life of the Virgin Mary*', in Arentzen and Cunningham (2019), 324–40

Cooper, J. Eric (1998), *Urban Centres in Western and Central Anatolia, 600–900* (unpubl. MPhil thesis, University of Oxford)

Cormack, Robin (1985), *Writing in Gold: Byzantine Society and Its Icons* (London: George Philip)

Cunningham, Mary B. (2011a), 'Messages in Context: The Reading of Sermons in Byzantine Churches and Monasteries', in A. Lymberopoulou, ed., *Images of the Byzantine World: Visions, Messages and Meanings. Studies Presented to Leslie Brubaker* (Aldershot and Burlington, VT: Ashgate), 83–98

— (2011b), 'The Use of the *Protevangelion of James* in Eighth-Century Homilies on the Mother of God', in Brubaker and Cunningham (2011), 163–78

— (2016), 'The Life of the Virgin Mary according to Middle Byzantine Preachers and Hagiographers: Changing Contexts and Perspectives', *Apocrypha* 27, 137–59

— (2019a), 'Byzantine Festal Homilies on the Virgin Mary', in Maunder (2019), 154–67

— (2019b), 'The *Life of the Theotokos* by Epiphanios of Kallistratos', in Arentzen and Cunningham (2019), 314–15

— (2021), *The Virgin Mary in Byzantium, c. 400–1000: Hymns, Homilies, and Hagiography* (Cambridge: Cambridge University Press)

Darrouzès, J. (1960), 'Épiphane de Constantinople', in *DS* 4.1, 862–63

— (1963), 'Épiphane, moine de Constantinople', in *DHGE* 15, 614–15

Davies, S. (1980), *The Revolt of the Widows: The Social World of the Apocryphal Acts* (Carbondale, IL: Southern Illinois University Press)
Dell'Acqua, Francesca (2020), *Iconophilia: Politics, Religion, Preaching, and the Use of Images in Rome, c. 680–880* (London and New York: Routledge)
Dolbeau, F. (2012), *Prophètes, apôtres et disciples dans les traditions chrétiennes d'Occident: Vie brèves et listes en latin*, SubsHag 92 (Brussels: Société des Bollandistes)
Domínguez, Óscar Prieto (2020), *Literary Circles in Byzantine Iconoclasm: Patrons, Politics, and Saints* (Cambridge: Cambridge University Press)
Dräseke, J. (1895), 'Der Mönch und Presbyter Epiphanius', *BZ* 4, 346–62
Dvornik, F. (1958), *The Idea of Apostolicity in Byzantium and the Legend of the Apostle Andrew*, DOS 4 (Cambridge, MA: Harvard University Press)
Efthymiadis, Stephanos, ed. (2011a), *The Ashgate Research Companion to Byzantine Hagiography*, vol. 1: *Periods and Places* (Farnham and Burlington, VT: Ashgate)
— (2011b), 'Hagiography from the "Dark Age" to the Age of Symeon Metaphrastes (Eighth–Tenth Century)', in idem (2011a), 95–142
—, ed. (2014), *The Ashgate Research Companion to Byzantine Hagiography*, vol. 2: *Genres and Contexts* (Farnham and Burlington, VT: Ashgate)
Ehrhard, Albert (1936–52), *Überlieferung und Bestand der hagiographischen und homiletischen Literatur der griechischen Kirche von den Anfängen bis zum Ende des 16. Jahrhunderts*, 3 vols (Leipzig and Berlin: Hinrich)
Elsner, Jás (2012), 'Iconoclasm as Discourse: From Antiquity to Byzantium', *The Art Bulletin* 94.3, Sept., 368–94
Esbroeck, Michel van (1994), 'Neuf listes d'apôtres orientales', *Augustinianum* 34, 109–99
— (1995), *Aux origines de la Dormition de la Vierge* (Aldershot and Brookfield, VT: Ashgate)
Flamion, J. (1911), *Les Actes apocryphes de l'apôtre André. Les Actes d'André et de Matthias, de Pierre et d'André et les textes apparentés* (Louvain: University of Louvain)
Flusin, Bernard (2011), 'Vers la Métaphrase', in S. Marjanović-Dušanić and B. Flusin, eds, *Rémanier, Métaphraser: Fonctions et techniques de la réécriture dans le monde byzantine* (Belgrade: University of Belgrade), 85–99
Foss, Clive with Tulchin, J. (1996), *Nicaea: A Byzantine Capital and Its Praises* (Brookline, MA: Hellenic College Press)
Gador-Whyte, Sarah (2013), 'Changing Conceptions of Mary in Sixth-Century Byzantium: The Kontakia of Romanos the Melodist', in B. Neil and L. Garland, eds, *Questions of Gender in Byzantine Society* (Aldershot and Burlington, VT: Ashgate), 77–92

Gero, Stephen (1973), *Byzantine Iconoclasm during the Reign of Leo III with Particular Attention to the Oriental Sources*, CSCO 346, Subs. 41 (Louvain: Peeters)

— (1977), *Byzantine Iconoclasm during the Reign of Constantine V with Particular Attention to the Oriental Sources*, CSCO 384, Subs. 52 (Louvain: Secrétariat du Corpus SCO)

Gerstel, Sharon (2012), '"Tiles of Nicomedia" and the Cult of St Panteleimon', in D. Sullivan, E. Fisher, and S. Papaioannou, eds, *Byzantine Religious Culture: Studies in Honour of Alice-Mary Talbot* (Leiden and Boston: Brill), 173–86

Getcha, Archimandrite Job (2012), *The Typikon Decoded: An Explanation of Byzantine Liturgical Practice* (Yonkers, NY: St Vladimir's Seminary Press)

Graef, Hilda (2009), *Mary: A History of Doctrine and Devotion*, rev. edn (Notre Dame, IN: Ave Maria Press)

Gregory, Andrew and Tuckett, Christopher, eds (2015), *The Oxford Handbook of Early Christian Apocrypha* (Oxford: Oxford University Press)

Gregory, J. (1998), *The Life of Herod: From the Jewish Antiquities of Josephus* (London: Everyman)

Grumel, V. (1958), *La Chronologie* (Paris: Presses universitaires de France)

Haldon, John F. and Elton, Hugh, eds (2018), *Archaeology and Urban Settlement in Late Roman and Byzantine Anatolia: Euchaïa-Avkat-Beyözü and Its Environment* (Cambridge: Cambridge University Press)

Hamblin, William J. and Seeley, David R. (2007), *Solomon's Temple: Myth and History* (London: Thames and Hudson)

Hartenstein, Judith (2015), 'Encratism, Asceticism, and the Construction of Gender and Sexual Identity in Apocryphal Gospels', in Gregory and Tuckett (2015), 389–406

Haskins, Susan (1993), *Mary Magdalen: Myth and Metaphor* (Old Saybrook, CT: Konecky and Konecky)

Hatzaki, Myrto (2010), 'The Good, the Bad, and the Ugly', in L. James, ed., *A Companion to Byzantium* (Maldon, Oxford, and Chichester: Wiley-Blackwell), 93–107

Heyden, Katharina (2009), *Die 'Erzählung des Aphroditian'. Thema und Variationen einer Legende im Spannungsfeld von Christentum und Heidentum*, Studien und Texte zu Antike und Christentum 53 (Tübingen: Mohr Siebeck, 2009)

Hild, Friedrich and Restle, Marcell (1981), *Kappadokien (Kappadokia, Charsianon, Sebasteia und Lykandos)*, TIB 2 (Vienna: Österreichischen Akademie der Wissenschaften)

Hinterberger, Martin (2014a), 'The Byzantine Hagiographer and His Text', in Efthymiadis (2014), 211–46

— (2014b), 'Byzantine Hagiography and Its Literary Genres: Some Critical Observations', in Efthymiadis (2014), 25–60

Hoeck, J.M. (1951), *Stand und Aufgaben der Damaskenos-Forschung*, *OCP* 17, 5–60

Høgel, C. (1997), 'Literary Aspects of Greek Byzantine Hagiography: A Bibliographical Survey', *Symbolae Osloenses* 72, 164–71

— (2002), *Symeon Metaphrastes: Rewriting and Canonization* (Copenhagen: Museum Tusculanum Press)

— (2014), 'Symeon Metaphrastes and the Metaphrastic Movement' in Efthymiadis (2014), 181–96

Holum, Kenneth G. (1982), *Theodosian Empresses: Women and Imperial Dominion in Late Antiquity* (Berkeley, Los Angeles, and London: University of California Press)

Horbury, William, Davies, W.D., and Sturdy, John, eds (1999), *The Cambridge History of Judaism*, vol. 3: *The Early Roman Period* (Cambridge: Cambridge University Press)

Humphreys, Mike (2015), *Law, Power, and Imperial Ideology in the Iconoclast Era, c. 680–850* (Oxford: Oxford University Press)

—, ed. (2021), *A Companion to Byzantine Iconoclasm*. Brill's Companions to the Christian Tradition 99 (Leiden and Boston: Brill)

James, Liz (2017), *Mosaics in the Medieval World from Late Antiquity to the Fifteenth Century* (Cambridge: Cambridge University Press)

Janin, Raymond (1925), 'Nicée. Étude historique et topographique', *EO* 24, 482–90

— (1937), 'Études de topographie byzantine', *EO* 36, 294–98

— (1953), *La géographie ecclésiastique de l'empire byzantin*, Pt. I. *Le siège de Constantinople et le patriarcat oecuménique*, vol. 3: *Les églises et les monastères* (Paris: Institut français d'études byzantines)

— (1975), *Les églises et les monastères des grands centres byzantins: Bithynie, Hellespont, Latros, Galèsios, Trébizonde, Athènes, Thessalonique* (Paris: Institut français d'études byzantines)

Jauss, H. (1982), *Towards an Aesthetic of Reception*, trans. T. Bahti (Minneapolis: University of Minnesota Press)

Johnson, Cale J. and Stavru, Alessandro, eds (2020), *Visualising the Invisible with the Human Body: Physiognomy and Ekphrasis in the Ancient World* (Berlin and Boston: De Gruyter)

Johnson, Mark J. (2020), 'Constantine's Apostoleion: A Reappraisal', in Mullett and Ousterhout (2020), 79–98

Johnson, Scott Fitzgerald (2017), 'Christian Apocrypha', in W. Johnson and D. Richter, eds, *The Oxford Handbook of the Second Sophistic* (Oxford: Oxford University Press), 669–86

— (2020), 'Apostolic Patterns of Thought, from Early Christianity to Early Byzantium', in Mullett and Ousterhout (2020), 53–66

Jugie, Martin (1944), *La Mort et l'Assomption de la sainte Vierge. Étude historico-doctrinale*, ST 114 (Vatican City: Biblioteca Apostolica Vaticana)

Junod, É. (1981), 'Origène, Eusèbe et la tradition sur la répartition des champs de mission des apôtres (Eusèbe, *HE* III, 1, 1–3)', in F. Bovon, ed., *Les Actes apocryphes des apôtres: christianisme et monde païen* (Geneva: Labor et Fides), 233–48
Kahl, G. (1989), *Die geographischen Angaben des Andreasbios* (*BHG* 95b und 102) (unpubl. PhD thesis, Stuttgart)
Kalavrezou, Ioli (1992), 'When the Virgin Mary Became *Meter Theou*', *DOP* 44, 165–72
Kazhdan, A., in collaboration with Sherry, L.F. and Angelidi, C. (1999), *A History of Byzantine Literature (650–850)* (Athens: National Hellenic Research Foundation)
—, with C. Angelidi (2006), *A History of Byzantine Literature (850–1000)* (Athens: National Hellenic Research Foundation)
Kennedy, George A. (1983), *Greek Rhetoric under Christian Emperors* (Eugene, OR: Wipf and Stock)
Krausmüller, Dirk (2011), 'Making the Most of Mary: The Cult of the Virgin in the Chalkoprateia from Late Antiquity to the Tenth Century', in Brubaker and Cunningham (2011), 219–45
— (2021), 'The Problem of the Holy: Iconoclasm, Saints, Relics, and Monks', in Humphreys (2021), 464–93
Krueger (2004), *Writing and Holiness: The Practice of Authorship in the Early Christian East* (Philadelphia: University of Pennsylvania Press)
— (2014), *Liturgical Subjects: Christian Ritual, Biblical Narrative, and the Formation of Self in Byzantium* (Philadelphia: University of Pennsylvania Press)
— (2016), 'The Hagiographer's Bible: Intertextuality and Scriptural Culture in the Late Sixth and the First Half of the Seventh Century', in Krueger and Nelson (2016), 177–89
Krueger, Derek and Nelson, Robert S., eds (2016), *The New Testament in Byzantium* (Washington, DC: Dumbarton Oaks Research Library and Collection)
Kurtz, E. (1897), 'Ein bibliographisches Monitum für der Verfasser des Aufsatzes "Der Mönch und Presbyter Epiphanios"', *BZ* 6, 214–17
Ladouceur, Paul (2006), 'Old Testament Prefigurations of the Mother of God', *St Vladimir's Theological Quarterly* 50.1–2, 5–57
Lafontaine-Dosogne, Jacqueline (1964; repr. 1992), *Iconographie de l'enfance de la Vierge dans l'Empire byzantin et en Occident*, vol. 1 (Brussels: Palais des Académies)
— (1975), 'Iconography of the Cycle of the Life of the Virgin', in P. Underwood, ed., *The Kariye Djami: Studies in the Art of the Kariye Djami and Its Intellectual Background* (London: Routledge and Kegan Paul), 161–94
Lanham, Richard A. (1991), *A Handlist of Rhetorical Terms*, 2nd edn (Berkeley, Los Angeles, and London: University of California Press)

Ledit, Joseph (1976), *Marie dans la liturgie de Byzance*, Théologie historique 39 (Paris: Beauchesne)
Leemans, J., ed. (2005), *More Than a Memory: The Discourse of Martyrdom and the Construction of Christian Identity in the History of Christianity* (Leuven: Peeters)
Lequeux, X. (2019), 'La recension longue de l'*Index apostolorum disciplinorumque Domini* du Pseudo-Dorothée: contenu, datation, postérité', *AB* 137, 241–60
Lichtenberger, A., Agtürk, T.S., Winter, E., and Zimmerman, K., eds (2020), *Imperial Residence and Site of Councils: The Metropolitan Region of Nicaea/ Nicomedia*, Asia Minor Studien 96 (Bonn: Dr Rudolf Habelt)
Lipsius, R.A. (1883–90), *Die apokryphen Apostelgeschichten und Apostellegenden. Ein Beitrag zur Altchristlichen Literaturgeschichte*, 3 vols (Brunswick: C.A. Schwetschke)
Livingstone, Elizabeth, ed. (1997), *The Oxford Dictionary of the Christian Church*, 3rd edn (Oxford: Oxford University Press)
Lourié, Basil (2010), Review of Heyden (2009), *Scrinium* 6, 436–39
Louth, Andrew (2007), *Greek East and Latin West: The Church AD 681–1071* (Crestwood, NY: St Vladimir's Seminary Press)
MacDonald, Dennis R. (1986), *The Apocryphal Acts of the Apostles*, Semeia 38 (Decatur, GA: Scholars Press)
— (1994), *Christianizing Homer: The Odyssey, Plato and the Acts of Andrew* (Oxford and New York: Oxford University Press)
Magdalino, Paul (2007), 'Medieval Constantinople', in idem, *Studies on the History and Topography of Byzantine Constantinople* (Aldershot: Ashgate), I
— (2018), 'The Liturgical Poetics of an Elite Religious Confraternity', in Shawcross and Toth (2018), 116–32
Magdalino, Paul and Nelson, Robert S., eds (2010), *The Old Testament in Byzantium* (Washington, DC: Dumbarton Oaks Research Library and Collection)
Mango, Cyril (1993–94), 'The Chalkoprateia Annunciation and the Pre-Eternal Logos', *Deltion tes christianikes archaiologikes etaireias* 4.17, 165–70
— (2000), 'Constantinople as Theotokoupolis', in Vassilaki, ed. (2000), 17–25
— (2002), 'A Journey Round the Coast of the Black Sea in the Ninth Century', *Palaeoslavica* 10, 255–64
Maunder, Chris (2008), 'Origins of the Cult of the Virgin Mary in the New Testament', in idem, ed., *The Origins of the Cult of the Virgin Mary* (London and New York: Burns and Oates), 23–39
—, ed. (2019a), *The Oxford Handbook of Mary* (Oxford: Oxford University Press)
— (2019b), 'Mary and the Gospel Narratives', in idem, ed. (2019a), 21–39
Mayer, Wendy (2008), 'Homiletics', in S.A. Harvey and D.G. Hunter, eds, *The Oxford Handbook of Early Christian Studies* (Oxford: Oxford University Press), 565–83

Mayor, Adrienne (2014), *Lives and Legends of Warrior Women across the Ancient World* (Princeton and Oxford: Princeton University Press)
Meltzer, F. and Elsner, J., eds (2011), *Saints: Faith without Borders. A Critical Inquiry Book* (Chicago: Chicago University Press)
Millar, F., Cotton, H.M., and Rogers, G.M. (2004), *Government, Society, and Culture in the Roman Empire* (Chapel Hill: University of North Carolina Press)
Miller, Patricia Cox (1983), *Biography in Late Antiquity: A Quest for the Holy Man* (Berkeley, CA: University of California Press)
Mimouni, Simon Claude (1995), *Dormition et Assomption de Marie. Histoire des traditions anciennes*, Theologie historique 98 (Paris: Beauchesne)
— (2011), 'Les *Vies de la Vierge*, état du question', *Apocrypha* 5 (1994), 211–48 = idem (2011), *Les traditions anciennes sur la Dormition et l'Assomption de Marie. Études littéraires, historiques et doctrinales* (Leiden and Boston: Brill), 75–115
— (2017), 'Jésus de Nazareth et sa famille ont-ils appartenus à la tribu des prêtres? Quelques remarques et réflexions pour une recherche nouvelle', in M. Vinzent, ed., *Studia Patristica* 91, vol. 17 (Leuven, Paris, and Bristol, CT: Peeters), 19–46
Mioni, ed. (1967), *Bibliothecai Divi Marci Venetiarum codices graeci manuscripti*, 3 vols (Venice: Istituto Poligrafico e Zecca dello Stato Libreria dello Stato)
Moulet, B. (2016), *Évêques, pouvoir et société à Byzance (viii*^{e}*–ix*^{e} *siècles). Térritoires, communautés et individus dans la société provinciale byzantine*, Byzantina Sorbonensia (Paris: Université de Sorbonne)
Mullett, Margaret E. and Ousterhout, Robert G. eds (2020), *The Holy Apostles: A Lost Monument, a Forgotten Project, and the Presentness of the Past* (Washington, DC: Dumbarton Oaks Research Library and Collection)
Murray, Robert (1975; repr. 2004), *Symbols of Church and Kingdom: A Study in Early Syriac Tradition* (Cambridge: Cambridge University Press; London and New York: T. & T. Clark)
Naffah, C. (2009), 'Les "histoires" Syriaque de la Vierge: traditions apocryphes anciennes et récentes', *Apocrypha* 20, 137–88
Nasrallah, L.S. (1999), '"She Became What the Words Signified": The Greek Acts of Andrew's Construction of the Reader-Disciple', in Bovon, Brock, and Matthews (1999), 233–58
Neville, Leonora (2019), *Byzantine Gender* (Leeds: ARC Humanities Press)
Panou, Eirini (2018), *The Cult of St Anna in Byzantium* (London and New York: Routledge)
Papaioannou, Stratis, ed. (2021), *The Oxford Handbook of Byzantine Literature* (Oxford: Oxford University Press)
Parry, Kenneth (1996), *Depicting the Word: Byzantine Iconophile Thought of the Eighth and Ninth Centuries* (Leiden, New York, and Cologne: Brill)

Paschalidis, Symeon A. (2011), 'The Hagiography of the Eleventh and Twelfth Centuries', in Efthymiadis (2011a), 143–71
Peeters, P. (1932), 'Les débuts du christianisme en Géorgie d'après les sources hagiographiques', *AB* 50, 5–58
Peltomaa, Lena Mari (2015), '"Cease Your Lamentations, I Shall Become an Advocate for You". Mary as Intercessor in Romanos' Hymnography', in Allen, Külzer, and Peltomaa (2015), 131–37
Pentcheva, Bissera (2006), *Icons and Power: The Mother of God in Byzantium* (University Park, PA: Penn State University Press)
Perkins, J. (1995), *The Suffering Self: Pain and Narrative Representation in the Early Christian Era* (London: Routledge)
Pervo, Richard I. (1987), *Profit with Delight: The Literary Genre of the Acts of the Apostles* (Philadelphia: Fortress, 1987)
Peschlow, Urs (2017), 'Nicaea', in P. Niewöhner, ed., *The Archaeology of Byzantine Anatolia: From the End of Late Antiquity until the Coming of the Turks* (Oxford and New York: Oxford University Press), 203–16
Peterson, P.M. (1958; repr. 1963), *Andrew, Brother of Simon Peter: His History and His Legends* (Leiden, New York, and Cologne: Brill)
Price, Richard (2004), 'Marian Piety and the Nestorian Controversy', in R.N. Swanson, ed., *The Church and Mary*, Studies in Church History 39 (Woodbridge: Boydell Press), 31–38
— (2019), 'The Virgin as Theotokos at Ephesus (AD 431) and Earlier', in Maunder (2019), 67–77
Prieur, J.-M. (1981), 'La figure de l'apôtre dans les actes apocryphes d'André', in Bovon (1981), 121–39
— (1989), 'La Vie d'André par Grégoire de Tours', in idem, *AA*, 551–651 (see Primary Sources)
— (1992), 'Introduction', in J.-M. Prieur and W. Schneemelcher, 'The Acts of Andrew', Schneemelcher (1992), vol. 2, 101–15 (see Primary Sources)
Rapp, Claudia (1998), 'Storytelling as Spiritual Communication in Early Greek Hagiography: The Use of Diegesis', *JECS* 6.3, 431–88
— (2010), 'The Origins of Hagiography and the Literature of Early Monasticism: Purpose and Genre between Tradition and Innovation', in C. Kelley, R. Flower, and M.S. Williams, eds, *Unclassical Traditions*, vol. 1: *Alternative to the Classical Past in Late Antiquity* (Cambridge: Cambridge University Press), 119–30
— (2015), 'Author, Audience, Text and Saint: Two Modes of Early Byzantine Hagiography', *Scandinavian Journal of Byzantine and Modern Greek Studies* 1, 111–30
Reynolds, Brian K. (2012), *Gateway to Heaven: Marian Doctrine and Devotion. Image and Typology in the Patristic and Medieval Periods*, vol. 1: *Doctrine and Devotion* (Hyde Park, NY: New City Press)

Robert, Louis (1980), *A travers l'Asie Mineure: poètes et prosateurs, monnaies grecques, voyageurs et géographie* (Athens: École française d'Athènes; Paris: Boccard)

Rowe, Galen O. (1997), 'Style', in Stanley E. Porter, ed., *Handbook of Classical Rhetoric in the Hellenistic Period, 330 BC–AD 400* (Leiden, New York, and Cologne: Brill), 121–57

Rowley, H.H. (1940), 'The Herodians in the Gospels', *JTS* 41, 14–27

Ruggieri, Vincenzo and Zäh, Alexander (2016), *Visiting the Byzantine Wall Paintings in Turkey* (Rome: Edizioni Orientalia Christiana)

Saranti, Eleni G. and Triantaphylopoulos, Demetrios D. (2013), *Ho Apostolos Andreas sten istoria kai ten techne*, Patra, 17–19 November 2006 (Patras: University of the Peloponnese)

Schmit, T. (1927), *Die Koimesis-Kirche von Nikaia* (Berlin and Leipzig: De Gruyter)

Scott, Roger (1990), 'The Byzantine Chronicle after Malalas', in E. Jeffreys with B. Croke and R. Scott, eds, *Studies in John Malalas*, Byzantina Australiensia 6 (Sydney: Australian Association for Byzantine Studies), 38–54

Ševčenko, Ihor (1977), 'Hagiography of the Iconoclast Period', in Bryer and Herrin (1977), 113–31

— (1981), 'Levels of Style in Byzantine Prose', *JÖB* 31.1, 289–312

Shawcross, Teresa and Toth, Ida, eds (2018), *Reading in the Byzantine Empire and Beyond* (Cambridge: Cambridge University Press)

Shoemaker, Stephen J. (2002), *Ancient Traditions of the Virgin Mary's Dormition and Assumption* (Oxford: Oxford University Press)

— (2005), 'The Virgin Mary in the Ministry of Jesus and the Early Church According to the Earliest Life of the Virgin', *HTR* 98, 441–67

— (2008a), 'The Cult of Fashion: The Earliest Life of the Virgin and Constantinople's Marian Relics', *DOP* 62, 53–74

— (2008b), 'Early Christian Apocryphal Literature', in S.A. Harvey and D.G. Hunter, eds, *The Oxford Handbook of Early Christian Studies* (Oxford: Oxford University Press), 521–48

— (2016a), *Mary in Early Christian Faith and Devotion* (New Haven and London: Yale University Press)

— (2016b), 'The (Pseudo?-) Maximus *Life of the Virgin* and the Byzantine Marian Tradition', *JTS*, n.s., 67, pt. 1, 115–42

— (2023), 'Mary at Mar Saba: The Late Ancient Origins of the Orthodox "Life of the Virgin" Tradition', *Journal of Orthodox Christian Studies* 5.2, 153–77

Simelidis, Christos (2020), 'Two *Lives of the Virgin*: John Geometres, Euthymios the Athonite, and Maximos the Confessor', *DOP* 74, 125–59

— (2023), 'Symeon Metaphrastes: Two Puzzles Reconsidered', *JÖB* 73, 1–23

Sode, Claudia (2001), *Jerusalem–Konstantinopel–Rom. Die Viten des Michael Synkellos und der Brüder Theodoros und Theophanes Graptoi*, Altertumswissenschaftliches Kolloquium 4 (Stuttgart: Franz Steiner)
Stewart-Sykes, Alistair (2001), *From Prophecy to Preaching: A Search for the Origins of the Christian Homily*, Suppl. *VC* 59 (Leiden: Brill)
Stoops, R.F., ed. (1997), *The Apocryphal Acts of the Apostles in Intertextual Perspectives*, Semeia 80 (Atlanta: Scholars Press)
Swain, Simon, ed. (2007), *Seeing the Face, Seeing the Soul: Polemon's Physiognomy from Classical Antiquity to Medieval Islam* (Oxford: Oxford University Press)
Taft, Robert F. (1986), *The Liturgy of the Hours in East and West: The Origins of the Divine Office and Its Meaning for Today* (Collegeville, MN: The Liturgical Press)
— (1998), 'Women at Church in Byzantium: Where, When – and Why', *DOP* 52, 27–87 = idem (2001), *Divine Liturgies – Human Problems in Byzantium, Armenia, Syria and Palestine* (Aldershot and Burlington, VT: Ashgate), I
Tissot, Yves (2015), 'Encratism and the Apocryphal Acts', in Gregory and Tuckett (2015), 407–23
Toniolo, Ermanno M. (1991), 'L'Akathistos nella Vita di Maria di Massimo il Confessore', in I.M. Calabuig, ed., *Virgo Liber Dei. Miscellanea di studi in onore di P. Guiseppe M. Besutti, O.S.M.* (Rome: Edizioni Marianum), 209–28
Tsafrir, Yoram, Di Segni, Leah, and Green, Judith, eds (1994), *Iudaea – Palaestina: Maps and Gazeteer, TIB* (Jerusalem: Israel Academy of Sciences and Humanities)
Tsironis, Niki (2000), 'The Mother of God in the Iconoclastic Controversy', in Vassilaki (2000), 27–39
Vailhé, Siméon (1902), 'Fr Diekamp: Hippolytos von Theben, Texte und Untersuchungen', *EO* 5, 190–91
Vassilaki, Maria, ed. (2000), *Mother of God: Representations of the Virgin in Byzantine Art* (Athens and Milan: Skira)
Velkovska, E. (1997), 'Byzantine Liturgical Books', in A.J. Chupungco, ed., *Handbook for Liturgical Studies*, vol. 1: *Introduction to the Liturgy* (Collegeville, MN: Liturgical Press), 225–40
Vuong, L.C. (2013), *Gender and Purity in the Protevangelion of James* (Tübingen: Mohr Siebeck)
Wenger, Antoine (1955), *L'Assomption de la très sainte Vierge dans la tradition Byzantine du VIe au Xe siècle*, Archives de l'Orient Chrétien 5 (Paris: Institut français d'études byzantines)
Weyl Carr, Annemarie (2001), 'Threads of Authority: The Virgin Mary's Veil in the Middle Ages', in S. Gordon, ed., *Robes and Honor: The Medieval World of Investiture* (New York), 59–94

INDEX

Abasgia 52, 60, 137
Abgar I, king of Edessa
  (4 BCE–50 CE) 52, 60, 137n151
Abraham (Abraam), Old Testament
  patriarch 77, 130, 158
Achaia 47, 49, 53–4, 61, 64, 140, 142
Acts of Andrew (*AA*) 4–6, 10–11, 35,
  38–42, 44–9, 55–7, 62–8, 72
Acts of Andrew and Matthias (*AAMt*)
  35, 47–9, 61–2, 71, 107n2,
  110n19, 112nn27–8, 126n88
Acts of the Apostles (apocryphal) 5n23,
  6, 45–9, 63, 70, 107n2
Acts of the Apostles (canonical) 36,
  45–6, 84n49, 98nn136–7,
  101n154, 102n160, 106n181,
  109nn13–14, 110n15, 119n60,
  133n132, 134n140, 135n143,
  139n165
Adam 6, 42, 128–9
Africanus, Julius Sextus 17n81, 25,
  26n131, 81n33
Aigeates, *anthypatos* or proconsul of
  Patras 4–5, 34–5, 38–9, 64–8,
  140–6
Alania (Salania) 37, 52, 60, 137
Alkamanas, servant of Stratokles 65,
  143
Amasia 50, 55
Amastris (Kromna) 37, 52, 59, 115,
  135n142
Amisos 10, 50, 58, 116n46, 122, 136
  church of Theotokos 122

Anastasios I of Antioch (d. 598) 27
Anastasios of Sinai (d. after 700)
  27
Andrew, the 'first-called' apostle 2–7,
  34–73, 94, 107–46, 155–8
  asceticism 6, 39–40, 48, 109, 119
  crucifixion 5, 54, 66–7, 145–6
  cult in Constantinople 73
  disciples of 119
  education 109
  feast-day (30 November) 70, 146
  icon (marble) of 3, 8–9, 43–4, 111,
  116
  miracles 110, 119, 121, 125–7,
  133–5, 137, 140–3, 146
  missions 34–8, 40–2, 49–68,
  107–46, 155–8
  physical description of 119
  relics 40
  sermons of 41–3, 111–13, 117–21,
  125, 127–33, 136
Andrew of Crete (ca. 660–740) 6,
  17, 22n108, 23n112, 27–8, 76,
  78n21, 101–2
  Homilies on Dormition 6, 28, 76,
  98n137, 101nn155–6, 102n163
  *Homilies on the Nativity of the
  Virgin* 17n81, 23n112, 76
  Kanon on the Nativity of the Virgin
  78n21
angels 19, 21n103, 24, 53, 64, 77n11,
  83–7, 100, 102–5, 109, 120–1,
  131, 133

Anna, mother of Virgin Mary 5, 16, 24, 28, 78–80, 100, 152
Antioch 27, 37, 51, 58, 107, 110, 123
Aphrodisian the Persian *see Legend of Aphroditianus*
Aphrodite, goddess 126
apocryphal texts 1, 5–6, 9, 11–12, 15–16, 19–20, 25–9, 44–9, 77n11, 79nn23, 82n38, 87n68, 90n89, 104nn172–3, 108, 110n17, 123n70, 126n86
Apollo, god 117n50, 124
apostles 2, 5n23, 19, 21, 24–6, 35–6, 38–40, 44–6, 49, 52, 54–6, 60, 63, 75, 85, 91, 95n123, 98, 100–10, 121–2, 123n70, 138, 152–4
Apotactism 6n27
Apsaros, fortress 60, 113
Apsaros, river 56
Arethas of Caesarea (d. after 932) 69
Argyropolis 41, 52, 61, 139
Armenian *Passion of St Andrew* 45, 63
Artemis, goddess 51, 59, 125
asceticism 5–6, 13, 20–1, 35, 39–40, 48, 81–2, 85n56, 86, 94n117, 101, 104, 107, 137
  all-night vigils 40, 157
  celibacy 39–40, 48, 83n47, 109, 143–6
  fasting 21, 81, 84, 93, 101, 122, 152
  genuflexion 21, 101
  hymnody 101, 120–1, 152, 154
  kneeling 40
  prayer 40, 67, 81–3, 84n49, 101, 111, 131–2, 152, 157
  sleeping on the ground 101, 152
  tears 101, 152
  virginity 23n112, 83, 85–6, 87n68
Asia Minor 1, 3, 6, 8–10, 34, 36–8, 41–3, 45, 49, 68, 73, 106n179, 123n70, 129n106

assumptionist 20
Astacos (Astakos), Gulf of 69
Athanasios, bishop of Alexandria (ca. 296–373) 20, 85, 86n60
  Letters to Virgins 20
Athens 65, 143
Augustine of Hippo (354–430) 6
authorship 7–11
Auxentios, monastery of Mt 7–8

Babylon 88n70, 147
baptism 41, 50–1, 57, 59, 93–4, 96, 103, 109–13, 116–18, 121–2, 125, 131–3, 142–4, 156
Barnabas, apostle 108
Bartholomew, apostle 51, 58, 97, 104, 123, 150
Bartholomew, Questions (or Gospel) of 82n38, 104
Basil of Caesarea 42, 77, 88, 114, 128n95, 147
beauty, physical 17–18, 81, 92, 149
Bethabara 93
Bethlehem 3, 24, 32, 78, 79n24, 82, 86–90, 148
Bethsaida 93–4, 95n123, 97, 108, 150
Bithynia 7–8, 10n42, 43, 48, 55–6, 59, 69, 123, 134, 151
Black Sea 2–3, 6, 34–7, 43–5, 48, 52, 55–7, 59, 61–2, 68, 73, 110n20, 113n32, 114n34, 115nn40–1, 116n46, 122n68, 134n141, 135n142, 137n152, 138n159, 138n163, 159
Booth, Phil 14
Bosphoros 36, 134n139
Bosporos, Black Sea 52, 61, 114, 138–9
Byzantion (Byzantium, later Constantinople) 41, 52, 55, 61, 67, 108n5, 139

INDEX

Caesar Augustus, Roman emperor
 (27 BCE–14 CE) 87
Caiaphas, Jewish high priest 98, 151
Cain and Abel 42–3, 50, 58, 121, 128–9
 seven punishments of Cain 42–3,
  128–9
calendars
 civil 85
 liturgical 12, 67, 84, 114n35, 115n39
 lunar 84–5
Cameron, Averil 46
Cana, marriage of 39, 94
cannibalism 4, 37, 47, 52, 57, 60,
 110n19, 112n28, 126n88,
 135n143, 139**
Capernaum 96
Cappadocia 50, 57, 89n81, 110
Caucasus 3–4, 34, 38, 41–2, 45, 49, 60,
 68, 70
celibacy *see* asceticism
Chalcedon 52, 55, 59, 69, 114n35,
 134nn139–40, 158
Charlemagne, emperor (800–14) 9
Cherson 37, 52, 61, 116n46, 138–9
Christ, Jesus
 appearance to his mother after the
  resurrection 16, 23–4, 30–1,
  100n151
 ascension 9, 20, 36, 51, 59, 84, 98n137,
  101–3, 104n173, 106, 133, 153
 baptism 93–4
 circumcision 89
 commandments of 43, 156–7
 crucifixion 99, 106n179, 118, 133, 151
 disciples (twelve) 16, 30, 84n49,
  93–8, 97–8n136, 106n180,
  119n60, 150–1, 153–4
 disciples (seventy) 55, 108n5,
  137n151
 passion 99, 109, 118
 physical appearance 17–18, 22, 92,
  149

 presentation in Temple 89
 resurrection 20, 109, 118, 133
 Second Coming 118, 133
 visit to Temple (aged twelve) 92
Christology 5–6, 74
Claudius Tiberius, Roman emperor
 (41–54) 122
Clement of Rome *see Clementine
  Homilies*
Clementine Homilies 6, 44, 95n119,
 107–8n3, 109n9, 118n57
Constantine I, emperor (324–37) 40,
 139n167, 140n170
Constantine V, emperor (741–75) 2–3,
 8, 43, 69, 111
Constantinople 1–2, 16, 40–1, 43–4,
 55, 61, 69–70, 73, 81n36,
 114n35, 122n67, 134n139,
 139nn167–70
 apostolic foundation of 40–1, 69,
  139n169
 church of Blachernai 81n36
 church of Holy Apostles 40
 church of Theotokos (legendary) 69,
  139n169
 libraries of 16
 monastery of Kallistratos
  7–8n32
 monastery of Stoudios 84n48
 patriarchate of 41
Constantios, emperor (337–61) 40
Constas, Fr Maximos 15
Coptic translation of *AA* 45, 63
Councils, Ecumenical
 Chalcedon (451) 86n60, 114n35,
  134n139
 Ephesus (431) 11
 Nicaea (325) 114n35, 115–16n44,
  123n74
 Nicaea (787) 2, 123n74
creation 6, 42, 51, 59, 93n108, 113n29,
 118, 120, 136

Crimea 350–4, 34, 52, 55, 61–2, 68, 114n34, 138–9
cross 23, 41, 51, 53, 59, 62, 66, 72, 99, 124, 126, 142n179, 144–5, 151
'seal' or make sign of 53, 126n86, 127, 144n186, 145
Cyril of Alexandria (d. 444) 77

Daniel, Old Testament prophet 131
Danube, river 69
Darrouzès, Jean 7
Daukomis (or Daukome), village near Nicaea 126
David, Old Testament king 16–18, 75, 77, 83, 91–2, 122, 130–1, 149
physical appearance 18, 149
De gestis in Perside see *Legend of Aphroditianus*
demons 4, 50, 52–3, 59, 65, 124, 131, 134, 143
devil (Satan) 42, 93–4, 107, 109, 120–1, 124n79, 127–31, 157
(ps-) Dionysios the Areopagite 19, 28, 85, 102–3, 105, 154
The Divine Names 19, 28, 85n59, 100–1, 103n167, 105n175
Doctrina Jacobi nuper baptizati 17n82, 26, 76n5
Domitian, Roman emperor (81–96) 91
Dorapin 37, 115
dormitionist 20
(ps-) Dorotheos of Tyre 40, 48–9, 55–6, 60n257, 70
dragons 37, 42, 51, 59, 124–6, 134n135
Drakontios, first bishop of Nicaea (?) 51, 59, 134
Dressel, Albert 25, 32–4, 66, 70–3, 75n1, 107n1
dualism 42, 46
Dvornik, Francis 40–1

Edessa 52, 60, 137, 150
Egypt 89–90, 130–1
Ehrhard, Albert 29
Elijah, Old Testament prophet 131–2
Elizabeth, mother of John the Baptist 16, 80, 82, 86–7, 90
Emmaus, Judaea 91
Encratism 6, 39, 46, 143n182
enkomion 69–70, 73, 76, 108
Ephesus 51, 58, 103, 106n179
Ephidama (Ephidamia, Iphidama), servant of Maximilla 64n274, 66, 140–1, 143, 146
Epiphanios 'Hagiopolites' 8–9, 11
(ps-) Epiphanios of Salamis 45–6, 48–9, 55–62, 108n5, 113, 114n33, 134n140, 139n169
Esbroeck, Michel van 14, 18
Ethiopians 56, 60, 70, 113n32
Eucharist ('divine mysteries') 110, 112n26, 122, 144
Euklia, servant of Maximilla 65
Eusebios of Caesarea (ca. 260–ca. 340) 17, 25, 45–6, 76, 89n82, 91n91, 102n164, 109n9, 110n17, 117n50, 137n151
Euthymios the Athonite 2, 13–15, 21, 29n152, 31, 40n198, 81n37, 94n117, 109n12
(ps-) Evagrios of Sicily, *Life of St Pankratios* 44–5, 107–8, 123n71
Eve 6, 42, 128
Ezekiel, prophet 85

feast-days (Christian and Jewish)
Consecration of the Tabernacle 84
Dedication of the Jewish Temple 79
Dormition (15 August) 6, 12, 19, 24, 29
Easter 31, 37, 122

INDEX

Nativity of Virgin (8 September) 12, 17n81, 29
Passover 92, 99, 123n69, 151
Pentecost 26, 36, 51–2, 58, 60, 98n137, 101n154, 123, 136
Tabernacles 97
Flamion, J. 47, 56, 71

Gabriel, Archangel 19, 21, 83–4, 86, 104
Gaius Caligula, Roman emperor (37–41) 122
Galilee 3, 36, 78–9, 82, 86–7, 91, 93–5, 97–8, 117–18, 125, 131, 133, 150
Galilee (or Tiberias), Sea of 10, 15n71, 95n119, 150
Garden of Eden 42
Gelasian Decree 46
gender 80n28, 137n154
genealogy 13, 16–17, 26, 28, 76–9
  priestly 17, 75n4
  royal 17, 75n4
Gennesaret (Gennesa), Lake of *see* Galilee, Sea of
George of Nikomedia (d. after 880) 14
Georgia *see* Iberia
Georgian *Life of the Virgin see* Euthymios the Athonite
Germanos I of Constantinople (ca. 650–ca. 730) 19, 98n137, 105n176
Gethsemane 4, 19, 24, 98n137, 101, 105
gods (pagan) 42, 114n36, 126–8, 136
Gorsinoi 38, 50, 60, 113
Gospels, canonical 17, 23–4, 31, 36, 45, 83n47, 84, 89n78, 90n83, 94n114, 95n119, 99n145, 100n151, 108n9, 109n12, 132n122, 133n128, 142n178
  John 23, 151
  Luke 17, 23, 77, 87n68, 91, 96n131, 97–8n136, 102, 145n191

  Mark 96n126, 97n136, 99n145
  Matthew 17, 26, 77, 84, 87–8, 97, 99n145, 106, 133n128, 150
Greece 6, 34, 61, 73
Greeks (pagans) 39, 41, 101, 112–13, 116, 122, 124, 126–7, 131, 136
Gregory of Tours, *Epitome* 48–55, 63, 70, 124n79

Hegessipus 25, 91n91
Hera, goddess 26–7
Herakleia, Black Sea 52, 59, 115n41, 134, 158
Herakleia, Thrace 52, 61, 139n170
heresies 9, 46, 77n11, 107n2
Herod I, king of Judaea 24–5, 32, 45, 89–90, 104, 117, 148, 154
  death of 89, 90n87, 104, 154
  sons, Alexander, Aristoboulos, and Antipater 25, 89, 148; Agrippa 154
  wife, Mariamme (Mariamne) 25, 89, 148, 154
Herodians 117n49
Hierotheos, disciple of Paul 102, 103n167
Hippolytos of Thebes, *Chronicle* 7n30, 27–8, 78nn16 and 21, 82n39, 102, 105n174
Holy Spirit 41, 93–4, 101, 104, 106, 112–13, 118, 122, 131, 133, 146, 152, 156–7
homiletics 1, 4, 6, 12, 19, 24–5, 27–9, 41–4, 68, 105n176, 158
Hyrkanos, John, high priest and ruler of Jews (134/ 5–104 BCE) 108, 117, 148
Hyssos, bay of 60, 137n153

Iberia 37, 50, 52, 55, 60, 113, 122, 137
Iconoclasm 2–3, 6, 8, 18, 21–2, 38, 43–4, 73, 111, 113–14

iconophilism 6, 8, 18, 21–2, 43–4
icons 2–3, 6, 8–9, 18, 21–2, 27, 43–4, 111, 113–14, 116, 142
idols 42, 51, 59, 121, 124–7, 130, 133, 142, 146, 155–7
Ignatius of Antioch (ca. 35–ca. 107) 23n112
Isaac, Old Testament patriarch 158

Jacob, Old Testament patriarch 75n3, 158
Jacob of Voragine, *Golden Legend* 30–1
James, monk and companion of Epiphanios 4, 8, 34, 37, 43, 111
James of Alphaeus, disciple, apostle and first bishop of Jerusalem 26, 30, 91, 95, 97, 100n147, 102, 106n181, 150, 152–3
  wife of 91
James 'the Hebrew' *see Doctrina Jacobi nuper baptizati* and *Protevangelion of James*
James of Zebedee, disciple and apostle 96–7, 104, 150, 154
Jephonias 24
Jerome (ca. 345–420) 6
Jerusalem 3–4, 6, 8–9, 11, 21, 37, 51–2, 55, 57–8, 60, 76, 79–80, 82, 87–9, 91–2, 96, 98, 101–6, 117, 122, 136, 147, 150–1, 154
Jews, Judaism 17, 24, 27, 39, 41–2, 50, 57, 86, 89, 93, 98, 101, 108, 110–13, 116–17, 122, 124, 127, 131, 135, 151
Joachim, father of Virgin Mary 5, 16, 24, 77–80, 100, 152
  vision in Temple 79
John the Baptist 16, 24, 36, 45, 78, 82–4, 90, 93–4, 109, 117–18, 131–2

John Chrysostom 40, 42, 88, 147
  Homilies on Epistle to Hebrews 40n201
  Homilies on Genesis 42nn207–8
  Homily on Nativity of Christ 88n73
  On Heresies 117n49
John of Damascus 6, 16–17, 27, 76n5
  Exposition of the Orthodox Faith 16–17, 78n16
  Homily on the Nativity of Christ 27
  On the Divine Images 113n30
(ps-) John the Evangelist, *Transitus* 24, 76
John Geometres, *Life of the Virgin* 13–15, 21, 29–31, 39–40n193, 81n37, 94n117, 95n122, 109n12, 115n37
John of Thessalonike, *Homily on the Dormition* 19, 24, 76
John of Zebedee, disciple, apostle and Evangelist 9, 21, 23–4, 28, 51, 54, 58, 63, 76, 93–4, 96–100, 104, 106, 123, 150–1, 154
  house in Jerusalem *see* Sion, Mt
Johnson, Scott Fitzgerald 46
Jonas, father of Peter/Simon and Andrew 108
Jordan river 93
Joseph, betrothed husband of Virgin Mary 5, 16–17, 20–1, 24, 28, 77–9, 82–4, 87–91, 94, 95n119, 97, 100, 104–5, 150, 152
  angelic revelation to 89
  sons and daughters of 16, 82, 84, 104
Joseph, son of Jacob 130
Joseph of Arimathea 30
Josephus, Flavius 25, 45, 89, 95n122, 129n102
Joshua, son of Naue (Nun) 130

Judaea 86–8, 93, 96, 102, 108n7, 118, 131–2, 147, 153
Judas of Alphaeus, disciple and apostle 82, 91, 95, 97, 100n147, 150
Judas the Iscariot, disciple 97, 109, 119n60, 132, 150
Jugie, Martin 18–19

Kallistratos, monastery of 1n1, 7–8, 11
Karousia 37, 115
Katzapos, rock of 125
Kazhdan, Alexander 28, 39n193
Klopas (Kleopas), brother of Joseph 78, 91, 100n149, 152

Laodikeia 37, 51, 58, 123
Latin versions 11, 30–1, 48
Lazica 51, 58, 122
Legend of Aphroditianus 26–7, 75–6, 81n31, 81n33, 88n75
Leo I, pope (440–61) 86
Leo V, emperor (813–20) 2, 8
Leo VI, emperor (886–912) 69
Lequeux, Xavier 55–7
Lesbios, proconsul of Patras 64–5
Letter of the Three Patriarchs 18n89, 22, 92–3n105
Leucius Charinus 63
literary sources 1, 22–9, 44–68
literary style 4–5, 10–15, 34–5, 44, 62, 67, 72–3
  didactic 4, 6–7, 11–22, 39–44
  dramatic 2, 10, 12, 44, 61–2ß
  narrative 4–5, 12–13, 15, 20–1, 25, 38–40, 44, 72–3
  novelistic 5, 35, 67
  panegyrical 5–7, 10, 12–13, 15, 68–70
  paratactic 10
  simple or koine 4, 78n17
Lives of the Virgin Mary 1–2, 13–15, 29–31

Lokous, rock of 125
Lycia 123, 156

Macdonald, Dennis R. 47–9, 71, 110nn17 and 19, 112nn27–8
Macedonia 53–5, 61, 69, 140
Magi, three 24, 26–7, 32, 88–9, 131, 147–8
Malalas, John 18
Mango, Cyril 3n14, 4, 36–7, 43
Manichaeism 6n27, 39
Manuel I Komnenos, emperor (1143–80) 30
manuscripts 7, 9n40, 11, 27, 29–34, 38, 47–8, 63, 68, 70–3, 161
maphorion *see* Virgin Mary
Markianos, bishop of Sicily 123
Marmara, Sea of 36, 43, 114n35, 115n41, 139–40n170
marriage 16, 28, 67–9, 83, 91, 143–4
Marriage of Cana 39, 94
martyrdom 2, 10–11, 34, 43–6, 55–6, 62–3, 66–8, 71–2, 91, 101–2, 106, 109n9, 114–15, 134, 140n172, 142n179, 145–6, 153
Martyrium prius (*Mart. pr.*) 55–6, 63–8
Mary Magdalen 16, 23, 30, 97, 99–100, 104, 152
massacre of innocents 24, 89, 117n50, 148
Matthew, disciple, apostle, and Evangelist 17, 26, 77, 84, 87–8, 97, 99n145, 106, 150, 154
Matthias, disciple and apostle 35–6, 38, 43, 47, 50, 57, 61, 109–13, 116, 119, 136–7
Maximilla, wife of Aigeates 4–5, 35, 38–9, 64–8, 140–6
menologion 12, 29
Menologion of Basil II 70
Mimouni, Simon 19–20, 22, 28–9

Mingarelli, Giovanni Luigi 25, 31–4, 75n1
miracles 2, 6, 45–6, 48, 57–61, 64–5, 97, 105, 110, 118, 130, 132–5, 137–8, 140–3, 146
monasticism 3, 6–8, 11–13, 15, 20–1, 29–30, 39–40, 43–4, 68, 71, 80n30, 81–2n37, 84n48, 111, 143n182, 146
Moses 41, 43, 112–13, 118, 122, 130–1, 136, 156, 158
Mother of God *see* Virgin Mary
Munificentissimus Deus of Pope Pius XII (1950) 18
Myrmidonia ('city of ants') 47, 110n19, 135n143
myrrh-bearing women 23, 30, 99–101, 133, 152
Mysia 37, 51, 58, 123
mystical (last) supper 99, 151

Narratio, anonymous 40, 48, 55–69, 72–3, 145n189
Nathan, son of David 16, 77
Nazareth 79, 82, 86, 89–92, 94
Neocaesarea (Neokaisareia) 37, 52, 60, 136
Nero, Roman emperor (54–68) 109n9, 142
Nicaea 37, 42–3, 51–2, 55, 57, 59–61, 114, 123–34, 155–7
  church of Theotokos 133–4n134
Niketas David the Paphlagonian, *Laudatio* 68–9
Nikomedia 43, 52, 55, 59, 114–15, 134, 158
Noah, Old Testament patriarch 129

Odessopolis 36
Odyssoupolis (Odessopolis) 37, 51, 58, 123n73
Olympos, Mount 123

orality 34, 111, 113–16
Origen (ca. 185–ca. 254) 17, 76n9, 90n83, 93n110
Orthros (morning office) 29, 144

Pamphilos *see* Eusebios of Caesarea
Pankratios, bishop of Sicily 44–5, 108n4, 123
papacy, Roman 69
Paschal the Roman 30
Patrai (Patras) 5, 10–11, 34, 38, 45, 48–9, 53–7, 62–8, 71–2, 140–6
  church of St Andrew 142
Paul, apostle 36, 40, 63, 102–3, 123, 139n169, 153
  wife of 102, 153
Pella (Peraia) 102
Peloponnese 3, 34, 140
Perinthus (Perinthos) 53
Persia 26–7, 32, 76, 88, 98n137, 123n69, 131, 147
Peter (formerly Simon), disciple and apostle 16, 36, 40, 50–1, 54, 57–8, 63, 94–5, 97, 108–11, 116, 123, 131, 150, 152
  mother-in-law of 16, 95, 109
  wife of 95, 100, 108–9n9, 152
Phasis, city and river 51–2, 56, 58, 60, 70, 113, 122, 137
Philaster of Brescia (d. ca. 397) 46
Philip, disciple and apostle 51, 58, 94, 95n123, 97, 123, 150
Philippi 53–5, 96
Philologos, first bishop of Sinope 139
Photios, patriarch of Constantinople (858–67, 878–86) 14, 63, 69
  Bibliotheca 63
Phousta 52, 60, 137
Phrygia 37, 51, 58, 123

Pilate, Roman governor of Judaea 118, 132
pilgrimage 36–8, 111, 113–15
Pinakes database 29–30, 70–1
Pisidia 123
Pontos 1, 3, 110, 122, 138
Prieur, Jean-Marc 47–9, 56–7, 63–4, 68–9, 71
prophets 17, 75, 85, 92, 112, 117–18, 120, 122, 130–2, 136, 157–8
Protevangelion of James 5, 16, 24, 26, 31, 76n5, 77n11, 79nn22, 25, 83n44, 86nn61–2, 87n68, 88n74, 90n83, 105n178
Psalters 31n158, 100n151, 122, 142n178

relics 1–3, 6, 8, 10, 14, 22, 36–8, 40–4, 50n245, 67, 69–70, 81n36, 114–15, 138, 142n179
thrones (καθέδραι) of the apostles 9, 43, 111n22, 116
rhetorical devices
 anaphora 5
 ekphrasis 4, 10, 15n71, 18
 exclamatio 5
 prosopopoeia 5, 62
 word play 10
Romanos the Melodist 12
Rome 30, 41, 44, 46n228, 69, 86, 91, 107, 109n9, 115n42, 142–3, 148

saints 1, 3, 8, 22, 29, 36, 43, 69–71, 114–15, 154
 Aniketos 115
 Anthimos 115n38
 Auxentios 7–8
 Drakontios 51, 59, 134n135
 Hyacinth 115n42
 Hypatios 115n44
 Indes 115n39
 Nikopsis of Zekhia 138

Panteleimon 114n36
Phokas 110–11n20
Photios 115n40
Zotikos 115
Salome, daughter of Hyrkanos 89n81, 148
Salome, midwife and cousin of Virgin Mary 78, 86nn61–2, 87, 91
Salome, mother of James and John of Zebedee 96, 99
Salome, previous wife of Joseph 82
Samaria 102, 123, 153
Samosata (Amousatos) 37, 52, 60, 136
Samuel, Old Testament judge and prophet 130
Schermann, Theodore 55–6
scribes 32–4, 72–3, 76n10, 88n71, 90, 92, 137n153, 148, 149n1
Scythia 56–7, 60, 123
Scythians 38, 50, 60, 110, 113
'seal' or make sign of cross *see* cross
Sebastopolis 50, 52, 56–7, 60–2, 113, 137
Seth, son of Adam and Eve 129
Shoemaker, Stephen J. 14, 19
Sicily 44–5, 108, 123, 156
Simelidis, Christos 2, 14–15
Simon the Canaanite, disciple and apostle 52, 60, 94, 97, 136–8, 150
Sinope 3, 8, 10, 35–8, 43, 47, 50, 52, 55, 57, 59–62, 71, 110–13, 116, 135–6, 139, 158
Sion, Mt 3–4, 6, 9, 16, 21, 23–4, 31, 96, 98–101, 106
 John's house on 6, 9, 16, 21, 23–4, 31, 96, 98n137, 99–101, 106, 151
Slavs 70
Sogdians (Kosogdianoi) 38, 50, 60, 113
Solomon, Old Testament king 77, 80

Sosios, citizen of Patras 64, 140
Sougdaia 52, 60, 137, 138n158
Sousania (Sousarmia) 50, 52, 60, 113, 137n153
Stachys, first bishop of Constantinople 41, 52, 61, 69, 139
star (that guided the Magi) 26–7, 32, 88, 131, 147
Stephen, first martyr 101–2, 102n161, 153
Stephen the Deacon, *Life of St Stephen the Younger* 7
Stratokles, brother of Aigeates 65–7, 72, 142–6
suicide 38–9, 67, 141, 145–6
Symeon, elder in Temple 89
Symeon, monk in Sinope 43, 111
Symeon, second bishop of Jerusalem 26, 91
Symeon the Metaphrast
  Commemoration of St Andrew 69–70
  Life of the Virgin 13, 29–30
Synaxarion of Constantinople (*SynaxCP*) 70, 79n26
Syriac narratives 13, 78n19

Tabula Imperii Byzantini (*TIB*) 37
Temple, Jewish 5, 15, 17–18, 20–1, 24–5, 32, 79–82, 89–90, 97, 104–5, 132, 148
  pictured as church 80n30, 90n84
Thaddaeus, disciple and apostle 97–8n136, 119, 137, 150
Theophanes, monk in Sinope 43, 111
Theotokos *see* Virgin Mary
Thessalonike 19, 24, 53–5
Thessaly 56n255, 61, 69
Theudesia (Theodosia) 52, 61, 138
Thomas, disciple and apostle 40, 63, 97, 101, 150, 152

Thrace 3, 41, 52–3, 55–6, 60–1, 69, 73, 139
Tiberius Caesar Augustus, Roman emperor (14–37) 122
Timothy, disciple of Paul 40, 102–3
Trajan, Roman emperor (98–117) 91n91, 115n42, 124
Trebizond 37, 51–2, 55, 58, 60, 122n68, 136
Tyana 36–7, 50, 57, 110
Tychikos, first bishop of Chalcedon 52, 59, 134n140
typology 75n3, 85

Vinogradov, Andrey 35–6, 49, 68–9, 71–3, 107n1, 155–8
Virgin Mary 3, 11–31
  age 15–16, 27–8, 79, 105
  annunciations 15, 23, 81–2, 84, 104
  asceticism 5–6, 13, 20–1, 80–1, 83–4, 101–2
  assumption into heaven 19–20, 102–5, 154
  burial 18–20, 105
  character 13, 80–1, 85, 87, 101–2
  Christological role 3, 12
  Christ's appearance to after the resurrection *see* Christ
  cult 22
  dormition (falling asleep or death) 18–20, 24, 28, 102–6, 154
  education 13, 80
  emotions 12
  entrance into Temple 15, 25, 79
  female disciples 16, 19–20, 81, 84, 95–7, 102, 153
  image of 26–7
  immaculate conception 85n56
  imprints of knees on floor of house at Mt Sion 6, 9, 101n156

INDEX 195

intercessory power 12, 21
maphorion 81
maternal relationship with Christ 12
menstruation 82n43
miracles 22, 101–2
physical appearance 13, 17–18, 26n133, 80–1
purity 83–6
spinning (Temple threads) 80
virginity 83n47, 85, 87n68, 148
vision in Temple 15, 81–2, 104
visitation with Elizabeth 21n103, 86–7

wall paintings 142n179
Wenger, Antoine 13, 18
women
   disposition in church (or Temple) 80n30, 90, 148
   female disciples *see* Virgin Mary

Zacharias (John the Baptist's father) 24, 32–3, 79, 82–4, 87, 117, 131, 148
Zalichos 52, 60, 136
Zebedee, father of James and John 51, 58, 93, 96–9, 104, 123, 150, 152, 154
Zekchia 52, 60, 137–8

www.ingramcontent.com/pod-product-compliance
Lightning Source LLC
Chambersburg PA
CBHW061446300426
44114CB00014B/1861